What the experts are say... .....

Jackson: The Rise and Fall of
The World's Largest Walled Prison
A history and a memoir
By Perry M. Johnson

"Perry Johnson has given a **front row seat** to the reader in discovering the **history of world famous Jackson Prison**. You will **feel as if you were working there** from the 1950's until the break-up of the massive facility. Beyond Perry's first-hand accounts, is a history of the prison which **students of criminal justice will find invaluable.** Countless stories of conflicts, projects, and accomplishments during Perry's tenure **make this book a rich combination of a memoir and history of Jackson.**"

  James A. Gondles Jr., CAE
  Executive Director, American Correctional Association

"I have always known Perry Johnson **to tell it "Like it is."** True to tradition, Perry tells it like it is and/or was in relating what he knows about the State Prison of Southern Michigan, commonly referred to as "Jackson." He tells what he has learned from **research, interviews, casual conversations and his own experiences. He has "lived" the prison** as a counselor, assistant to the warden, deputy warden, warden, corrections department deputy director and director. **I know of no one with as much knowledge of the prison as Perry** and fortunately, with this writing he has shared that knowledge. **Whether you think you know something about Jackson, or admit you are not familiar with it, you will find this book informative, exciting and entertaining.** Enjoy it!

  Robert Brown
  Former Director Michigan Department of Corrections

"I worked at Jackson Prison thirty years ago and would **have thought that place could never be captured in words.** But Perry Johnson has done it. **He brings to life** the people and events from inside those prison walls. Anyone who appreciates **both meticulously researched history and tales ranging from the humorous to the macabre will be captivated by this account.**"

  Pam Withrow
  Former Warden Michigan Reformatory and
  Warden of the Year in North America

Jackson: The Rise and Fall of The World's Largest Walled Prison
A history and a memoir

Jackson: The Rise and Fall of
The World's Largest Walled Prison
A history and a memoir

Perry M. Johnson

Jackson: The Rise and Fall of The World's Largest Walled Prison
A history and a memoir

Copyright © 2014 by Perry M. Johnson

Perry M. Johnson
Cover design by Penny Shanks

Second printing January 2015

ISBN-13: 978-0692261569

Cover photo by permission iStockphoto LP

www.jacksonprisonhistory.com

Love is above all, the gift of oneself.
--Jean Anouilh

To Uyvonne--

The love of my life and true partner for more than 60 years.
You held my hand on a lifetime's journey beyond our
childhood imaginations.
You taught me and our children how to practice a giving and
compassionate life. You are my best friend for all time. This book
would not have been possible without your generous
ongoing support and patience.
For all those reasons, and more, this book is dedicated to you.

Table of Contents

Foreword

This book is subtitled "A History and a Memoir." An even more accurate description might have been "A History Illuminated by a Memoir." For almost three decades (nearly half of its existence), Perry Johnson was intimately involved in the operation of the State Prison of Southern Michigan at Jackson.

Starting there as a lowly counselor in 1955, he would, before his career was over, serve the prison as the Deputy Warden, Administrative Assistant to the Warden and Warden – before moving on to oversee all of Michigan's prisons and eventually becoming Director of the entire Department of Corrections. It would be no exaggeration to say that he knew Jackson Prison inside and out.

To the reader's benefit, the recounting of this career is not merely a recitation of events, but also an evaluation of their meaning and context. It is a tale told with humor and compassion. As is inevitable in any history of an old-line prison there are stories involving extreme violence and cruelty – but these are leavened with others that are genuinely funny.

Nevertheless, this book not only gives a dramatic depiction of life behind the walls of the world's largest walled prison, it is also a serious history of that prison's birth, and development before Perry Johnson appeared on the scene. As it turns out, much that went on during that period had been obscured by time but also much had been hidden for good reason. As he says in his introduction, in his career at the prison, Perry had heard many fragmentary stories:

> ...of the prison's turbulent and violent history and the clandestine political corruption which surrounded that past...Many of those involved had worked very hard to see that these dark matters would remain hidden, but over the years I heard the hints and echoes of those events through rumor and old men's tales, and thought someday I might try to separate truth from myth so as to tell the real story of Jackson Prison. After retirement, that day finally arrived and that task—this book—was begun.

The task was begun--but only begun. It took Perry ten full years of dogged study and research in the State's library and archives, poring through old committee reports, meeting minutes, departmental and governmental publications and memoranda, as well as, often conflicting newspaper accounts, to get at the real story behind long-buried events.

Some of these occurrences have been the subject of earlier investigations, which he is careful to cite, but even in these instances much that is new may now be coming to light for the first time. In any case, this is, and was intended to be, a well-documented and serious history and not a recitation of mere hearsay.

So – a history illuminated by a memoir. A memoir, but the subject is Jackson prison, not Perry Johnson. The reader will form some impression of the author from his work, but as a friend of more than 40 years, let me tell you a little more about him.

Perry was born in a log cabin – literally – in the wilds of Alberta Canada in 1931. When he was a small child, his parents moved to a farm near Lakeview Michigan, where he grew up. This was during the depression and his family, like others at the time, was quite impoverished. Some idea of the situation in which he was raised may be gained from the fact that, until he enrolled at Michigan State University, he had never used a telephone. But to say that he was both bright and hard-working would be an understatement. I know that he does not care to have his horn blown here or elsewhere, so I will list only a few of his distinctions and achievements:

In 1977 he was the first recipient of the *Award for Distinguished Service to the State* given at the annual National Governors' Conference. In his chosen field of corrections, he has served on the Board of Directors of The American Correctional Association, and as President of that Association, he helped develop standards for correctional institutions which have resulted in the upgrading of many of North America's prisons. His accomplishments were recognized by his peers by giving him the E.R. Cass Award, the highest honor in the profession.

When Perry became Director of Corrections in Michigan his style of management was quite a change for the agency. Corrections departments are by their nature militaristic in command structure and that did not change, but Perry wanted management done by the book. And there was no book. Therefore, he set to work creating an organized set of policy directives and operational procedures for all areas of the agency. This was a task which took a great deal of effort and a long time to complete, but with the department growing so large and the times so litigious, it was necessary to have written documentation to support actions likely to be challenged.

One result of this effort was that these documents made it clear to staff just what their duties and job obligations were. While this would seem to be valuable information for training purposes, it held people accountable for their performance and actions, and many people did not care to receive this information, Perry was not popular with that contingent of employees, but was respected by those who approached their work more professionally.

Perry introduced many other changes in making the department a more modern and professional operation. Classification of prisoners had heretofore been much at the mercy and personal bias of those making the decisions. He introduced an objective system of classification to determine the security level needed for each prisoner, as well as a set of risk factors to assist parole and community placement decisions. Other major changes he introduced in his career are described in the narrative that follows. Sadly, not all the progressive moves he initiated have survived the political winds, which later prevailed, but overall the department was much changed and improved.

All through his career, his wife Uyvonne, whom he met when both were in grade school, was there as a loyal support. They had five children together, and if you want to take a portrait today of the whole family, children, grandchildren, and great-grandchildren, you had better bring a camera with a wide-angle lens. In addition, if you want to make a list of all the accomplishments of this progeny, you had better bring a pen with a lot of ink.

Jackson prison was indeed a confusing place. You could get lost trying to navigate your way around it. I remember, on one of my first visits to Jackson, coming through the entrance sally port[1] into the rotunda, seeing a prisoner pushing a cart full of cardboard boxes into

---

[1] The primary modern meaning for **sally port** is a secure, controlled entryway, as of a fortification or a prison. The entrance is usually protected by some means, such as with a fixed wall blocking the door which must be circumvented before entering, but which prevents direct enemy fire from a distance. It may include the use of two doors such as with an airlock.--*Wikipedia*

the rotunda from the opposite entrance. Rushing after him was another prisoner, shouting "No! No! No! — this is *not* the sub-hall office! – How'd you ever get *into* prison, anyway?

So even some of those who lived there found the place intimidating and confusing. You will need a guide. You are about to get a very good one.

-Bill Kime
Former Deputy Director, Michigan Department of Corrections,
Program Bureau

Jackson Prison circa 1955 *Photo by permission Archives of Michigan*

Introduction

AS A VERY YOUNG MAN MORE THAN 50 YEARS AGO, I passed for the first time through the massive steel gates at Jackson Prison. Even though the state legislature renamed the prison the "State Prison of Southern Michigan" (SPSM), out of deference to the citizens of Jackson city who wished not to be identified with the prison's periodic scandals, to most it forever remained "Jackson Prison." At that time it was said with perverted pride to be the "world's largest walled prison." Warden William "Wild Bill" Bannan often dramatized this immensity by pointing out that he "could sleep you in a different cell every night for more than fourteen years and you would never sleep in the same one twice."

As a prison counselor on that spring day of 1955, I had no idea that passage through those clanging gates would be but the first of several thousand I would make over the next thirty years. Nor that one day, I would be sitting in the front office as the Warden overseeing this almost unmanageable mélange of stone, steel, and humanity. Nor did I then have more than the sketchiest notion of the prison's turbulent and violent history or the clandestine political corruption that surrounded that past.

1

Many of those involved had worked very hard to see that these dark matters would remain hidden, but over the years, I heard the hints and echoes of those events through rumor and old men's tales, and thought someday I might try to separate truth from myth to tell the real story of Jackson Prison. After retirement, that day finally arrived and that task—this book—was begun.

The uncovering of the prison's hidden past has taken countless hours of poring through archived historical documents and has acquainted me with a cast of characters ranging from the mobsters of Detroit's Purple Gang (some of whom I remember well from my own prison years) to corrupt prison officials and political operatives of all stripes. Acquaintance also, I should add, with a good many exemplary citizens. Some of these intrigues, tragedies, riots, and sometimes-noble efforts occurring in recent years, I recount from personal knowledge; I have documented all others to the extent possible.[1] However, before I turn more chronologically to the prison's historical beginning, let me recount my own impressions and experiences upon my first introduction to Jackson Prison.

I started there as a counselor in 1955 and, because the Warden mandated it, attended a prison guard school for two weeks, and then spent a week working as a prison guard. Guard school trainers described the prison as just another place to work—not unlike a Ford auto plant but with very exacting rules. Media images from a catastrophic 1952 riot were fresh in our minds, and news accounts over the years had painted Jackson as grim, ominous, and chaotically dangerous. I am not sure what I expected to see when our class of eight finally went "inside" through the massive, interlocked steel gates for our training orientation. The prison certainly was an overwhelmingly immense and complex place yet it was surprisingly orderly.

Stepping from the gate area we entered the rotunda, which contained the control center of the prison and was the province of the commanding officer called the Hallmaster. He was a burly, scarred, and pockmarked veteran whose piercing glare intimidated all but the hardiest souls. His domain was a rotunda as large as one in a big city

---

[1] Johnson served at SPSM as prison counselor in the 1950s, prison administrator, and Deputy Warden in the 1960s, and Warden 1970-72.

train station, which it resembled with its terrazzo floor and three-story high ceiling.

A balcony lined with small offices and work areas surrounded the rotunda. Tucked to the left of the security gate landing was a gun turret with rifle ports looking something like a deer blind made from steel boilerplate; they told us that the turret was added after the 1952 riot. I was somewhat reassured to see that it was unmanned on this morning. A chest high, marble clad, L-shaped counter some 40 feet long dominated the north wall and enclosed an area called the hall office. Behind this counter were desks for the control center officers and mounted to the wall was a massive "count board" containing more than 5,000 one by three-inch cards representing the cell location of each prisoner. A small set of bleachers backed up against the far wall was, of all things, a shoeshine concession operated by inmates. The scale of all this dwarfed the people in it—it had an aura of grandeur.

In the rotunda, the nerve center of this massive prison, I saw that most of the workers were inmates—this symbiotic relationship between the keepers and the kept seemed incongruous to me then. There were clerks and runners (messenger carriers) all spiffy in their sharply pressed white shirts, prison blues, and a half-dozen buglers with brightly polished horns. A prisoner's day commenced with the bugler's rendition of reveille and ended with the lights-out call of taps, bugle calls also signaled meal and recreation lines. The Hallmaster, a lieutenant, a sergeant and a few officers rounded out the rotunda's usual permanent cast of players.

Roll calls and assignments for round-the-clock shifts were held in the rotunda every day. Every civilian employee and anyone else with business inside the prison passed through the security gates and rotunda. Shop and maintenance supervisors checked their assignment keys in and out with security at the hall office. An occasional miscreant, having fallen afoul of prison rules, was hauled before the Hallmaster to determine his fate pending a disciplinary court hearing. There was a constant hum of activity.

After the hall office, we continued further on into the prison. We moved first into one of the north blocks, where the individual cells were back to back, like row upon row of stacked cages, five tiers high, 52 to a side on each tier—simply named "Five Block." The cells were identical six by nine feet reinforced concrete boxes, with steel barred fronts opening onto suspended walkways called galleries. Under Michigan law at the time, "one man to a cell" was the rule so these north side blocks held more than 2,000 prisoners; Five Block alone held some 500—a big population for the three officers on duty to control.

Five SPSM Block, east side, circa 1955
Photo by permission Archives of Michigan

Each cell contained a toilet, washbasin, bed, and for most prisoners, all their worldly possessions. Headphones were provided for listening to one of three public radio channels (an inmate disk jockey and commentator was the main local attraction). The galleries fronting all north side cells were narrow, with railings to separate prisoners from the wide gap to the outer shell of the cell house, the walls of which contained banks of casement windows for ventilation and light. Windows opening into the outside world rather than the prison yard were protected from the escape-minded by steel bars but occupants of the upper galleries could at least look out over the parked cars and across Cooper Street to the pastoral countryside and fantasize about freedom. We were told that some distraught inmates sought freedom another way by jumping over the fifth gallery railing— "flyers" they were called—and that no one had yet survived the 40-foot fall.

Some people have the impression that prisoners spend almost all their time in their cells, but this is not so, except for a few confined for punishment or protection in segregation units. During the day, most are involved in work, school or other activities. The movement of thousands of prisoners to meals, recreation, and work reminded one of a bustling city. While an officer could let an individual prisoner in or out of his cell with a key, most coming and going involved groups, and the locking systems which controlled the cell doors for these groups in those days were mechanical, with long iron levers, called 'breaks,' unlocking a gang of around 25 cells each. In this cellblock of 500, there were 20 such levers.

It was physically impossible for three officers, two on the galleries and one at ground level or 'base,' to scamper about unlocking the 500 cells. Instead, inmate 'break boys' did the unlocking upon signals from the officers, a practice that was abandoned in later years due to litigation. (One of the reasons prisons have become more expensive to operate is that staff now must do many of the tasks formerly performed by prisoners. While these changes were economically costly, they arose in part from the internal corruption and abuse inherent in the old system.)

The blocks south of the rotunda differed from the north blocks in that instead of back-to-back cells in the center of the block, cells faced each other across a wide interior gallery. The quality of their construction, including the locking systems, was inferior, but in most other respects, they were quite similar.

While the cellblocks were where the prisoners lived and spent their nights, let us zoom out for a moment to see the prison as a whole and view some of the activities, which occupied prisoners' days. The exterior walls of the cellblocks themselves provided part of the prison's "security perimeter." A massive concrete wall some 34 feet high provided the rest of that perimeter, extending from where the blocks ended. A railroad entrance penetrated the wall on the east to allow delivery of coal and industrial material and shipment out of finished products. A vehicle sally port of interlocking gates through which dozens of trucks, heavy equipment, and occasional emergency vehicles gained access to the prison opened to the south.

The 52 acres enclosed in this security perimeter contained all the necessities for feeding, clothing, and housing over 5,000 prisoners, and for repairing and maintaining the prison—including factories, a hospital, recreation facilities, classrooms, farms and a power plant. A large recreation area and ball diamonds were located in the north yard where more than 2,000 prisoners thronged on a typical summer weekend. The prison auditorium—a theater seating hundreds, complete with stage and balcony was located in the south yard. This classically designed auditorium was scarred by fire and smoke—vestiges from the 1952 riot—providing stark contrast between the noble and the savage. Warden Bannan vowed it should remain unrepaired as a reminder to the prisoners of their folly.

In short, the prison was a complete walled city—sheltered by some 5,000 acres of prison property. Outside the prison's secure perimeter was "The Trusty Division"—a minimum-security operation housing more than 1,500 prisoners in "outside" cellblocks and farm barracks. These inmates provided labor for a complex agricultural business on the prison's thousands of acres of farmland.

Prisoners performed most of the services necessary to the daily life of the prison, including preparation of meals served in the "big top" dining hall, laundry, janitorial, nursing, and clerical services. There were, as unlikely as it may seem, even inmate locksmiths. Prison staff supervised all of this work—at least theoretically.

More interesting to me at the time were the factories where the prisoners produced goods for state use, (the thriving 1920s private sector sales of prison-made goods now being illegal.) A metal stamp plant was making license plates and road signs. Other shops were producing garments and shoes for both guards and inmates. A tailor shop fitted and pressed the garments. There was a cannery and a textile factory.

Of these, the textile plant fascinated me most since, like most Michiganians, I had never seen one before. This massive three-story affair along the north wall was some two-football fields in length, with a width of nearly one hundred feet. Giant bales of raw cotton came by rail and left as finished garments and dry goods. Spinning the cotton into thread for weaving done to the continuous din of clattering looms with shuttles whacking back and forth was the first step in the textile process. This racket combined with the hiss of misting spray used to reduce the explosive hazard from the clouds of dust and lint billowing from the process cast a foggy cacophonous gloom over the rows of looms and workers. I cannot imagine any Free World factory having a greater sense of production urgency. The textile supervisors pointed out prisoners who had worked there continuously for many years and had become very skilled and almost indispensable.

The sheer mass and complexity of the prison would come to intimidate many who attempted to operate it over the years. I would learn that understanding Jackson Prison was akin to peeling an onion. Most apparent was the immense bureaucracy required to operate such a complex enterprise, a bureaucracy complicated by the politics of personal and institutional ambition. Often not visible, but just as intractable, were layers upon layers of intrigue, kinships, personal obligations, and individual agendas on the part of both prisoners and staff. In such a massive institution these undercurrents created a culture, among both prisoners and staff, quite different from that in Michigan's other prisons. It was ever the case that when anything went awry at Jackson, or the latest egregious scandal was uncovered, the reaction of staff in other prisons was a collective rolling of eyes and a sigh of, "There goes Jackson again, what else would one expect?" .

Of course, on that first visit I had no premonition of these events or the occurrences which would give rise to them. So let me turn now to a relation of that history. It is filled with many stories that are fascinating in their own right, some of which may with this telling, only now be seeing the full light of day.

--Perry Johnson

Warden Harry L. Hulbert, circa 1923
Photo by permission Archives of Michigan

Chapter One
In the Beginning—the Harry Hulbert Era

OVER THE YEARS, THERE HAS BEEN MUCH SPECULATION about how Jackson prison came to be so immense and why it perpetually cycled between disrepute and disorder on one hand and hopeful programs and productive industry on the other. Once built, the question as to whether it might just be too massive ever to be properly managed was raised repeatedly over its existence.[1] Were its problems a curse of design or

---

[1] Warden George Kropp while serving as secretary for the prison board in 1933 took notes for a meeting to consider ways to compartmentalize the 'new prison' to make it more manageable reported here from discussions with his Administrative Assistant Perry Johnson.

just a developing legacy? Who conceived it, planned it and brought it into being? What problems already present in the old prison had survived transplant to the new? Answers to these questions require the following of an often obscure and erratic paper trail.

There had been a prison in Jackson since the mid 19th century, but before the turn of the 20th century, it had become hopelessly obsolete, deteriorated, and required replacement. The new prison saw its incubation when the Jackson Board of Health condemned the East Wing of the old prison in 1912[2] and it gained traction several years later with the appointment of a Special Joint Legislative Committee to Investigate Jackson Prison[3] and the subsequent creation of a Board of Control on the Proposed New Michigan State Prison. The Board of Control consisted of three members from a Detroit architectural firm and the Warden of the old prison, Harry Hulbert.

By this time, there was a consensus of both the legislative committee and the Board of Control that the old prison was a wretched and dilapidated facility, which no amount of renovating could salvage. Built in the 1850s on a twenty-acre parcel at the north end of Mechanics Street, it was later hemmed in by the city of Jackson. The inmate cells were without plumbing, running water, or adequate ventilation, and only 74 of 1,250 had access to daylight. The inmates were locked in each night with only a crude chamber pot. The Planning Proposal described the "shame of the bucket system" and the pungent stench by 6 a.m. each day in the poorly ventilated cellblocks that caused both officers and inmates to gag and vomit. Health problems compounded the prisoners' plight. There was a prevalence of tuberculosis and venereal disease: it was reported that 26% of prisoners in the old prison had VD, mostly syphilis. The Board of Control called the prison the "black hole of Calcutta"[4] and it issued a Planning Proposal in 1920 for replacing it with a new prison. The legislative committee report issued on April 1, 1919 said:

---

[2] Blaney, Charles A., Merriman, Mark, Eaman, Frank D. and Hulbert, Harry L. "Report of the Board of Control on the Proposed New Michigan State Prison" Planning Proposal, 1920, p6.

[3] *Ibid.* p2.

[4] *Ibid.* p14.

There is absolutely no question but what Jackson Prison should be moved from its present location in the city of Jackson. This Committee has considered this subject very thoroughly, and recommends that said prison be located on what is known as the "North Farm" in Jackson County, which is about three miles from the city. This farm is an ideal location for an institution of this nature, is well and favorably located, having good railroad facilities, and being supplied with an abundance of good water. The removal should take place gradually, and in conformity with a well-defined plan, both as to its building and financing.

The Planning Proposal called for the new institution to provide for 1,500 inmates with space to allow adding 1,000 in the future. It was to be located close to the railroad on the east and Cooper Street on the west with the cellblocks oriented north and south to maximize sunlight for the prisoners.[5] The new site would be a spacious 50 acres as compared to the 20-acre site of the old prison. A schematic drawing attached to the report showed the layout of a 1500 bed prison on the proposed site—it was somewhat similar in design to the much larger prison actually built (which had 5,280 individual cells.)[6] The legislature subsequently passed an appropriation of $5,000 for building the new prison, a figure that grew to $7,671,329 by 1928 as the construction proceeded.[7] By 1927, Governor Green estimated the total construction cost would be $12 million dollars (however, we found no final accounting filed after the prison's completion in the mid-thirties). An undated memo from Hulbert's nemesis, M. E. Brogan, found in the

---

[5] Blaney, Merriman, et al., *op. cit.*, p27.

[6] *Ibid.* p6.

[7] Jackson, H. H. *The Michigan State Prison, Jackson 1837-1928.* Jackson, Michigan: Michigan State Prison, June 30, 1928, p63.

Attorney General's files[8] said: "Warden Harry L. Hulbert stated to Governor Groesbeck that he would save the state architect's fees in connection with construction of the new prison. Which he did but at great cost of mistakes and waste." Could it be that Hulbert alone was the mastermind behind the final prison? He certainly was a major force in its construction and strongly influenced programs, prison industries and the institutional culture transplanted from the old prison to the new prison by both prisoners and employees.

Politically Positioned for Power

Harry Hulbert was a sturdy, muscular man with craggy good looks that gave him a commanding presence.

He was a trained engineer with experience managing construction projects prior to becoming Warden; he had an entrepreneurial flair and considerable political savvy. He also had a reputation as an ambitious, hard-drinking, short-tempered, two-fisted manager with a streak of cruelty. Governor Sleeper appointed him the Warden of the old Jackson Prison in 1918 at the urging of the then Attorney General Allen Groesbeck (Groesbeck went on to become Governor in 1920 and served three terms through 1926.)

Warden Hulbert also became head of Prison Industries in 1923 and was appointed the Director of Construction for the New Prison in June 1924. Thus, for a time, he simultaneously held three paying jobs (Warden, Director of Prison Industries, and Director of Construction) making his salary the highest in the state.[9] Hulbert's political loyalty went personally to Groesbeck and his branch of the Republican Party— not to the Party as a whole. During this time in the 1920s, the Republicans had become accustomed to dominating Michigan politics, as they had done since before the Civil War. Generally, they held all statewide offices and both houses of the legislature, having lost the governorship only twice in 70 years. In fact, the first official meeting of this nation's Republican Party was in Jackson City, in June of 1854,

---

[8] Attorney General--Criminal Division Files, *Special Investigations of SPSM*, Michigan Archives, Box 1, File 4.

[9] Bright, Charles, *The Powers That Punish: Prison and Politics in the Era of the "Big House," 1920-1955*. Ann Arbor, Michigan: The University of Michigan Press 1996, p83.

so the party's roots run deep in the state. Given the party's dominance, the important political factions within the party fought their battles during the primaries, with the winner practically assured of election in the fall. Tradition was that after each election the spoils went to the winners, so after each bi-annual election, there were patronage jobs, contracts, and political favors doled out and constituents kept happy through the next campaign. Warden Hulbert had the power to hire, fire and set salaries for hundreds of prison staff so he could accommodate many of the Governor's patronage obligations. He could give contracts and direct purchasing for both the old prison and construction of the new, to friends of the administration. In addition, the largess of the prison farms and prison labor were at his disposal. He was a highly visible advocate for the Governor throughout all of Jackson County. Surviving records show Groesbeck urging him to firm up his county organization, get the propaganda out, determine voter sentiment, and prepare to get the primary vote.[10] Even in Groesbeck's primary defeat in 1926, Hulbert delivered the Jackson County vote.

Ever eager to please his boss, Hulbert provided prison labor for Governor Groesbeck's signature program of road building. Designed to meet both the needs of the exploding auto industry and the wishes of the public, this program was a politician's pork-barrel dream. In all, during Groesbeck's six years in office, more than 6,000 miles of state and county roads received a concrete surface, another 3,000 miles of highway were added, and 240 bridges built. Prison labor built only a portion of all this, but much of the concrete was supplied at below market cost from Hulbert's prisoner-operated Chelsea Cement plant. Groesbeck learned that prisoners could also be used for leverage; when confronted with a county contractor he disliked or local labor costs he thought too high, the Governor was prepared to bypass them with gangs of prisoners working from transient road camps constructed and maintained by Hulbert.[11]

---

[10] Adrienne Eaton, John Knox, Frank Sudia, Marianne Carduner, Roy Doppelt, Jody George, Ellen Leopold, Charles Bright, *A History of Jackson Prison, 1920-1975,* East Lansing: Michigan State University 1979, p30.

[11] Bright, Charles, *The Powers That Punish, op. cit..* p53.

The prison's 4,000 acre farm system provided Warden Hulbert with access to quantities of meat and produce which he passed on to friends and the politically connected. Cases of canned goods were routinely shipped to Prison Commissioner Porter, the Secretary of State, and the local Senator from Jackson, among others, and large quantities of beef, pork and chicken were checked out to the Warden's house according to prison records.[12] In one party honoring Governor Groesbeck, the prison steward recalled that 45 inmate-waiters served steaks to 370 guests while the prison band played waltzes.[13]

Despite Hulbert's political value to Groesbeck there were some flare-ups between the two, both being volatile personalities. They settled their differences in a meeting in January 1923 and Groesbeck subsequently wrote that Hulbert was "an ideal choice for prison building because he was a construction man in civilian life and had much experience directing labor."[14] Shortly afterward, as noted above, the governor appointed Hulbert as Director of Construction in addition to his warden and prison industries responsibilities. Hulbert would design and begin building the very prison recommended by the Board of Control of which he was the state's sole member, the other three being private architects.

Prison Crowding—Increasing Urgency

When Hulbert became Warden of the decrepit old Jackson Prison in 1918 Michigan was experiencing the onset of a flood of prisoners, which would seriously stress and complicate his prison operation. With the signing of the armistice that year, young men in the crime prone age group were coming home from the Great War, and demographic changes and new laws would bring still more prisoners. Moreover, in 1918 Michigan would lead the nation with the enactment of prohibition laws, which would eventually bring a further tidal wave of new lawbreakers to prison.[15]

---

[12] *Ibid.* p58.

[13] Eaton, Knox, Sudia, et al. *op. cit..* *p24.*

[14] Woodford, Frank B., *Alex J. Groesbeck,* Detroit: Wayne State University Press 1962, p174.

[15] Engelmann, Larry, *Intemperance: The Lost War against Liquor,* New York, N. Y.: The Free Press, 1979, p159

To cope with the immediate prison-crowding problem, when he became Warden, Hulbert assembled surplus army barracks sufficient to house 400 inmates on prison farmland two miles north of Jackson—named the Jackson Prison Annex.[16] During the early 1920s, he built a number of other wooden barracks for inmate housing outside the prison; added numerous road construction camps; and built housing for inmates operating both the Chelsea cement plant and a brick and tile factory in Onondaga. As a result, minimum-security placement flourished under Warden Hulbert—about one third of the prison population was housed outside the walls of the old prison. As productive workers, these were true 'trustees' not under armed guard. Ironically, this emergency housing also provided merciful relief from the miserable conditions behind the walls.

Despite these measures, crowding would torment Hulbert throughout his tenure. In December 1921, Governor Groesbeck issued a circular[17] to all circuit court judges requesting they defer, as far as possible, further commitments to state prison and later in 1923, a desperate Hulbert wrote Groesbeck, "I am doing all in my power to prevent trouble (from crowding) but I need your help."[18] However, perhaps more telling, was this quote from Governor Groesbeck's journal entry of January 2, 1923: ". . . met with Frank Eaman (parole commissioner) and Harry Hulbert . . . Hulbert obstreperous and several times talked about resigning because paroles were not coming fast enough. This was destructive of discipline, he said because of crowded prison conditions. Told him I recognized this quite as well as he did and that I was tired listening to him talk about resigning. That he could tender his resignation as soon as he wished and that I would run the prison." [19] Hulbert did not resign but his willingness to annoy the governor suggests that he was deeply concerned about his crowded prison—a problem he was sure would be resolved finally with the building of the "new prison."

---

[16] Attorney General—Criminal Division Files, *op. cit.* Box 2, document titled "History for Conspectus," unknown, p5.

[17] Woodford, *op. cit.*. p162.

[18] Bright, Charles, *op. cit.*. p34

[19] Woodford, *op. cit.*. p163.

Leadership Style

Trying to evaluate Hulbert's seven-year reign as Warden presents an enigma. He was ahead of his time on some issues, for example, he undoubtedly had more trustees outside prison walls than any system in the United States at the time.[20] He advocated a quirky self-governing honor system for minimum-security prisoners—actually operating a brick plant eighteen miles from the prison on an honor system and without guards. He organized a school system using a combination of inmate teachers and correspondence courses. The Warden's Association at the American Prison Congress in 1922 elected Hulbert as their president and considered him an expert on prison industries.

However, his "bullpen" for prison discipline was barbaric. His management style was dictatorial and abrasive. During drinking bouts, which seemed uninhibited by prohibition, he was sometimes out-of-control and subordinates had to restrain him. He was secretive and imposed stringent censorship on both inmates and staff.

Hulbert's accomplishments were diminished by a drumbeat of accusations of impropriety and outright graft. These charges included drug trafficking with prisoners, embezzling inmate benefit funds, selling paroles, abusing both prisoners and staff, 'cooking the books' and bizarre behavior. Hulbert was the subject of Judge Williams' 1926 one-man grand jury[21] established to investigate waste and corruption, but he escaped indictment.

Freedom for Sale

Governor Groesbeck centralized the parole system in 1921; this overhaul reduced the paroling powers of local judges and created a Commissioner of Pardons and Paroles. This commissioner reported directly to him but Groesbeck retained the power to parole, frequently sitting in on parole hearings, and receiving recommendations directly from wardens.[22] Thus, Warden Hulbert had direct access to recommend for or against the parole—a favorable recommendation only helped the inmate but an unfavorable one spelled denial. To the

---

[20] Attorney General--Criminal Division Files, *op. cit.* Box 1, File 1, "1924 Report to the Prison Commission" unsigned.

[21] Bright, Charles, *op. cit.*. pp 94-95.

[22] Bright, Charles, *op. cit.*. p11.

extent the Warden's subordinates could influence his recommendation to the governor they too had clout in the parole process. Furthermore, any elected official or politically powerful citizen with access to the governor's ear could influence a parole, or at least make that claim. From the prisoner's perspective, there were no guidelines for earning parole. Granting parole was a purely arbitrary decision that denied half of the eligible inmates, so the convict's precious freedom hinged on a mysterious process concerning which he could see no rhyme or reason. This made it easy for hucksters to step in with real or perceived influence, for a price giving the prisoner some hope of controlling his destiny. If paroled, the convict considered the money well spent, if denied he felt double-crossed.

Blackie Henderson's case from Hulbert's 1926 Grand Jury investigation is representative of how the scam worked. Blackie had been paroled from Jackson after serving seven years on a 20 to 40 years sentence for armed robbery and was living in Chicago when the grand jury obtained his sworn statement, dated June 9, 1926.[23] That statement is condensed as follows:

> Chaplain (William) Hopp had it fixed with Dr. Scudder to release me on payment of $1200. My wife, Gertie, first deposited a 4.25 carat diamond ring valued at $2500 with Chaplain Hopp as security about Christmas '25. Later she went from Detroit to Jackson and redeemed the ring for $1200 cash. Gertie ran a 'sporting house' in Detroit where she had twenty girls and Chaplain Hopp was a frequent visitor. My wife gave up this house shortly after my parole.
>
> I was paroled January 29, 1926 and told to stay out of Michigan. Chaplain Hopp told me to keep my mouth shut or I would be returned to prison—no matter what state I was in. When my parole was granted, Dan Courtney put me on the train to Chicago and told me never to come back.

---

[23] Attorney General--Criminal Division Files, *op. cit.* Box 1, File 1, Henderson statement.

> For five years, while I was serving at Jackson, my wife sent $75 per month in care of Chaplain Hopp, and I had to take it out in trade with the chaplain for morphine—he (Hopp) charged me $75 per one-half ounce. I know the money was sent regularly on the 15th because I received my allowance of dope each month per my agreement with Chaplain Hopp.

Other prisoners testified that Hopp monitored inmate accounts and whenever significant money appeared he would dicker for a parole sale.[24] Because Warden Hulbert and Chaplain Hopp were considered thick as thieves generally and they frequently made joint recommendations for parole,[25] convicts were convinced that the Warden was also profiting from selling paroles, although no direct funneling of money to Hulbert was found.

Drug Trafficking and other Hustles

One of the most lucrative hustles of the Hulbert era was drug trafficking. The drugs of choice in Jackson prison in the 1920s were morphine, cocaine, and alcohol: these were reported to be prevalent within the walls. Blackie's claim that Chaplain Hopp was his source for morphine was but one of many allegations of scandalous conduct against this man-of-the-cloth who, from inmate accounts, was a sort of early incarnation of Elmer Gantry. The Committee of Jackson Prison,[26] an underground inmate group defying censorship rules, made a series of allegations in general but focused a blistering attack on Chaplain Hopp. They accused Hopp of selling paroles as well as double-crossing inmates, pressuring inmate wives for sex, and owning a blind pig and brothel in Detroit. Sgt. Ludwig of the Detroit Police Department confirmed the latter charge.[27] Numerous other inmates

---

[24] Bright, Charles, *op. cit.*. p98.

[25] *Ibid.* p99.

[26] Attorney General--Criminal Division Files, *op. cit.* Box 1, File 1, Underground letter from "The Committee of Jackson Prison" p3.

[27] *Ibid.* Statement Sgt. George Ludwig, Detroit PD., November 26, 1924.

identified Hopp as their source for drugs.[28] John Kline, twine plant supervisor, and Hulbert's brother-in-law, E. D. Deane, who ran the inmate store,[29] were also named as major conduits for drug trafficking and dealing in contraband. Hulbert was suspected through guilt by association because it seemed improbable that so many skullduggeries could have been afoot without some knowledge on his part. However, no police agencies conducted any criminal investigations; only the broader-ranging grand jury looked at the charges, with jurors complaining that prosecution was so shoddy as to constitute a sham and cover-up.[30]

The grand jury also investigated Hulbert's shady financial dealings. Early in his administration, he converted the co-op inmate store into a community store operated by his brother-in-law. This was an operation patronized by both employees and prisoners and its poorly audited profits went to the inmate benefit fund—an account which later audits revealed was used by Hulbert as a personal slush fund. In 1921, according to its previous president, Hulbert changed an inmate organization called the *Pathfinder's Club*, into the *Good Fellowship Club* and designated himself as president, secretary, and treasurer. He then expropriated their $600 balance and added $1,000 from the inmate benefit fund.[31] It is unclear whether Hulbert pocketed money directly or just ran purchases benefiting him through the inmate benefit fund accounts. Nevertheless, it is clear that both inmates and numerous staff considered Hulbert a crook.

Erratic Behavior

Warden Hulbert had a reputation of erratic behavior coupled with hard drinking. One such incident occurred during Thanksgiving week 1924[32] when prison farm foreman, John Clancy, acting on a tip from

---

[28] *Ibid.*

[29] Bright, Charles, *op. cit.*, p100.

[30] Attorney General--Criminal Division Files, *op. cit.*. Box 1, File 1, Statement Dan Ziegan, Grand Jury Foreman.

[31] *Ibid.* Statement by J. N. Rogers, February 1925.

[32] Riley, Deputy, *State Prison of Southern Michigan, Record of Punishment*, volume 10, page 892, Michigan Archives (Records

one of his inmates named Woods, went in search of reported contraband liquor near the property. Finding none, he hurried back to the farm office. Shortly afterward, the phone rang greeting him with an obscene harangue. Thinking it was just some drunk he hung up. Soon the phone rang again and this time he recognized that it was Warden Hulbert, who was very angry about something. Soon a relief officer came, ordering Clancy to bring inmate Woods to the Warden's office. Hulbert called Woods into his office and after some conversation, Clancy heard Hulbert say, "You're a Goddamn liar. I'll knock your damned head off." Woods yelled as if struck. At this point Clancy went into the office saying, "If there is anything to be said to Woods for telling me about the jug then say it to me." Hulbert then turned his full fury on Clancy saying, "I'll take care of you right now," and threw off his coat and lunged at him. Clancy reported, "I knocked him down. Then he got up. He tore off his collar, and ripped off his vest, saying, 'I have licked a good many men in the west and I won't take that from you.' I told him to come ahead. Instead, Deputy Riley and Ryan stepped between us. Behind them he kept on calling me names."

Clancy continued, "I told him that if he would set down and not act like a drunken fool I would explain it all to him. He sat down and I told him about the liquor jug. Then he sobered up and I told him I was through . . . then he said he wanted to see me privately. Then the Warden told me that he had something better for me that he did not want me to quit. He said we had both been hasty and he figured he got a little the worst of it and he wanted me to stay until spring . . . I told him I would stay."

A sober Hulbert apparently possessed a bit of charm offsetting his irascible conduct when under the influence.

The rough, tough, and gruff Warden met his match on at least one other occasion. It seems that after several escapades with female employees, gossip reporting noticeable intimacy between him and his secretary, Doris Horsfall, came to Mrs. Hulbert's attention. Understandably annoyed, she ordered Ms Horsfall's immediate

---

Herbot sentenced to one day detention 11-30-1923 and committed suicide 12-1-1923).

discharge and made it known that thereafter *she* would hire the Warden's private secretary.[33] Hulbert meekly complied.

Culture of Violence

Warden Hulbert's infamous bullpen and other punishment methods were common among American prisons at the time, and to some extent were merely a reflection of Jackson Prison's history and culture. Moreover, violence sanctioned at the top often encourages illegitimate excesses in which prisoners are maimed or killed, and this did occur under Hulbert.

In 1855 Agent (warden) William Hammond reported that in Jackson Prison, whipping is allowed but that other modes of punishment such as cold shower baths, ball and chain, shackles and the iron cap are (generally) sufficient.[34] Being 'chalked' in one's cell, solitary confinement, restrained in the "circle door" and being thrown in the bullpen more or less completed the punishment menu. Agent Hammond recorded 'only' ninety-three whippings that year, about one for every ten prisoners, so one wonders how many whippings these other methods prevented. One notable report of whipping followed the riot of 1911 when the prison Board of Control ordered flogging of 90 alleged ringleaders.[35]

It is not hard to imagine the discomfort of being hosed with cold water or wearing an iron cage (cap) locked on one's head but whippings were particularly brutal. Here the miscreant is shackled by his wrists high up on the whipping post and then flailed with a leather 'bat' for a specified number of blows. The bat was a heavy perforated leather strap attached to a handle that allowed for a two-handed swing. Until the early 20th century, blows were applied to the convict's bare back but because so many men became gruesomely scarred, the legislature mandated that the back be covered. The prison's solution to the new law was to use a sheet soaked in salt water. Whipping ended in 1924, Hulbert's last year as Warden.

---

[33] Attorney General--Criminal Division Files, *op. cit*, Box 1, File 3, Brogan Statement.

[34] Jackson, H. H., *op. cit.* p 31.

[35] *Ibid.* p 57.

A dungeon was built in 1857 to carry out Michigan's alternative to the death penalty—a sentence to life in solitary confinement.[36] Four years later, it held 20 men, of whom seven had become insane, a condition that prompted Chaplain Fox to resign because his health suffered from visiting inmates in solitary. The legislature then agreed that the dungeon was barbarous and inhumane and authorized removing the convicts and putting them to work. Inexplicably, the dungeon then housed insane prisoners until 1885, but punishment of solitary confinement continued on to the new prison.

The circle-door was the most severe official punishment in the 1920s—it was used to punish those already in solitary confinement. This device was a half-circle iron cage, which was hinged inside the cell door compressing the inmate between the door and the cage with room to stand, but not turn or sit. Sentences could be for as long as sixty days that called for ten hours per day in the circle door with one hour off and a diet of bread and water.

However, the worst unofficial punishment of all was being thrown into the bullpen with a dozen of the prison's most violent and nasty convicts.[37] As in the case of Inmate Lewis White who died in May 1924, a death certified as suicide by prison physician, Dr. McGregor, despite overwhelming evidence to the contrary. According to testimony from night officer George Webster, White was placed in the bullpen containing nine other convicts who then murdered him.[38] Webster went on to say, "This was because he was characterized as a rat." W. E. Bailey,[39] an embalmer, reported: "When deponent first saw the body of deceased Lewis White, his throat was cut practically from ear to ear . . . that the body indicated a stab over the heart which pierced the heart . . . That deponent was present at the autopsy conducted by Dr. G. A. Seybold and that both deponent and Doctor doubt that the deceased had committed suicide."

---

[36] *Ibid.* p25.

[37] Attorney General--Criminal Division Files, *op. cit.* Box 1, File 1, 8 B, Statement of Leslie Wolford, July 20, 1926.

[38] *Ibid.*

[39] *Ibid.* Statement of W. E. Bailey, May 13, 1924.

Although the circumstance indicated callous indifference by officials in throwing Lewis to the wolves, and pre-meditated murder by his assailants, the prison took no administrative or legal action.

Therefore, this was the culture of violence that Hulbert and other prison officials were accustomed to—they believed disorderly convicts deserved such punishments and more. Even annoying a "keeper" could get a prisoner in trouble—on one occasion, it is alleged Hulbert beat up a 75-year-old prisoner just for "mumbling" when questioned.[40]

According to the Anonymous Committee,[41] prison life was often a reign of terror as described in their letter to the 1926 Grand Jury:

> Men die under exceedingly peculiar circumstances . . . a coroner's jury visits the prison (to comply with the law) but never goes to a trouble of an actual inquiry—preferring to smoke a cigar or two after which a verdict is rendered. So often they (inmates) vanish . . . and they return just as mysteriously as they vanish, hideous wrecks of their former selves, and on their way to the insane asylum at Ionia.

Another example occurred on Thanksgiving week in 1924 when Anna Zabinski received notice that her husband, Bernie (Brownie) Herbot, a farm trustee, had committed suicide in the "bullpen" at Jackson prison. She was understandably distraught but disbelieved this account because she had visited Brownie a few days before and found him in the best of spirits. With attorney in tow, she gathered what information she could, and then contacted the coroner demanding an investigation of her husband's death.[42] The mystery of Brownie's transfer from the farm to the bullpen was somewhat explained by his supervisor, John Clancy[43] who testified that while at Warden Hulbert's office on the Wood case he saw Brownie and "he looked as if he had been hit and had been crying. This is the last time I saw Brownie alive.

---

[40] Bright, Charles, Ellen Leopold, et al. *loc. cit. p24.*

[41] Attorney General--Criminal Division Files, *loc. cit.* Box 1, File 1, Letter from The Anonymous Committee.

[42] *Ibid.* Jackson County Coroner's Report.

[43] *Ibid.* Statement of John Clancy, January 23, 1925.

Warden Hulbert said, 'take that son-of-a-bitch and put him in the bullpen,' referring to Brownie." Apparently, the Warden believed Brownie was untruthful about a booze jug. Subsequently duty officer George Webster[44] reported in a sworn statement:

> At 6:30 p.m. inmate Brownie came to the East Wing (bullpen) and was told to go to Deputy Riley's office. He came out of the Deputy's office and was put in the bullpen and about 9:00 p.m. the same evening, he was found dead by Night Captain Butler, Captain Pettit and myself. His shirt was removed, one sleeve tied about his neck and the rest of the garment fastened to the bars. His knees were barely resting upon the floor and his legs below the knees were bent backward . . . There was no indication of strangulation, no marks about the neck. His eyes were closed and not protruding . . . I assisted in taking the body down one of the deceased's arms was so flexible as to indicate it had been fractured between the wrist and elbow.

The embalmer, W. E. Bailey[45] stated that the suicide claim for Brownie was unlikely, and the coroner ordered his disinterment with the statement: " In an examination of Anna Zabinski (wife) I am satisfied that there is just cause to believe that Herbot came to death by means of violence wrongfully done to him by some person or persons unknown and that post mortem examination of the body will materially aid in prosecution." However, the sheriff refused to execute the order and took no further action, thus leaving Dr. McGregor another certified suicide and leaving Anna to wonder and weep.

Why didn't courts intervene in such blatant cases brought before the coroner or grand jury? Because, until the late 1960s, both federal and state courts maintained a hands off posture regarding prison matters. This policy was spelled out in no uncertain terms by Circuit Judge Charles Collingwood in March 1922 when he wrote: "to my mind, the prison should be inaccessible to the public, nothing should be

---

[44] *Ibid.* Statement of George Webster, February 20, 1925.
[45] *Ibid.* Statement of W. E. Bailey.

known of its workings and among criminals generally it should be regarded as equal to, or worse than, a death sentence."[46]

Unbridled power to operate Jackson prison in a setting isolated from judicial redress or police inquiry, and a partisan political climate dedicated to keeping all embarrassing skeletons hidden from public view is a sure formula for abuse.

However, not everyone in the prison business back then was cruel or corrupt. There were honest and honorable employees. Officer George Webster had the courage to violate the prison code of silence and testify honestly and forthrightly. Farm foreman John Clancy not only defied that code but also had the courage to challenge his Warden to prevent the abuse of inmate Woods, who was not only a convict but also black—about as servile a condition as one could be subjected to in those blatantly racist times. Certainly, other decent people, like Webster and Clancy, worked at the prison but never made the news. The problem was that these harsh, but officially permitted, practices continued for years, as would illegitimate excesses. These problems were carried over from the old prison to the new, bubbling to the surface from time to time for years to come.

It was not until the political winds began to shift, as enemies of Governor Groesbeck (and consequently, Hulbert) gathered force for the coming 1926 gubernatorial campaign that the horrific treatment of the prisoners began to surface.

Contract System to Prison Industries

During the prison's early years it was assumed that the agent (Warden) was not capable of both operating the prison and its workshops so the state had contracted with private parties to do the latter.[47] Under this "contract" system, the workshops were provided rent-free by the state with the contractor furnishing machines and raw material. One of the first contracts, which started May 1, 1847, called for "120 convicts @ $.345 per day to manufacture woolen goods, carpeting, farming tools, saddle trees, hames and harness trimmings, steam engines and boilers, barrels and copper ware."[48] Many more

---

[46] Bright, Charles, *op. cit.*, p94.

[47] Jackson, H. H., *op. cit.* p21.

[48] *Ibid.*

contracts would follow over the years. Initially the prisoners earned nothing, but soon contractors discovered that productivity increased markedly with a little incentive pay "under the table." The new prison board in 1865 discovered this practice and ordered it stopped, but imagine their chagrin when a month later a disenchanted convict burned the workshops to the ground at great loss to both the state and the contractors.[49] During the ensuing years, there were prevalent reports of prisoner abuse, dangerous work places, kickbacks, and collusion between convicts and contractors. These reports, coupled with protests from competing businesses undercut by cheap prison labor, resulted in legislation outlawing the renewal of existing contracts or the granting of new ones.[50] At the same time, the new Michigan constitution passed in 1908 gave a green light to prison industries run by the state.[51]

By 1918, the old prison was adjusting to the phasing out of the nineteenth century contract labor system and substituting state-run farms and fledgling industries. It was Hulbert's vision[52] that a profitable "industrial prison" was possible which would provide the work that he considered vital to good prison discipline while at the same time defray prison costs—a vision that would shape prison industries at the new Jackson prison for 70 years.

In 1921, to pursue his industrial prison concept, Hulbert persuaded Governor Groesbeck to agree to a deal in which the state would provide $300,000 from the general fund for operating Jackson prison for each of the next four years.[53] The balance of funds for running the prison and expanding industries was to come from profits, thus leaving the Warden the freedom to develop jobs wherever and however he could. It was a creative idea but the pressure to produce the required profit would indirectly cost Hulbert his Warden's job.

Therefore, by 1918 the table was set in Michigan for Hulbert to realize his dream despite the strong undercurrent of opposition to the use of convict labor, opposition that would spread nationwide, resulting

---

[49] *Ibid.* pp15-17.

[50] *Ibid.* p16.

[51] *Ibid.* p55.

[52] Warden Hulbert's Presentation to The American Prison Congress, 1922.

[53] Bright, Charles, *op. cit.* p87

in federal and state laws limiting the sale of prison made goods.[54] That Hulbert's vigorous production and marketing would undoubtedly contribute to the passage of restrictive laws after his time was a consequence he failed to anticipate.

From 1918 to 1925 prison industries and farms under Hulbert were a virtual beehive of productivity, not only from the existing programs but also through the establishment of new ventures with products marketed nationally to both the government and the private sector. Among the products, Jackson Prison manufactured were 50 kinds of brushes and brooms, soap, tombstones and grave markers, and aluminum cooking utensils. The metal stamping plant was set up in 1921 and began producing license plates and road signs for Michigan and other states.[55] The farm livestock numbered 135 milk cows, 700 hogs, hundreds of poultry, and 116 draft horses. Hulbert expanded cannery output to market over 400,000 cans of vegetables annually to grocers and institutions.[56]

In 1918 Hulbert moved the Michigan State Brick and Tile Factory from inside the prison walls to Onondaga, eighteen miles distant, where inmate trustees operated it profitably, using brick clay stripped from clay pits on prison farmland. However, boycotts by Michigan's bricklayers union, which refused to use prison made bricks, contributed to the demise of this industry by 1925.

He arranged to lease the Chelsea cement plant in 1923 and bought it outright for $500,000 a year later. It operated with prison labor under the name "Michigan State Cement Industry" to support road construction along with convict road gangs.[57]

Nevertheless, during the 1920s binder twine was the prison's most profitable product; a new mixture of sisal, manila and hemp made Jackson prison twine of high quality at a competitive price. To take

---

[54] The Hawes-Cooper Act, Federal legislation in 1929, banned prison-made goods from interstate commerce after 1935 and the Michigan Munshaw-Frey Act of 1935 restricted the in-state sale to governmental entities.

[55] Woodford, *op. cit.* p167.

[56] Bright, Charles, *op. cit.*. p85.

[57] Woodford, F, *op. cit.* p217.

advantage of this, Hulbert ran the plant "day and night" to produce 14 million pounds annually.[58]

Prison industries, with the exception of the binder twine mill, were in direct competition with Michigan businesses or labor and therefore a source of friction. Hulbert hit upon the idea of bringing a textile factory to the prison to expand in an area less threatening to local business since there was none in the state. The need for clothing for prison and mental hospital inmates assured a demand for these products in addition to potential domestic markets. He proceeded to study textile mills in the east, where the industry was dying as factories followed cheaper labor to the southern states, and he then bought surplus looms from Massachusetts and New Hampshire. The textile operation Hulbert set up in 1922, producing finished goods from raw cotton, was moved to the massive textile factory he designed in the new prison—a periodically modernized factory still in operation to this day.

This industrial expansion resulted in the employment of three quarters of the prison population by 1925—nearly half outside the walls[59] using virtually all of the prison's available work force, the remainder being medically unemployable, in detention or needed for institutional assignments. This would be a record of full employment never again achieved following Hulbert's tenure. Furthermore, profits from prison industries paid for the industries expansion and contributed a million dollars toward the prison operation. Hulbert was at the apex of his career—he was now drawing a salary from three jobs. He valued this at $25,000--$15,000 salary and $10,000 maintenance[60] at a time when the average wage in Michigan was $1,000.

Not only was Hulbert's cheap convict labor enraging private business and labor unions but both he and Governor Groesbeck were accumulating enemies and formidable political opposition. Hulbert was dictatorial and abrasive, making him many enemies among his staff and vendors, and his high visibility made him a convenient vehicle with which to politically damage the governor. In addition, Governor Groesbeck had a similar hard-driving, dictatorial style (which had

---

[58] Bright, Charles, *op. cit.* p84.

[59] *Ibid.*

[60] Attorney General--Criminal Division Files, *op. cit.* Box 1, File 1, Harold DeWitt Statement, p3.

earned him the nickname "little Mussolini" among party insiders)[61] making him vulnerable to his political enemies. A coalition comprised of former governor Sleeper and Hulbert's predecessor, Warden Smith, along with Fred Green, were taking aim at defeating Groesbeck, a task they accomplished; Fred Green became governor in 1926.

Among Hulbert's most persistent gadflies during this time was Robert Reece—a former employee who either resigned under duress or was fired—who was credited with amassing material on corruption and parole peddling. After failing to get the *Lansing State Journal* to publish his waste and corruption claims, Reece found an ally in the *Jackson Times*, which circulated a citizen's petition in 1925 to initiate a grand jury—headed by Judge Benjamin Williams.[62] The grand jury's investigation of parole peddling got nowhere but Reece was undeterred. In the midst of this aura of suspicion, Warden Hulbert reported losses in his 1924 annual report—a matter of sufficient concern to bring the Joint Legislative Committee to Jackson "to put to rest any suspicions."[63] Governor Groesbeck was unsatisfied and ordered an audit. Hulbert was furious and obstinately opposed the audit. He threatened the bullpen for any inmate clerks/accountants providing information to the auditors; in meetings with the governor and auditors, the discussions were "heated" and he used "foul language towards Auditor Emery."[64] Evidence from Judge Williams' grand jury made it clear that Hulbert's "stonewalling" came to no avail. Roy Beebe, inmate shipping clerk, testified that in 1923,[65] a prison industries banner year, 14 million pounds of twine was manufactured and shipped to 10 states and prior to being sold were incorrectly entered as accounts receivable. Further, that he could show from books that multiple railcars of twine were shipped, billed, loaded and unloaded four times with cancellation and renewal of insurance and handling charges. Beebe went on to testify that during 1924 two and a half million pounds from 1923 remained unsold. This carry over inventory was

---

[61] Bright, Charles, *op. cit..* p54.

[62] *Ibid*, p97.

[63] *The Jackson Citizen Patriot,* February 19, 1925, p1.

[64] Attorney General--Criminal Division Files, *op. cit.* DeWitt Statement, p19.

[65] *Ibid,* Roy Beebe Statement.

then sold off at fire sale prices significantly less than the higher sale price originally listed in 1923 as revenue, thus, creating a deficit on the books. Without audit reports, the extent of Hulbert's fiscal problems is unclear but it is certain that part of the problem came from this overstating of twine mill profits. Governor Groesbeck's agreement that Hulbert could use industries profits to supplement the prison budget made the temptation to do so understandable because it would allow Hulbert to proceed with industries expansion and pet projects with the intention, or hope, that the inevitable deficit could be made up in subsequent years. It was a scheme doomed to failure.

Hulbert therefore lost the Warden's position in February 1925 when Governor Groesbeck appointed Harry Jackson to succeed him but he was admonished to "straighten out the prison books before stepping down"[66] and he was eased out as Director of Prison Industries. He would stay on as Director of Construction for the new prison. His principal legacy undoubtedly lies in the prison industries he created, and the factories he designed in the new prison. They were the unmistakable foundation of the Michigan State Industries, as they exist to this day.

---

[66] *Jackson Citizen Patriot*, January 25, 1925, p1.

Chapter Two
Building the New Prison

HARRY HULBERT BEGAN PREPARATION FOR BUILDING the new prison in mid- 1924 by laying out the 50-acre site according to the approved 1920 Planning Proposal he helped develop. The prison site was located on a two hundred acre polygon bordered on the west by Cooper Street, on the south by Parnell Road, with a railway to the east; it was nestled in the southwest corner of the prison's 4000 acre North Farm three miles north of the city of Jackson. Although the site was logistically ideal, located with road and rail close by, its swampy terrain would prove forever troublesome. Architects for the Planning Proposal originally estimated that the project would cost about $6 million to build which could be partially offset by selling the old Jackson Prison and the West Farm for about $2 million. Further, they argued that "the new prison will tend to pay for itself as its revenues will be much greater than the present antiquated prison affords . . ."[1] Hulbert would design and start building the new prison with prison labor and without using an architect—cost saving measures he had promised Governor Groesbeck.

The initial design called for up to 2,500 cells in blocks running north and south oriented to gather morning and afternoon sunshine, making an intentional and dramatic change from the sunless, gloomy cells in the old prison. However, much of this advantage was lost when

---

[1] Blaney, Charles A., Merriman, Mark, et al. *op. cit..* p27.

the plan mysteriously doubled in size shortly after construction started. This occurred May 25, 1925, in a meeting with Governor Groesbeck wherein the Prison Commission initiated a program change recorded in their minutes as: ". . . Superintendent Hulbert was instructed to build the cell blocks across the front as planned and carry out the same construction on each side for 600 feet..." [2] In effect, this added ten acres and six cellblocks with more than 2,000 cells and required dynamiting 300 feet of newly poured wall, re-rods and footings into 200 tons of rubble to make space for the cell blocks. Instead of a prison for 2,500, the new prison would boast 5,280 individual cells when completed. It appears the idea for doubling the new prison's size and cost originated with Governor Groesbeck, who had a reputation for making impulsive, unilateral decisions, and it occurred at a time when he was preparing for the 1926 gubernatorial election and was under political fire from the *Detroit Free Press* for a "soft parole policy."[3] If he 'toughened up' on paroles, as his campaign promised, the prisoners denied had to be housed somewhere and already the population at Jackson Prison had doubled in just five years and would soon exceed the planned capacity of the new prison (2,646 in 1926).[4] Therefore, the Prison Commission implemented changes without legislative approval. Thus the responsibility for building the "world's largest prison" at Jackson clearly lies with Governor Groesbeck although his reasons for doing so remain speculative.

By late summer of 1924, the new prison site was swarming with several hundred inmate workers assigned to grade, fill, provide drainage, and lay out foundation plans. Under an intra-agency account the old prison was compensated $1.50 per day for inmate workers—the prisoners were paid a few cents depending on their skill[5] and most were housed close by in existing Prison Annex barracks. It was reported that

---

[2] *Attorney General—Criminal Division Files, op. cit.* File 1, "Prison Commission Minutes," May 25, 1925.

[3] Woodford, Frank B., *op. cit.*. p170.

[4] Warden Harry Jackson, "Michigan State Prison Statistical Report 1926".

[5] Porter, William, Records of the Executive Office 1921-1926 November 26, 1926, Letter from Prison Commissioner William Porter authorizing pay for 197,371 days (at $1.50).

up to 45 "heavy teams" (made of draft horses weighing a ton or more each) and six tractors, all driven by inmates, were working the site. They poured the first concrete for the footing of the prison wall that December. It would be a massive structure rising 34 feet above ground, tapering from two feet to 14 inches at the top and resting on footings several feet deep and four feet wide. With the completion of ten perimeter cellblocks, this secure perimeter would enclose 57 ½ acres. Cellblocks one through five, the power plant, textile dye plant, the hall-master control building, and the kitchen and bakery were completed in 1927.[6] It must have been a chaotic beginning.

All the while this building frenzy was underway, Hulbert's nemesis, former employee Robert Reece, was making claims of waste and incompetence, if not outright corruption. When his efforts to get his claims published in the *Lansing State Journal* were thwarted, he turned to the now defunct *Jackson Times* and garnered the newspaper's support to demand a grand jury investigation.[7] Finally, Circuit Judge Benjamin Williams constituted himself a one-man grand jury in May of 1926, a move openly welcomed by Governor Groesbeck's gubernatorial opponent, Fred Green.[8] Thus, the construction enterprise and Hulbert's role in it became the subject of rumor, scandal, and political espionage. To give a flavor of the grand jury proceedings a summarized sample of pertinent testimony follows.[9] It comes from Richard Simmons, a mechanical engineer with an impressive resume and fine career, testifying on February 11, 1927, to a somewhat incredulous examiner:

> Q. What was your objective in dropping your regular job to work for Harry Hulbert?

---

[6] Attorney General--Criminal Division Files, *op. cit.* Box 2, titled "History for Conspectus," unknown.

[7] *The Detroit News*, May 2, 1934.

[8] Bright, Charles, *op. cit..* p97.

[9] Attorney General--Criminal Division Files, *op. cit.* Box 1, File 3, Richard Simmons Statement, February 11, 1927.

A. I went to work at the new prison for a purpose at the instigation of other parties, to find out what I could and report. I started July 24 and quit in November 1924.

Q. Why quit so soon?

A. Because I found out what I wanted and by then I knew Hulbert was on to me. I found that the bearing value of the soil is insufficient for the loads imposed. It is glacial terminal moraine with a high water table. No proper test borings or load tests were conducted.

We do not know whether Simmons was spying for Reece or the Fred Green political opposition; however, Hulbert's suspicious nature, requiring all employees to sign a secrecy pledge, was obviously justified.

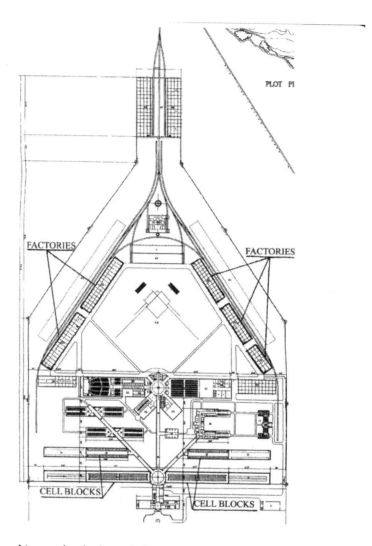

Enhanced 'new prison' schematic from the 1920 Planning Proposal courtesy Michigan State Library (The Cell Blocks would be facing west with the back railroad entrance coming from the east and factories located along the north and south diagonal walls.)
Drawing courtesy of Library of Michigan

The State Prison of Southern Michigan that was actually built, circa 1955
Photo by permission iStockphoto LP

Guy Cronkhite testified that he quit his teamster supervisor job at the new prison because of excessive waste. He described taking his crew down to fill trenches ahead of the form builders preparing to pour the wall stating:

> . . They had oceans of plank there of all dimensions, scattered all over, their horses continually going lame by stepping on nails. . . . I stopped the whole outfit and told him (Construction Superintendent Heiderman) we were covering up near a whole lumber yard. He told me that it was none of my business.
>
> I could not use these planks or timbers but had to take the team back a mile to get new oak plank . . . (on another occasion) it looked wicked to me to see all kinds of army wagons, always built the best that can be built, . . . They laughed at me again, and drew them out and burned them, twelve or 15 of them one day and they had been doing it for three or four days .

. .(and more) They wasted a lot of cement, didn't use it when it began to set, then dumped it into these holes . . . the inmates would watch their chance . . .they would take any way possible to get rid of sacks of cement to save them the work of counting and piling them.

Cronkhite, the foreman handling the teams, claimed that even though 25 sumps were pumping water he had to pull three teams from the mud and three horses had to be shot. When asked whether the site was fit to carry such heavy buildings Cronkhite opined: "No, I cannot understand why it was chosen to begin with, when a boy I used to hunt all over the back end . . . and had to go over it with a boat."[10] Others reported that "waste was endemic," and that massive amounts of usable lumber were simply burned, but that it was impossible to estimate the total amount because the books were "fudged."[11] As Leslie Wolford, inmate clerk, explained it, he was ordered to falsify records showing quantity and price to cover shortages on supplies for construction of the new prison and bring them into balance with Lansing records.[12] The intimation being that Hulbert was either incompetent or was wasting material to make more purchases from suppliers and thus benefit from kickback fees—a practice commonplace in the 1920s and the most likely explanation for both Hulbert's secrecy and the blatant waste.[13]

Fred Green, whose furniture business contract at the Ionia Reformatory was the last under the old system, defeated Governor Groesbeck in November 1926 but, surprisingly, he kept Harry Hulbert on as Director of Construction. He "shocked everyone" when in 1927 he estimated the cost to completion for the new prison would be more than $12 million, double the original guess—[14]apparently no attention had been paid to the cost of doubling the size of the prison two years prior. However, because of the stream of complaints about shoddy

---

[10] *Ibid.* Statement of V. Guy Cronkhite, April 11, 1927.

[11] Bright, Charles, *op. cit.. p90.*

[12] Attorney General--Criminal Division Files, *op. cit.* Box 8B, Wolford Statement.

[13] Bright, Charles, Ellen Leopold, et al. *op. cit.* p19.

[14] Bright, Charles, *loc.cit.*

workmanship, and the settling and cracking of both the prison wall and massive buildings, suggested poor planning, the new Governor Green requested an independent evaluation. Harry Conrad, a private engineer, was dispatched to do this. On February 1, 1927, he reported that:

> Taxpayers need not fear faulty design, workmanship, or construction--as the work to date is 'superfine' single cells, hot and cold running water--push button control vitreous china water closets (more conveniences than some of our finest hotels). Terrazzo floors and glazed brick wall seemed unnecessarily ostentatious for a penitentiary. Critics waxed wistful before the enormous walls -- admired by those who know a beautiful piece of work when they see it."

The North Wall in 2010. *Photo by permission iStockphoto LP*

Building the New Prison

The prison wall did not sink into the swamp and stands secure to this day some 100 years later. Obviously, Robert Reece's complaints were exaggerated.

Therefore, Reece missed his target again—there was no grand jury indictment of Harry Hulbert although the Warden was obviously wearied by the constant public attacks and grand jury hearings. On April 8, 1927, he handed in his letter of resignation. Governor Green and John Minor, new prison commissioner, urged him to stay—their support a mystery in light of the scandal and bad publicity that surrounded this protégé of their political enemy Groesbeck. However, one week later, he again tendered his resignation effective May 1, stating: "I have served my state and its taxpayers for nigh onto nine years, and I have tried to give them the best there was in me."[15] Whether Hulbert's steadfast support from the prison commission, who initially opposed his removal as Warden despite his 'cooking the books,' and from both governors, had anything to do with dividing the 'spoils of patronage' may never be known, much to Robert Reese's disappointment.

Charles Frazier replaced Hulbert as Director of Construction in 1927. Little is known about Frazier but construction of the new prison went unabated following Hulbert's plan—this progress was reported in a prison document titled *History for Conspectus* written sometime after 1937 by persons unknown;[16] it is excerpted for brevity as follows:

> The textile factory, detention block (15 Block), and Warden's residence were completed in 1928. The next year Cell Block 7, the laundry and the main prison garage were built. Construction reached a high point in 1930 with the building of Cell Blocks 8 and 9; the new Administration Building; a 200 bed hospital; a school, auditorium and stores building; a massive dining room (that would later be divided to provide a gym); and a metal stamping plant and

---

[15] Bright, Charles, Ellen Leopold, et al. *op. cit..* p28.

[16] Attorney General—Criminal Division Files, *loc.cit.* "History for Conspectus."

cannery. In 1931, Cell Block 10 and a residence and garage for the Deputy Warden were completed. Cell Block 16, for trusties outside the walls, and Receiving, Shipping, Storage, and Sanitation facilities (for bed and furniture repair, sanitizing of mattresses for re-issue, and distribution of cleaning supplies) were completed in 1932.

Politics and the Great Depression created a delay in completing the new prison. Democrats were swept into office with the 1932 landslide election of Franklin Roosevelt. When William Comstock became Michigan's governor, he fired Warden Harry Jackson, and appointed Peter Gray, Lansing's mayor, to replace him. Construction slowed until 1934 when, faced by budget cutbacks, the Prison Commission declared, somewhat prematurely, that the new prison was complete, abolished all jobs connected with its construction, and transferred the remaining prisoners from the old prison. Thus, the old prison was abandoned July 1934, after 97 years of service[17] and the transfer of the culture and tradition from the old prison was complete. The net cost estimates by the planning architects proved to have been incredibly understated. Compounding the cost problem was the fact that the old prison proved unsalable and the State did not sell the West Farm. In addition, laws preventing the sale of prison-made goods would eventually block anticipated prison industry revenues so the ideal of a "productive, profitable prison industries" was never realized.

---

[17] *Ibid.*

HARRY H. JACKSON
Photo courtesy of the Michigan Department of Corrections

Chapter Three
The Warden Jackson Era

IN JANUARY 1925, GOVERNOR GROESBECK REMOVED Warden Harry Hulbert for "cooking the prison industries' books" and replaced him with Harry Jackson, the governor's commissioner of public safety. Although Governor Groesbeck lost his reelection bid within months of this appointment, Warden Jackson would keep his post for nearly another 20 years before finally leaving under a cloud of scandal. Thus, the time referred to as "the Warden Jackson era" constituted almost a quarter of the prison's history.   Knowing nothing of the prison's culture, traditions, procedures or pitfalls—his background consisting of a brief stint as head of the State Department of Public Safety while on loan from the Traffic Division of Detroit Police Department[1]—Jackson's only recourse was to learn on the job. Hulbert, furious over his dismissal, was not helpful to Jackson's transition; in an investigation by the State Police, a letter dated February 16, 1927, alleged that Harry Hulbert had encouraged inmate construction workers to protest Deputy Warden McCoy's tough restrictions of their movement and activities by rioting, while no riot ensued, the report must have been unsettling to Warden Jackson.[2] So Harry Jackson was left to learn how to run a prison from his key staff: Deputy Warden Leonard McCoy, the tough disciplinarian; Prison Records Supervisor, D. C. Pettit who was also the inmate recreation and special events director and a slick operator by most accounts; and the prison chaplain, William Hopp, soon to be named as a principal in drug and parole selling.[3] Undoubtedly, the whisperings of key inmate staff, so called 'convict politicians,' and 'snitches' also contributed to the greening of the new Warden. Thus, Jackson was thrust into the Warden position in a massive replacement prison, which was still being constructed by prisoners being supervised by his unhappy predecessor. This gave him two partial prisons, (the old Jackson and the new) managed with staff of uncertain loyalty, more than half of whom were prisoners.

In addition, problems in general were mounting. The prison population would reach an all-time high within the year; Jackson city newspapers were blasting the previous administration with allegations of corruption, waste and wrongful deaths (which prompted a grand jury investigation) while prison industry was under attack from labor and business interests. Moreover, this era would be one of extraordinary

---

[1] Jackson Citizen Patriot 3-9-1925 Harry Jackson was on loan from the Detroit Police Department He was Inspector in Charge of Traffic. Groesbeck to appointed him Commissioner of Public Safety (became Michigan State Police later.) After accepting the position of Warden at SPSM, Detroit Police Department asked his long term intentions. Getting no answer, he was dropped from status in Detroit Police Department.

[2] Attorney General--Criminal Division Files, Special Investigations of SPSM, Box 1, File 1, Sgt. Loomis MSP letter 2-16-1927.

[3] Insight to Leonard McCoy's tenure was gained from his nephew, Lieutenant Lee McCoy in discussions with the author during the 1950s while both were employed at SPSM.

national crises: the stock market crash of 1929, the Great Depression, political upheaval and World War II—all of which had an impact on the prison operation.

In 1924, organized labor boycotted products made at the prison's Onondaga brick and tile factory—the first precursor of public resistance to using prison labor under Hulbert's new prison industries system. The state tore down the factory in 1929, though it had continued to make bricks for state use until then. This industry had been fueled by the abundance of high quality light blue clay on prison farmland—during the previous 65 years nearly one million cubic yards were mined for use by Bennett Sewer Pipe Company, Vitrified Products, and the prison itself, activities that would cease by the 1930s.[4] Governor Green sold the Chelsea Cement Plant in 1929 and closed the road camps. This eliminated more than 300 inmate jobs, but because there was full prison industries employment during the twenties, that loss could be absorbed. Nevertheless, the trend was ominous for the future of prison labor.

As Warden Jackson took office in 1925, there were already rumblings in Congress to curtail the sale of prison-made goods. The Prison Commission and local congressmen lobbied against the bill and sent Harry Hulbert, recognized as a national expert on prison industries, to testify before Congress in 1927, but to no avail. Thus, the federal Hawes-Cooper Act passed; allowing individual states to prohibit sales within their borders of any goods made by prisoners of another state; and in 1935, the Ashurst-Sumners Act made it a crime to transport prison-made goods interstate. Michigan followed these federal laws with the Munshaw-Frey Act of June 1935 that made it illegal to sell prison-made goods to the public within the state, thus making Michigan government, including the prison, the only customer for its products.

With the nation plunging into the Great Depression and its horrendous civilian unemployment, there was no sympathy for employing prisoners at the expense of honest citizens. The Prison Commission reacted by instructing Warden Jackson to reduce prison industries workers to a 40 hour workweek. Going even further in 1931, Governor Wilbur Brucker urged reduction in prison spending, cutting back in prison industries, and halting construction of the new prison.

---

[4] Evellyn Stringham, *Jackson Citizen Patriot* January 12, 1964.

The result of all this was that prison employment gradually had declined from providing work for every able bodied man under Harry Hulbert's industries enterprise in 1924, and the Munshaw-Frey Act of June 1935, immediately put many more prisoners out of work.[5] The result of all this was that an industries/work employment rate of 80% under Hulbert shrank to some 15% by the middle 1930s.

Warden Jackson had skillfully negotiated his course through the Republican Administrations of Governors Groesbeck, Green, and Brucker, but in 1932, the Democrats swept the land for the first time since Woodrow Wilson's presidency, and elected William Comstock governor.[6] The Democrats, lacking institutional experience in governmental transition, left Jackson's status in limbo for months. The first indication of change was Governor Comstock's May 1 appointment of Democrat activist Reverend Albert Ewert as Chaplain to replace Chaplain Richard McLain.[7]

Chaplain Ewert would prove to be a major influence with the new administration and presented quite a contrast to the scandalous Chaplain Hopp, or to Chaplain Larkey, who in 1932 served 10 months for embezzling money from Jackson prisoners. Ewert,[8] an ordained Episcopal Priest who first became interested in prison reform from Leavenworth's Warden Coggin in 1916, was a Democratic activist

---

[5] Captain Timothy Chapman discussing Munshaw-Frey impact in Marquette, "in 1936 on Friday we were making overalls for Sears and the next Monday nothing—and the inmates in the garment factory were out of work."

[6] Two years at the Prison and two on the Farm: Warden Bill Bannan, a great storyteller, during his administration in the 1950s, frequently told of working during the political patronage era of the 1930s as Democrats and Republicans switched control. It went something like this: "...we just expected to work two years at the prison if our party won or two years on the farm if it didn't.... the process was very simple, you come to work the day after the winner takes over and if there is a pink slip on your time card you're fired!--no questions, no conversation. Your chances depend on how many jobs the winner has to pay off."

[7] The *Detroit Free Press*, April 14, 1933.

[8] All information about Chaplain Ewert is from the Albert Merritt Ewert Collection in the Archives of Michigan.

advocating repeal of Prohibition and who was a passionate crusader for true indeterminate sentences, which take sentencing power away from judges. He viewed himself as fighting "the old concept of brutality," and became a friend of prisoners, his philosophy being, "After all, isn't it better to believe in man and sometimes be wrong, than never to believe at all?"[9] He would make an unsuccessful bid for Congress; serve on the committee establishing the Department of Corrections in 1937, and was appointed by Governor Murphy as Deputy Assistant Director of Probation in 1938. He later received a Civil Service promotion to Director of Probation, where he served until retirement in 1952.

Warden Peter Gray

On Saturday July 1, 1933, Governor Comstock's appointment of Peter Gray as Warden to replace Harry Jackson became official. Gray was a printer by trade and had served as city clerk, and for two years as mayor of Lansing, but had no criminal justice experience. The *New York Times,* in an article entitled "Michigan Prisons Pawns of Politics" (January 28, 1934), viewed the appointment with derision. On his first day, Warden Gray announced that the next Monday he would release all prisoners from segregation, leading 17 year veteran Deputy Warden McCoy to announce his retirement. Gray then designated recreation director Delisle (D. C.) Pettit as acting Deputy Warden, and shortly after that Assistant Deputy Warden M. S. Hatch resigned. Later Gray would have his first meeting with deposed Warden Jackson, who was very ill,—Jackson stayed in the Warden's residence until August 1, 1933. [10]

On Sunday, the day after his appointment, Chaplain Ewert introduced Peter Gray to 2,200 inmates gathered in the prison auditorium—the Warden would assume his new office during the following week and for the few intervening days designated Ewert as acting Warden.[11] In his address to the prisoners, Warden Gray assured

---

[9] Chaplain Ewert's Page, Radio Address, Sept. 24, 1933—Station CKLW, Detroit and Windsor

[10] *Jackson Times,* July 3, 1933.

[11] *Ibid.*

them that everyone would start with a clean slate with his Administration, therefore he would release the men in segregation on Monday, and he advised them that their recreation director D. C. Pettit would now be Deputy Warden, which brought "enthusiastic cheers and hats thrown in the air."[12]

While prisoners may have enthusiastically supported D. C. Pettit's ascension to Deputy Warden, it would create considerable controversy in other respects. Pettit's duties for nearly a decade under Warden Jackson had combined personnel functions, record office supervision, and service as director of recreation. In his personnel function, and as a staunch Republican, Pettit had forced employees to contribute to the campaign of Governor Brucker, Comstock's opponent. As record office supervisor, he processed new admissions and releases, so he knew many inmates personally and possessed a remarkable memory for names and prison numbers.[13] As director of recreation, Pettit was in daily contact with many inmates, including some prolonged trips away from the prison with entertainer groups such as the Harmony Kings and the 'Negro Dance Team' who performed as far away as Petoskey.[14] So now Pettit found himself in an enviable position in that he alone had great knowledge of the workings and history of the prison, while Warden Gray, Chaplain Ewert, and the soon to be hired Assistant Deputy Timothy Danaher (proprietor of the Stowell Hotel,) had no prior knowledge of Jackson prison whatsoever.

Complicating the management culture even further was the Warden's decision to use prisoners in sensitive staff positions. Most notable was the assignment of Chaplain Ewert's private secretary and right hand man, Henry Thorpe, to be the Warden's driver, spokesperson, and press secretary. Convict Thorpe was dressed in civilian business clothes and became the prison's contact with the outside world. Shortly thereafter, newspapers charged that inmates Cromer (Ewert's new clerk) and Thorpe had 'Czarist' powers and arranged firing of ten loyal Democrat guards. No one claimed to know the reason though Thorpe did the paperwork. It is unclear whether

---

[12] *Ibid.*

[13] This information was from Warden Kropp in conversations with Deputy Johnson in the 1960s.

[14] *Jackson Times*, July 3, 1933.

inmates were settling scores with disliked officers, or if they were under orders from Pettit. Tips began to come to the press. One was that Warden Jackson placed Thorpe in detention the previous October for returning from a driving trip to Detroit drunk with a bottle of whiskey in his pocket. The Jackson newspapers reported that Thorpe had served prison terms in Indiana State Prison, Huntsville, Texas, and Ellis Island, New York in addition to Jackson. Thorpe was called "the chief stool pigeon" and Pettit admitted to *Jackson Citizen Patriot* reporter Carl Muller that inmates Thorpe and Cromer were his leading contact men with the inmate body.[15] Pettit was very skillful in operating a cabal consisting of inmate politicians, informants, and petty grifters to provide intelligence about prison intrigue, to maintain order, and for profit. Warden Gray was undeterred by the publicity and both Thorpe and Cromer remained on assignment.

In August 1933, Warden Gray commented to the *Jackson Citizen Patriot*, "We Democrats may not be around for a long time but while we're here we will show 'em a thing." To make his point he said he had fired 73 prison employees.[16] In the fall of 1934, Gray stated that he and Pettit had been discussing the possibility of converting 1,200 Trusty Division inmates to staff type jobs because the state would not pay for civilians. Because of the transition under way in closing the Old Jackson prison and the wholesale move to the new one, it is difficult to analyze the actual seriousness of the staffing shortages at the time. However, the *New York Times* cited an Osborne Association finding, based on a January 1934 inspection that there was "...no significant improvement in discipline, punishments, medical service, education...that 40 percent of the inmates in Jackson...were idle."

In an effort to reduce inmate unemployment, Chaplain Ewert developed an Arts and Crafts program whereby inmate entrepreneurs could set up small, legitimate businesses known as concessions. The Arts and Crafts Program was not considered a violation of Munshaw-Frey the next year because of a loophole that did not prevent individual prisoners from selling goods on the open market. It was an immediate success. In September 1935, the *Detroit News*[17] carried the report of an

---

[15] *Jackson Citizen Patriot,* August 1933.

[16] *Ibid.*

[17] Bright, Andrienne, Knox, et.al, *op. cit.,* p37.

inmate earning $100 a month through sales of jewelry while hiring other inmates at 15 cents a day—in 1944 one inmate earned $5,141. That year over $100,000 in sales was reported from the 100 such concessions in operation and one concession had been sold for $500. Unfortunately, this created something of a public uproar, but it is unclear whether this was because something sinister was suspected, or just because convicts "should not have it so good." However, strict limits were imposed on earnings and on the number of inmates who could be hired. Eventually the department abolished the concession system substituting a new program called Hobby Craft. It is doubtful, however, that the Arts and Crafts Program ever employed more than two or three hundred prisoners, including extras hired by concessionaires.

During the 1930s, boxing champions held rock star status and the most popular of all was Jack Dempsey. His visit to Jackson Prison in 1934 was a major event. While there, he addressed an assembly of inmates in the theater/chapel and then refereed two prison boxing matches—two very good fight cards, according to the prison newspaper *Spectator:* Spencer v Mitchell and Lapacoloa v Curro.[18]

During July 1934, the last inmate transferred from old Jackson Prison to the new and the old prison closed. That provided the occasion for the commission to declare the new prison completed and abolished all jobs connected with its construction. The prison industries plants and facilities were finished; they were not used to capacity due to limited markets, but in 1934 did start to make a profit for the first time.

The first recorded escape from inside the new prison occurred on December 15, 1934 when two lifers scaled a cellblock wall.[19] Warden Gray blamed the escapes on a pre-election statement by Republican Frank Fitzgerald and Attorney General Harry Toy to the effect that they would "bear down" on paroles and only grant parole where there was error in the inmate's trial. Police captured the escapees without harm to the public and the prison staff installed iron spikes at roof edge to discourage future climbers.

---

[18]*The Spectator* July 30, 1965, 1-16, Vol. 35, Jackson, Michigan: State Prison of Southern Michigan.

[19] Durst, Don, *Jackson Citizen Patriot*, 1975.

In their final report in December 1934, the Prison Commission claimed the prison saved taxpayers $500,000 but we could find no fiscal analysis to confirm their claim. Since Governor Comstock was defeated in November by Frank Fitzgerald, Warden Gray's observation, that "we Democrats may not be around for a long time" proved prophetic.

On January 1, 1935, Governor Fitzgerald replaced Warden Gray with Charles Shean, a retired former Ionia Reformatory Warden, and one time Jackson Deputy Warden under Hulbert. Both Warden Shean and his successor retained Deputy Warden D.C. Pettit, a Republican appointed by Warden Gray. Warden Shean then recruited George (G.I.) Francis from his former Ionia staff to serve as Education Director at Jackson. Both Francis and Pettit would become contentious figures in subsequent years.

Education Director G.I. Francis' main responsibility was similar to that of a superintendent of a public school system except that he had few staff teachers, with most teaching provided by literate inmates who were given at least minimal training and structure. The program was called the "day school." The prison's first schoolteacher was hired in 1885 by reform Warden H.F. Hatch.[20] Initially, inmate schooling was restricted to night classes or cell study and correspondence courses— limitations that were imposed by the lack of classroom space and the full employment practices which forced prisoners to study on their own time so as to not interfere with the work day. This changed in the new prison with the provision of classroom space and the depletion of prison industries jobs. The "day school" introduced at the new prison in 1929 by Warden Jackson, had since expanded. Academic and vocational school programs would increase in size and quality over the next thirty years.

The new prison's first inmate insurrection came in December 1935. It was labeled by the local media as a "food riot" when about 800 prisoners protested against the serving of an offensive pea soup on several successive days. Guards soon quelled the disturbance and moved suspected ringleaders to solitary confinement so they could enjoy bread and water for a few days.

---

[20] Bacon, Ila J., *The State Prison of Southern Michigan 1837-- 1959*, Jackson: Unknown, April 21, 1959.

Harry Jackson returns—Dr. David Phillips

Nearly 15 months later, while attending a Rotary Club luncheon in Jackson, the 59-year-old Warden Shean suffered a fatal stroke.[21] Following Warden Shean's death Governor Fitzgerald picked former Warden Harry Jackson to replace him. Jackson filled out Fitzgerald's term and lasted six months into the term of Democratic Governor Murphy. During 1936, Warden Jackson established the prison's first guard training school; hired its first psychiatrist, Dr. David Phillips; restructured the prison classification system to include social and job history; and created a trial board for hearing inmate misconduct charges instead of leaving these for unilateral disposition by the Deputy Warden.[22]

Governor Fitzgerald endorsed the establishment of the guard training school as a move toward professionalizing the guard force by putting an emphasis on skill rather than politics. The idea would morph into a training academy at Jackson that served all institutions.

As the new psychiatrist, Dr. Phillips' job description would prove impossible to adequately carry out. He was first a member and then chairman of the prison classification committee, which had to review and classify fifty to seventy-five new commitments every week. He had to deal with periodic parole board requests for psychiatric evaluation of parole candidates and was required to handle referrals of mentally ill inmates. Consequently, staff criticized him from time to time because his evaluations tended to be superficial and repetitive.

To those of us who knew him, Dr. Phillips was a sometimes charming but always truly unforgettable character.[23] He was a sturdy, short man with a full mustache and an infectious smile working over a perpetual cud of tobacco, and he had a constant litany of stories, some off color but all funny. His creative disposal of the tobacco juice produced became legendary. Visitors to his office would have the

---

[21] *Portland Observer,* Obituary, March 26, 1936.

[22] Bright, Eaton, Andrienne, Knox, et.al., *op. cit.,* p103.

[23] Dr. Phillips was known by the author for many years including time in deer camp and these observations come largely from those memories.

experience of seeing him pull out the lower desk drawer, remove a Coke bottle, and expertly squirt a stream of tobacco juice into it through a gap in his front teeth. (I was impressed by this outstanding feat of marksmanship but the secretaries taking his dictation absolutely were not.)

The legend regarding this habit was firmly established some years before I knew him: This happened when the good doctor was accompanying three parole board members on the 400-mile car trip from Lansing to Marquette for hearings at the Branch Prison. It was an unseasonably hot day in June and, of course, cars then were not air conditioned, so the windows were down for ventilation. Dr. Phillips sat in the front passenger seat with the Parole Board Chairman, A. Ross Pascoe directly behind him. Pascoe was a tall stately man, always prim and proper, whose high starched collars and three-piece suits befitted his position and bore little resemblance to Dr. Phillips' rumpled attire. As the journey dragged on along old gravel highway 127 toward the ferries at the Straits of Mackinaw, Dr. Phillips unthinkingly squirted a liberal and toxic stream of tobacco juice out his side window – an emission that, when it hit the slipstream, immediately and entirely returned through the rear window onto Chairman Pascoe. No one ever explained how the good doctor managed to survive alive for the rest of the trip, but the others present entertained staff for years by recalling the event. Not, however, when Chairman Pascoe was present.

Following the 1937 reorganization act that formed the Department of Corrections, the department transferred Dr. Phillips to the Central Office. He and Chaplain Ewert were strong advocates of true indeterminate sentencing and traveled the state speaking on the subject. They argued that crime was similar to a mental illness; therefore, the criminal's sentence should be an indeterminate commitment for "treatment" and when finally "made well" in the judgment of therapist, the prisoner should be released to the community. Using this model, Michigan enacted the "Criminal Sexual Psychopathic Persons (CSP)" act in 1939 providing for sex offenders "commitment to the State Hospital Commission...until fully and permanently recovered from such psychopathy..." The law also granted the commission "...the right to release such person on parole... as his condition merits..." However, in the face of the courts questioning its legality, Michigan repealed the law in 1968. The

51

principle weakness of Michigan's CSP law was that it failed to provide treatment promised by the act, in effect warehousing offenders to serve a life in the state hospital without the due process rights of criminal laws.

The 1937 Corrections Act

Frank Murphy, a former Detroit mayor and governor of the Philippines, defeated Governor Fitzgerald in November 1936, continuing the alternating party control of the Governor's office every two years during the 1930s and early 1940s. Governor Murphy initiated two landmark legislative acts with significant implications for Jackson Prison. His hope was to remedy the chaos created by this perpetual patronage upheaval. The first was the 1937 Corrections Act that organized prisons, probation and parole within a single department headed by a director, and the second was the 1938 Civil Service Act aimed at substituting an employee merit system for the traditional spoils system.

The governor had appointed an old friend, Detroit Recorder's Court Clerk Hilmer Gellein, as Chairman of a study committee to develop the legislation for the Corrections Act. Membership of the committee included Chaplain Albert Ewert, Professor Arthur Wood (a Republican member of the Jackson Prison Commission,) Leslie Kefgen, and others. When the new Corrections Act took effect in July 1937—Gellein became Corrections Director and Ewert Assistant Director of Probation. Gellein fired Warden Harry Jackson, and Joel Moore became Jackson's replacement. Moore was a former professor and administrator with the Federal Bureau of Prisons.

JOEL R. MOORE
1937–39
Photo courtesy of the Michigan Department of Corrections

Warden Moore, whose federal experience had acquainted him only with well-structured prison management and adequate prison industries employment, found the endemic idleness at SPSM appalling, as well as its laissez faire approach to security. Inmates confined inside the walls could pass through any exit gate (front, railroad or vehicle) using only a "detail" signed by Deputy Pettit with an attached "mug shot" picture card. Those thus qualified included maintenance workers, locksmith mechanics, front house porters/counter men, and drivers on various errands downtown, including some that were unsupervised. The control of the flow of inmates from the Trusty Division passing freely in and out through the security gates on errands to the inside was even more casual. This made unrestricted introduction of contraband simple as well as the moving of ill-gotten gains from gambling and graft.

Curious citizens also had relatively free access to the prison and could even bring private cars through the gates, sometimes for illicit repairs. Warden Moore put an end to this practice for the duration of his tenure.

The federal prisons Moore came from had full inmate employment due to their sales monopoly with federal agencies, whereas in Michigan there were industry jobs for less than 10 percent of the prison population—a condition he was only able to improve by some five percent by the addition of a Salvage Department. He lamented, "More industrial labor is a crying need . . . and at least a third of institutional assignment could be shifted ..." if industries labor was available.[24]

Whereas Harry Jackson had added a psychiatrist, Dr. Phillips, to an all custody-staff classification committee, Warden Moore went much further and included a physician, the education director, vocational director, a social worker, and a chaplain to the committee, with Dr. Phillips serving as the Chairman. This may seem progressive, but with 50 to 75 inmates requiring classification every week, it was largely a waste of talent needed elsewhere.[25]

Warden Moore, who considered it "barbarous," eliminated 15 Block detention, known as the "bullpen," and substituted for it a form of indefinite segregation in Nine Block. Labels such as "000" and "blue hold card," which designated varying levels of restriction were used and inmates were classified according to the need to manage their behavior or for being protected from others. Subsequently, 15 Block would become the "shot block" for inmate big shots or, as they preferred, "the Aristocrats."

Near the end of Moore's tenure, on the day after Thanksgiving, November 25, 1938, two inmates used hacksaws to cut their way to

---

[24] Bright, Eaton, Andrienne, Knox, et al, *op. cit.* p40.

[25] As a counselor and member of the classification committee prior to the opening of the Reception Guidance Center the author speaks from personal experience.

freedom through a ventilator leading from a cell block to an outside wall and freedom.[26]

Unintended Consequences of the Civil Service Act

Governor Fitzgerald won the return election contest with Frank Murphy in 1938, so Warden Moore was out and Harry Jackson was back for the third time. Governor Fitzgerald died three months later and the Lt. Governor, 79-year-old Luren Dickinson succeeded him.

Governor Dickinson's administration would be notable for the enactment of the 1939 "ripper" amendment to the 1938 Civil Service Act. Under the Civil Service Act all prison employees were covered by its protection, but the ripper amendment removed most professional and supervisory positions from this coverage, thus making them "at will" appointments vulnerable to the old political spoils system. This, of course, applied to all of state government causing general outrage which prompted a citizen's initiative to amend Michigan's Constitution. This initiative passed in the 1940 election and a new Civil Service Commission was put in place the following January. Classification of employees began immediately—Harry Jackson was certified to his position as Warden, but when G.I. Francis became certified as Deputy Warden, this forced D.C. Pettit's demotion to assistant deputy.[27] This was a bitter pill for Pettit, a twenty-year veteran who had served as deputy Warden for the past six years. Adding insult to injury, he would have to surrender the deputy's residence for much less prestigious housing. It was a major annoyance to Warden Jackson as well, since he was helpless to prevent the demotion of his trusted deputy and protégé since 1925. He resolved this problem by ignoring Deputy Francis and continuing to rely on Pettit.

The Civil Service Commission's demotion of Pettit was unfathomable to many at the prison because he was popular with both staff and prisoners and was very knowledgeable about the whole prison operation and in fact, according to later Warden George Kropp, Pettit, not Harry Jackson, really ran the place.[28] The Treatment Director,

---

[26] Durst, *op. cit.,* 1975.

[27] Bright, Charles, *op. cit.*, p151.

[28] Comments from Warden Kropp to Johnson during his years as Adm. Asst. and Deputy Warden in the 1960s.

Vernon Fox, also commented on the matter, saying, "G.I. never spoke a civil word to me and D.C. never a harsh one. The inmates supported D.C. because he was humane and courteous to everybody while G.I. was caustic and personally ambitious." [29]

While Pettit had support of the staff and the Warden, G.I. Francis aligned himself with the Parole Board and the Lansing office.[30] This proved to be the beginning of a schism between the local administration and the Lansing office that would grow and fester for several years.

One Bad Sunday

November 5, 1939, began as a humdrum Sunday at the prison; a football game was in progress and the 2 p.m. shift change was underway when Warden Jackson, who was having a relaxing shave in the prison barbershop, glanced out the window to the north and saw the shadow of a man, an escapee, coming down Five Block's outside wall. He leaped from the chair, and with the barber apron around his neck and his face half lathered, ran into the main lobby full of families waiting to visit prisoners. As he reached the front door he turned back to get a gun from the front desk while Inspector Boucher rushed by, followed closely by Deputy Warden Carpenter.

Seeing two escapees on the ground next to Five Block, Inspector Boucher brandished his revolver and ordered them to put their hands up. Just then, three inmates in a car coming out of the parking lot roared up behind the inspector. As he swung his attention to them, a gun barrel poked out of the car's window firing a fatal round into Boucher's left side. The escapees fired a second shot at the prison lobby widows and two pellets struck visitor Dorothy Roberts in the face. No one else was harmed, but the lobby visitors all threw themselves to the floor.

In the meantime, Deputy Carpenter's inmate driver brought his car and they pursued the escapees north on Cooper Street in a high speed chase that ended in a crash after about three miles. Carpenter had shot out a rear tire on the fleeing vehicle, no mean feat with his

---

[29] Fox, Vernon, *Violence Behind Bars*, 1956, p152.

[30] Wood, Ike, *One Hundred Years at Hard Labor*, Au Train, MI: KA-ED Publishing Company, June 1985, p36.

wimpy 32-caliber revolver. The three escapees were unharmed and fled on foot. One was carrying a 12-gauge shotgun, more than a match for a small pistol, but Deputy Carpenter faced them down and they chose to surrender rather than commit another murder.[31] Officers captured the sixth and last escapee on the roof near the cornice, which he was using to anchor a rope intended for his descent.

The *Detroit News* reported that the six escapees were then beaten so badly that the press was not allowed to photograph them when they appeared at inquest the next day.[32] The six escapees were at large less than half an hour but the security weaknesses uncovered, and the psychological impact from having lost the first employee in Jackson's 100-year history, would leave a permanent imprint.

It was a well thought out escape plot and would provide an excellent example of how inmates can study a prison's practices and operations and find weaknesses. In this case, the route used by tower guards going from the inside rotunda to the roof and then up to One Post, the highest point in the prison, was the focus of the escapees' plan. They had observed that to get to One Post, officers came through security gates, used an elevator to go up four stories to office space above the rotunda/hall office, and then exited the office to cross the roof to the Post. They did so three shifts a day every day. (The One Post route was key to the escapees getting onto the roof because officers entered all the other gun-towers from outside the prison security perimeter.) Undoubtedly, by listening carefully, inmates had gotten a picture of how the double security doors leading from the upper office area out onto the roof worked.

Once on the roof, they needed a rope to descend 50 feet to freedom. Rope is in short supply within a prison for obvious reasons, but post officers used rope to reel up their meals from a Trusty Division food cart. When the prisoners gained control of the gun post, they would also have access to rope. Finally, they stole a getaway car from the parking lot right in front of the prison. By getting an upper gallery prison cell facing the parking lot inmates studied the parking lot traffic through a high outside window and identified the cars parked by One

---

[31] *Jackson Citizen Patriot,* November 6, 1939, p1, 2.

[32] Bright, *op. cit.,* p138.

Post Officers. They took one of them hostage, got his keys and then knowing exactly where his car was parked, were able to make a quick getaway.

They timed their plot to take effect during shift change on a Sunday, to give them the best chance for success. There were fewer guards on duty; recreational activities in the big yard would provide a distraction; there were few civilian staff or inmates to contend with; and, most critically, shift change was the only time that the officer on One Post came down to unlock the door to the roof. When the day came, the culprits first overpowered, tied, and gagged both Sociologist McLain working in the office space above the rotunda and the regular inmate elevator operator. Inmate Sawaya (who later confessed killing Boucher) took over the elevator just before the 2 p.m. shift change. When the 2 p.m. post relief officer, Glenn Ferrand, entered to go up for the shift change he noted the substitute elevator operator but suspected nothing amiss until he stepped out at the top where inmates armed with knives took him hostage. He was stripped of his uniform and the keys to the inside security door, then tied and gagged while inmate Lawman donned his uniform for the shift change about to take place.

Officer Russell Day, coming off duty and assured that the inside door was secured, unlocked the roof door. Inmate Lawman, in an ill-fitting officer's uniform, took him hostage. Now both officers were hostages, tied up, gagged, and locked into the vestibule between two locked security doors with no keys, and the six inmates were free on the roof with keys to Officer Day's car and the abandoned gun tower with its weapons and the all-important rope. They had brought along a bent piece of pipe to tie onto the rope as a grappling hook.

While the escape plot seemed to be going exactly according to plan, what the prisoners did not know was that Dr. McLain had managed to free himself and was calling Inspector Boucher to report the escape in progress. Immediately their scheme came unraveled, giving them only a few minutes of freedom at the cost of Inspector Boucher's life and new first-degree murder charges for each of them. From that day forward all employees and visitors entering the prison were required to leave their personal car keys with the security gate officers. The access to One Post was changed to eliminate the inside route from Six Block.

The Impact of World War II

Republican Harry Kelly defeated Democrat Murray Van Wagner for the governor's office in November 1941 and would go on to serve two terms (1942 through 1946). On December 7, 1941, Japan attacked Pearl Harbor, sweeping the United States into World War II and shifting the nation into fulltime war production and military mobilization. The war provided Jackson prison more opportunity for prisoner employment but presented a serious challenge in recruiting and retaining guards to staff the prison.

In 1942, the State Administrative Board gave the green light for sale of war materials requested by the federal government, and Michigan's Munshaw-Frey Act was amended accordingly.[33] Soon the moribund prison industries operation was going full throttle—growing prisoner employment from some 10% to nearly 90%. The textile mills began operating three shifts; the cannery expanded its line of canned goods; the garment factory produced underwear, socks, bedding and some uniforms; the metal plants produced brass casings for cannon shells, as well as fabricating some assault boats for the navy. The prison print shop printed coupon books for rationed goods under the authority of the Office of Price Administration. Inmates collected employee contributions for War Bonds, which they transferred to local Jackson city banks. According to the Sunday, August 29, 1943 issue of the prison newspaper, *The Spectator,* staff raised the first National Service flag (awarded to prisons for their achievement in war material production) in the chapel at SPSM. Undoubtedly, producing materials for the war effort and earning wages which were high by prison standards was good for inmate morale and helped keep peace during otherwise unsettled times.

Maintaining sufficient qualified custody staffing during the war years was most difficult. First, full mobilization of young men to the armed services drained the workforce available to everyone else; then better paying war production work tempted prison staff to leave entirely or to moonlight in these war production jobs, adding to their

---

[33] Correction Commission minutes November 10, 1942.

stress.[34] The consequences were dramatic—from 1937 to 1944 the guard force dwindled by 10% while the prison population increased by 25%. Warden Jackson complained bitterly that the "quality of new recruits was the poorest I have ever had."[35] Trying to maintain acceptable performance and conduct by culling the misfits amounted to having to replace poor with nothing—as personnel officer Lloyd Holtsberry often said, after interviewing new recruit applicants "sometimes it would be better to hang a uniform on my coat rack." However, the scandal we are about to recount—the worst of many in the prison's history, and one that would cost the Warden and his top staff their jobs, cannot be blamed on the guards or the lack thereof.

---

[34] During the author's years at SPSM (1955-1972) senior officers recounted their own experiences moonlighting and trying to stay awake on shift after working on war production in the City of Jackson. While moonlighting or working their farms, as well as working at the prison was, and still is fairly common, it was far more intense during the war years.

[35] Eaton, Andrienne, Knox, et al, *op cit,*, p48.

Chapter Four
The Tipping Point

"THE NUDE BODY OF PRETTY, RED-HAIRED LAURA FISCHER, an Austrian-born textile worker, was found on Christmas Eve of 1944 in a partially filled bathtub in a New Orleans hotel room."[1] She had been drugged and drowned. The room was registered to one D. J. Stafford. Two months later, police found the body of a second attractive red head, Blanche Zimmerman, age 38, under similar circumstances in a Chicago hotel bathtub. The room this time registered to J. H. Hanan of Dallas. Because the modus operandi and handwriting were similar in both cases, the police suspected a repeat killer, and the newspapers labeled the subsequent manhunt "the greatest since the days of John Dillinger."[2] Finally, Nancy Boyer, another pretty redhead, was shot to death after a party in Washington. Her escort was "J. H. Hannan of Dallas" but this ended the series, because the Washington D.C. police found that Stafford, aka Hannan/Hanan, was actually smooth talking Joseph D. Medley, a fugitive from Jackson Prison whose absence the prison authorities had neglected to promptly report.[3] Medley was arrested, convicted, sentenced to death, and executed in Washington D.C. Thus, he never returned to Michigan but his case triggered a massive investigation of Jackson Prison which would ultimately bring down the entire administration.

---

[1] "Medley Confession Sought in Three Slayings" *The Detroit Times*, March 21, 1945, C-17.

[2] *Ibid.*

[3] *Ibid.*

Originally, Medley was in Jackson serving a 20 to 60 year sentence for armed robbery, and in 1936, he was transferred to maximum security at the Marquette Branch Prison because of an escape conspiracy. Surprisingly, and for reasons we do not find in the record, he returned to Jackson only nine months later.[4] Even though he remained housed within the walls of the main prison, in a few years he became part of the inmate elite (called "convict-aristocrats" by fellow inmates) which status provided him with much freedom of movement inside and outside the walls. He was one of several prisoners to attend the wedding of Assistant Deputy Pettit's son in 1943 and an infamous photograph taken that day at the deputy's house shows him, along with several notorious gangster-convicts, sitting in Pettit's [dark] red Plymouth convertible.[5] Pettit periodically "detailed" Medley to work at his deputy's state residence where officers reported the inmate returning to the prison intoxicated but since he was considered untouchable, officers took no action fearing reprisals from Pettit. After his arrest in Washington DC, he would boast to Captain Mulbar: "I had the run of the place and could come and go about as I liked."[6]

Shortly prior to his escape, Pettit had placed him in charge of the prison's war bond program for both inmates and employees. He collected cash from employees and orders from inmates, and periodically visited the downtown Jackson war bond office.[7] Patriotic fervor was running high, even among inmates, at this late period in WW II--a fervor fired by reports of the Battle of the Bulge in the European Theater and of Japanese kamikaze attacks in the Pacific. The urgency of this war effort may well have precluded critical examination concerning the execution of prison bond drives, but in any case, the war bond program would become an instrument in Medley's escape.

The prison administration's initial investigation of Medley's escape was an obviously muddled cover-up in which an officer, Lt. Freeland, was made a scapegoat and fired but later returned to duty with two-weeks loss of pay. Frustration in Lansing with this mess, and

---

[4] Attorney General, *Investigation of Jackson Prison. 1945-47,* Box 11 8-13-1945 p3. Gilman and Sheridan,

[5] *Ibid.,* box 11, file 4 photos.

[6] *Jackson Citizen Patriot,* July 25, 1945.

[7] *Ibid.,* file 3, Freeland statement.

the mounting publicity nightmare led to the assignment of S. J. Gilman, the Corrections Department's Central Office special investigator, and Det. Lieutenant Joseph Sheridan, of the Michigan State Police, to conduct an investigation. The break in that investigation came from an anonymous tip saying that they should go see Lieutenant Howard Freeland to get the real story of the escape. That tip put them on the path to the following information.[8]

The day of Medley's escape was Monday, November 27, 1944. At six o'clock that morning, Lieutenant Freeland, following Assistant Deputy Warden Pettit's order, transported Medley from the prison to Jackson city, some three miles distant, ostensibly to pick up advertising literature for the prison war bond drive, with a detour to Freeland's home so that he could change out of his uniform. They then went to the home of Joseph Poirier, the inmate fund accountant. While there, Poirier furnished Medley with a suit of civilian clothes belonging to a former inmate, Ray Fox, who had been Pettit's clerk until his release the week before. On the way out the door, Freeland overheard Poirier's wife prophetically comment, "Joe, you have got to stop monkeying with these inmates or you are going to get in trouble."

After getting breakfast in town, Freeland dropped Medley in front of the War Bond Office in Jackson, just before its 9 a.m. opening. Being a night shift officer, Freeland then went home to get some sleep. This left Medley on his own until he was to be picked up that evening. But Medley failed to show at the appointed time and place, so Freeland went to Poirier's house hoping to find him there. No luck. Lt. Freeland then went on to work his shift and a now panicked Poirier began searching Jackson's bars and brothels for Medley. Finding nothing, he gathered up Freeland and both went to Pettit's home to report the escape. Pettit then joined Poirier and they went back again to check the city's dens of iniquity and found no trace of Medley. It was now clear that they must report Medley's escape to Warden Jackson. At this point, Pettit and Poirier warned Freeland not to mention the civilian clothing furnished to Medley. Thus, the cover-up began.

It was now well past midnight and still no trace of Medley. Finally, it occurred to the three that perhaps they should check the war bond money back at the prison. Unfortunately, the only person

---

[8] *Ibid.*

knowledgeable enough to audit that fund was its founder, Inmate Howard Prine, a 4th offender lifer then working at the East Lansing State Police Post—so in the early morning Poirier got him on the phone and pleaded for help which Prine readily agreed to provide. Poirier and Pettit jumped into a state car, rushed to East Lansing, and had Prine on the job before 8 a.m. Here is inmate Prine's account of what he found:[9]

> When I arrived at the prison that day (28th) after Medley's escape I found the little cash box that we used to keep in the booth tightly locked with a padlock--I twisted it off and opened it up. I audited the orders and found eight persons who had paid Medley money for war bonds between the last Friday of November and the following Monday. The prison had closed all business functions for Thanksgiving Holiday, so Medley took advantage of this situation (that no one would discover the theft until after his escape.) There were $850 he accepted and $49.50 in war savings stamps missing.

According to Lt. Freeland, inmate rumors had it that Medley lost and then won hundreds of dollars shooting craps over that Thanksgiving weekend. Nevertheless, it is obvious that he had carefully planned the escape and that gambling had nothing to do with it. After all, Medley could afford to be a reckless gambler that weekend knowing that if he won he had cash to take along on his Monday escape and any loss would merely leave uncollectable "chits."

Investigators Gilman and Sheridan, knowing they were working on a hot political case, had kept Corrections Commissioner Haynes and State Police Commissioner Olander informed. With this break in the case, Commissioner Olander notified Attorney General John Dethmers, in accordance with his instruction whenever State Police investigations led to another state agency. Dethmers immediately took over, ordered the Department of Corrections to cease investigating, and stipulated that his office would handle it with the assistance of the Michigan State

---

[9] Attorney General, *Investigation of Jackson Prison*, 1945-47, box 2, file four, 36-70, statement by Inmate Howard Prine.

Police.[10] He did specify, however, that S. J. Gilman would continue on the case but must be relieved of all Corrections duties until the investigation's completion. From that point, it officially became the *Investigation Regarding the Administration of the State Prison of Southern Michigan.* Testimony would be sworn providing the possibility of perjury charges for false statements; confidentiality would be promised, but employees' names would be on file with Civil Service should there be subsequent claims of harassment or reprisal by the prison administration for any perceived employee cooperation. A court stenographer would record and transcribe all hearings.

Assistant Attorney General Harry W. Jackson would represent Attorney General Dethmers and swear in all witnesses. Captain Harold Mulbar, commander of the State Police Bureau of Criminal Investigation; S.J. Gilman, Special Investigator, Department of Corrections; Detective Lieutenant Joseph M. Sheridan, of the MSP; and occasionally James Valentine, Detective MSP, made up the investigating task force. [11]

The investigators took some testimony in Sault St. Marie, Marquette, Detroit, and Lansing, but most statements were taken at the Jackson State Police Post. However, the proximity of that Post to the prison had the unfortunate consequence that both employees and trusty inmates could observe witnesses coming and going, thus providing fodder for the prison 'grapevine'—a rumor mill already abuzz with mysterious suggestions that the January murder of Senator Hooper was somehow connected to Jackson Prison. Captain Mulbar inadvertently added a bit of intrigue in a March 29, 1945 exchange with a hostile witness, Charles Watson, during which he exclaimed:[12] "We have been instructed by the court--by Judge Leland Carr, by Mr. Kim Sigler, the Special Prosecutor, that we are not to discuss any part of this case (Hooper Grand Jury) without their approval, and violation of that

---

[10] Gilman and Sheridan, *op. cit.* 2-4.

[11] *Attorney General, Investigation of Jackson Prison, 1945-47,* March 20, 1945, box 1, file 1, The hearing's purpose, members present, and protection of the witness restated in each witness testimony document.

[12] *Ibid.,* file 2, 46.

would hold me in contempt of court." (The Senator Hooper murder case is discussed more fully in Chapter 5 that follows.)

Sigler was hoping to ride the 'Hooper murder case' straight to the Governor's Office in the fall election by making himself the white knight cleaning up crime and political corruption.[13] However, Dethmers, also a gubernatorial hopeful, was not going to squander the political advantage he himself might gain from cleaning up the Jackson prison mess. Pressure was on the investigation task force to begin work immediately, since both parties wanted their stories out in August before the fall elections. The first interview was in the morning of March 20, 1945—and interviews continued for nearly three months during which there were interrogations of more than 100 inmates, some recent parolees, a few citizens, and several dozen employees.

As witnesses testified, rumors, leaks, and publicity fueled the urgency for completing the investigation and resolving the prison's mess. In June, a dramatic escape of SPSM inmates further damaged the prison's image: two inmates, one serving life and the other 50 years for assault, managed to construct compartments for their concealment in containers used to ship war production shell casings to a Grand Rapids factory. Somewhere between Jackson and Grand Rapids, they cut their way out of the truck and made good their escape. June 14, 1945 the *Grand Rapids Press* commented:

> . . . the fact that both have been caught will not lessen public curiosity as to how these two men could have enjoyed freedom of movement necessary to accomplish such an elaborate escape . . . (further) that the report of the current inquiry into alleged maladministration (at SPSM) will be scanned with interest for any disclosures it may make . . .[14] The newspaper went on to tie this escape to the Medley case, . . .the kind of custodial leniency that made his (Medley) escape possible was said to be a too common practice at the prison . .

---

[13] Bright, *op. cit.*, p186.

[14] "Packing Box Incident" *Grand Rapids Press*, June 14, 1945.

Five days later, after the *Grand Rapids Press* report, Dethmers requested a briefing memo updating the investigation.[15] He then made four major press releases during the following weeks. The attorney general's charges in these releases came under five broad categories: lack of control and wild parties; contraband cash and casino culture; privileged inmate aristocrats; sex; and catering to the old Purple Gang.

Lack of Control and Wild Parties

There were plentiful accounts of inmates going downtown to shop, visit brothels, visit certain employees for a few drinks or dinner, or attending wild parties with prison brass and then staggering back to the prison, obviously intoxicated. So Medley's having been dropped unsupervised on the city streets of Jackson, while shocking to the security minded, was not that unusual and it was not surprising that he, like some others, didn't come back.

Inmate Manuel Dennis explained how it worked for him:

> I talked Bobby Parker (employee in Poirier's office) into taking me downtown, then I made out a detail and had D. C. (Pettit) sign it. Went with Parker to the Regent Café for lunch, had a couple of beers, went to a store and bought a pair of shoes, and then had Parker drop me off at 631 E. Michigan (brothel). I learned about the "houses" from other inmates in 16 Block who had employees take them down. Riley, (recreation director), Poirier (inmate accounting), and Officer Fuller were employees who would take you down. We got dressed out in civilian clothes so we wouldn't be recognized as inmates. I didn't give Parker anything but generally officers don't expect to

---

[15] Attorney General, *Investigation of Jackson Prison*, 1945-47, *op. cit.* Box 1, file 11, Harry W. Jackson memo June 19, 1945.

do it for nothing. This was my third trip—about once a month.[16]

Inmate Harold Brosamer's venture did not go so well—Jackson City police arrested him on the street and convicted him of prison escape, which he explains this way:[17]

"I was a full trusty on the West Farm and I and other inmates frequently had verbal permission from the night officer to go visit houses of prostitution. The only stipulation was to return to the farm before the 4:00 a.m. count when the new officer came on duty. Some other guys without this privilege ratted on me."

The night officer admitted to Deputy Francis that he gave the inmate verbal permission, but thought he did no wrong.

Inmate Arthur Little recounted a livelier tale, which is pieced together here from his voluminous testimony after he was transferred to Marquette:[18]

> I slept at the farm when I worked as a houseboy at
> D.C. Pettit's but at that time, Mike Selik (Purple
> Gangster) slept in a basement room and his girlfriend,
> Naomi, stayed there as kind of a guest of Mrs. Pettit.
> Mike often served as bartender at drinking parties
> and I remember going with them on a party leaving
> Saturday afternoon and returning Sunday night—
> Mike and Naomi, Pettit's driver Johnson and people
> from Detroit were in the party. I managed to get
> quite drunk. Early on I found $200 Mike had stashed
> at the house which gave me a little capital to work
> with. I made at least 15 trips into town; once I just
> called a cab from the little store near Pettit's house;
> sometimes I called a friend from Jackson to pick me
> up; once I borrowed Carl Dexter's car and I generally

---

[16] Attorney General, Investigation of Jackson Prison, 1945-47, *op. cit.*, file 1, 6-24.

[17] Bright, *op. cit.* 343-350.

[18] Attorney General, Investigation of Jackson Prison, 1945-47, *op. cit.*, file 11, unnumbered notes by witness name.

would be gone from 9 p.m. to 4 a.m. I just went drinking and visiting houses of prostitution.

Another weak link in the prison's security came from the proliferation of inmate drivers who, though sometimes supervised, often were not. Here is inmate Henry's account of one incident in which he and inmate Martin attended a Detroit Tigers ballgame:[19]

> Q. How would you get the state car to go to the ball game?
> A. We got permission from Pettit—told him we were going fishing—he would call a car up for us. We would go pick up Pete Emerson (employee) and go to the ball game—Emerson would stop at a restaurant and get something to drink but he never went to O'Larry's Bar (Purple Gang owned). We happened to meet Mike Selik (Pettit's former houseboy now out of prison) and then went to O'Larry's bar where Mike loaded our car from the back door. At least three cases of whiskey and fancy foods (probably kosher food of which the Purples were fond). They sealed everything at Mike's (O'Larry's). The car was completely loaded—including the back seat. We took the back road back. It was after dark (11 p.m.) and I helped unload it to Pettit's basement—six or eight boxes. He had a bar in the basement.

Accounts from inmate Purple Gang members, such as Ray Bernstein and the two Keywell brothers, would have been at least as entertaining but they chose to make identical statements, in essence taking the "fifth" as the Purples were wont to do over the years.[20] They would admit to nothing except to receiving special food from O'Larry's Bar; they denied whiskey trafficking. The task force reported that all three, "were detoured to D. C. Pettit's office and advised by Pettit that they didn't have to appear at the investigation." Though self-serving,

---

[19] *Ibid.*, note by witness name.
[20] *Ibid.*

Pettit's advice was technically correct in that they were not compelled to appear by subpoena, so the investigators could not bring charges for obstructing justice.

D. C. Pettit's drinking escapades, the parties he threw at his state residence, and his favoring of privileged inmates were legendary and testified about to the task force by both inmates and staff. Robert Burdette, Pettit's closest neighbor, told of loud drinking parties on Pettit's porch only a few hundred feet from Burdette's house. The Hillbillies, an inmate quartet detailed from the Peak Farm, provided music for these parties until the wee hours. Burdette said his family did not socialize at Pettit's because theirs was a different lifestyle.[21] This would be but salacious gossip except for the corrupting entanglement of free-world hoodlums donating booze so long as their convict buddies got to share in the fun.

Pettit appeared to head a clique of other hard drinkers: Joseph Poirier (inmate accounting), Inspector Walter Wilson and Recreation Director Richard Riley—all Warden Jackson loyalists—were seen on the job under the influence from time to time. Moreover, the Warden himself was not exempt from implication in this corruption. Alfred Kurner, an inmate 'aristocrat' assigned to Cassidy Lake who had subsequently escaped, testified that he made three trips to SPSM delivering whiskey which he obtained from O'Larry's and on the last trip delivered 25 cases right to Warden Jackson at the Warden's residence. He said, "The Warden came out with a great big dog when I pulled in with the panel truck."[22]

Further evidence was gathered from civilians such as Betty Furstenberg, a bartender and waitress at O'Larry's from June 1944 until March 1945. She identified various inmates from mug shots and personal knowledge. She identified Pettit's drivers, Johnson and Henry, as inmates picking up packages, and she personally packed boxes of special foods for "big shot hoodlums" at the prison. She testified to seeing the Keywell brothers, Ray Bernstein, and Mike Biagini, all inmate Purple gangsters who should have been locked up instead drinking in the bar 75 miles from the prison. She also saw

---

[21] Attorney General Investigation of Jackson Prison, 1945-47, file 1, 89-99.
[22] Ibid.

Warden Jackson and Assistant Deputy Pettit drinking there and observed Mike Selik giving bottles of liquor to Riley (the recreation director).[23] Chief Engineer Loran Johnson reported the massive accumulation of liquor bottles from the prison's sewers accumulating at the disposal plant. This was circumstantial evidence in that these bottles could only have come from the cell blocks and/or the state residences of the Warden and Deputy Warden. (Pettit's residence was not connected to the sewer system.)

Contraband Cash and Casino Culture

While free whiskey might seduce the hard drinkers among the prison staff, cash money would prove to be an even stronger corrupting force. It facilitated many inmate escapades and provided fuel for gambling and bribery. In recognition of this risk, prison rules were straightforward: cash money was contraband; prison scrip (a coupon type book issued to the inmate by serial number) was the only legal tender; and the Inmate Accounting Office must control any money from home or the prisoner's job. However the investigators soon learned that a flourishing inmate cash economy existed inside the walls of Jackson. Rules were not enforced because the enforcers also stood to benefit from this illicit economy.

Al Fingle, institutional parole officer, wrote in a March 23, 1945 letter:

> Henry, the inmate porter for the Warden's Office, on different occasions attended baseball games in Detroit . . . I have seen Henry carry as much at $40 to $50 in his billfold prior to attending . . . In case you wonder why I didn't do anything about it . . . I knew it was useless to enforce rules that should apply . . . Many an officer had to close his eyes when he saw certain privileged inmates violate prison rules. It was not uncommon for an officer . . . to be transferred to other duties in the prison if he attempted to discipline

---

[23] *Ibid.*

inmates who carried more influence with the officials than did the officer.[24]

In describing how gambling concessions worked, inmate Walter Knowles acknowledged:[25]

> I had (poker) concessions for the whole yard and blocks except 11 Block—that was Ray Fox's (Pettit's chief clerk.) I had four poker games running constantly and had my own dealers. Of course I would have to pay Mr. Pettit, but what I consider small amounts—$15, $20, to $25 per week—not much but constant income." (Guard pay at the time was only eight dollars a day.)

Officers and inmates alike claimed gambling was especially open on holidays—in addition to poker tables, craps and bookmaking were popular. Just as in casinos, the operators took the "house cut." Inmate Crane testified that he had seen as much as $3,000 in the hands of a few inmates and "as much at $200 being faded in a dice game." Bookmaking on horseracing and sports events was modeled after that of organized crime in the streets of Detroit.

Inmate Charles Weaver specialized in loan sharking and expected about a 20% return on his money. He said he bought the "details" necessary to operate through the Hall Office for a couple of bucks. Inmates also had money from relatives or friends brought into the prison by accommodating officers—for a delivery fee of about 20%. It was also alleged that prison misconduct records were expunged for a fee, much to the aggravation of the Parole Board, which placed emphasis on a prisoner's conduct during his sentence. Special details for privileges in the gymnasium or auditorium were a bit pricier— Inmate Timothy Baxter claimed he paid from $5 to $25 to Bob Hart, director of entertainment, for those. Inmate Eugene Powley was one of

---

[24] Attorney General Investigation of Jackson Prison, 1945-47, Fingle letter to A. Ross Pascoe, March 23, 1945.

[25] *Ibid.*, File 9, 70.

several to explain how Big Moe, a hall office clerk, sold favorable cell assignments for three dollars.[26]

Work assignments, moves to the Trusty Division, and transfers to Marquette could cost much more and were handled through D.C. Pettit's office. Inmate Reginald Crane claimed to have paid money to Pettit six times; sometimes to buy cells and on one occasion he had to borrow $5 from the chaplain to put together $20 to buy a trusty assignment for a friend.[27] Crane explained that he could bypass the prison's classification committee because Pettit's office controlled transfers and assignments. Indeed, at the time of the investigation, nearly half of the inmates in the Trusty Division were there without the knowledge of classification. Lt. Leonard McCoy stated, "Pettit picks men for the Trusty Division—some are long termers and lifers."[28] Apparently, the interests of money trumped the interests of proper classification.

In response to an early warning that the investigators were beginning to focus in on Jackson's underground cash system, the prison issued a notice to inmates that after May 1, 1945, all cash money would be confiscated if found.[29] This created a brief amnesty period during which inmates turned in some $4,000—the balance, of course, remaining underground. At Marquette, a short time later, Lt. Charles Aho reported finding $694 in the property of Ted Bentz as he came off the transfer bus from Jackson.[30] We do not know the actual volume of cash inside the walls, but it is clear that privilege and circumstance were for sale during this era, and cash was king. The majority of inmates were denied this bonanza or were victims of it. Nevertheless, those who were benefactors of the cash and casino culture comprised a rather large and influential group.

Privileged Inmate Aristocrats

Inmates acquired "aristocrat" status in several ways, but primarily through prison assignments that offered access to inside information

---

[26] *Ibid.* File 9, 25-82.

[27] *Ibid.* File 1, cards by name.

[28] *Ibid.* File 2, 10-21.

[29] *Ibid.* B 11, File 3.

[30] *Ibid.*

and the opportunity to grant favors. Others gained that status simply by collaborating with corrupt staff. These privileged elite shared in any ill-gotten gains and in a pinch could achieve their ends by resorting to bribery, the threat of blackmail, and intimidation—all facilitated by their insider status. Many were skilled double agents, serving as snitches for the prison staff and as spies for prisoners. Guards felt helpless to enforce rules because of the powerful symbiotic connection between "inmate aristocrats" and the prison administration.[31] The task force found that conditions at Jackson amounted to "the inmates running the asylum."

Big Moe, whose real name was Jurcyzyn, worked directly under the Hallmaster as the "move clerk" in the prison's Main Hall Office. He was a facilitator for cell assignments and transfers. Standing a massive six foot three inches and dressed in crisply pressed whites, as all hall office inmate staff were, he practically oozed importance. He was the logistician for the prison population, matching inmates with empty cells, and preparing "move slips" and transfer lists perfunctorily authorized by the duty Captain, Inspector Wilson, or Assistant Deputy Pettit. This documentation was essential for keeping track of the whereabouts of each of the prison's 5,000 plus inmates. It was also the basis for posting their cell location on the Master Count Board, a system of accounting for a virtual cascade of humanity. This included new commitments coming in and transfers going out by the hundreds each week as well as all the in-prison moves dictated by changing work assignments, or by inmate requests (often to avoid enemies or seek lovers), and moves arising from an upgrading of privilege or demotion for misconduct. Thus, Big Moe's job required mastery of suffocating detail, which his superiors had neither the inclination nor time to accomplish. So he was granted wide latitude so long as the job was done—latitude which included a pass to go anywhere anytime throughout the prison. Both inmates and officers identified Big Moe as the one to see in order to pay two or three dollars for a desired cell. Moe even went into quarantine to snare the new commitments, so a few went directly from quarantine to the honor block.

Officer Newton Shafer testified[32] that:

---

[31] *Ibid.* File 11, Harry W. Jackson memo June 19, 1945.

[32] *Ibid.* File 17, Shafer statement.

(Big) Moe is a convict politician who gets better clothes, more privileges and has a 'big shot' complex. Want a cell change? See Moe and he will do it for a couple of dollars. When I was first back from the army, I attempted to put Big Moe, the hall office clerk, in the hole for insubordination but he did not go. I went to the warden and he still did not go so I went back to the warden and he called Inspector Wilson. Wilson fronted for (defended) him. Warden Jackson said he should do his five days—but he never went.

Such conspicuous immunity from discipline only served to cement Big Moe's status as an "aristocrat" in the minds of both staff and prisoners. Nevertheless, Raymond Fox, long time chief clerk in D.C. Pettit's office, undoubtedly became the most powerful inmate politician of the era. He was serving a life sentence for armed robbery imposed by Judge Skillman in 1928; a sentence the Judge would reduce in 1944 after a running snit with the Parole Board for not paroling him under provisions of Michigan's ten-year lifer law.[33] Inmate Fox was released November 21, 1944, just six days before Medley's escape. He served D.C. Pettit for years as office manager, a go-between for bribe payments, as an aide-de-camp, and as an enforcer for years, but he also found time to free-lance on his own and manage a gambling concession in 11 Block. The office, located between the hall office and a security gate to the yard, was a supermarket for the privileges most cherished by prisoners—privileges such as being out-of-cell after hours, receiving special meals, playing sports, getting gym time and even going downtown as Medley did, which required a "detail" signed by Pettit. All key jobs in the prison and transfers to another prison, to the Trusty Division or to one of the farms, required Pettit's approval. In addition, both Medley and Fox were conduits for the elaborate spy system Pettit employed for control.[34] Since no illicit activities of any significance

---

[33] Attorney General, *Investigation of Jackson Prison, 1945-47*: Box 1, File 1, 22-24, Pascoe statement.

[34] *Ibid.* Pascoe testimony, file 1, p399.

could go on without Pettit's knowledge and concurrence, the gambling concessions and rackets were subject to being "busted" and put out of business by competitors who maintained his favor.

Fox's handiwork appeared repeatedly in snippets of testimony among the hundreds of documents. He was clearly the "boss convict" backed by his muscle and the authority of Pettit's office. Howard Prine, war bond organizer and former clerk in Pettit's office testified: "I divorced myself from Deputy Pettit's office because Ray Fox was so dictatorial and abusive." When inmate Donald Cahill, wedding photographer, had the audacity to take the infamous photo of Fox and ten fellow hoodlums in Pettit's red convertible at the marriage of Pettit's son, Fox ordered all copies destroyed. Realizing their political value, Cahill smuggled some out but did not challenge Fox's order directly.[35] Later, as Medley and Fox returned to the prison from the wedding a bit under the influence, Fox chastised Medley for "fooling with some woman at the Pettit wedding." This later led to some fisticuffs (officers noted that Medley sported a classic shiner for some time afterward.)[36]

Fox was even more devious in other dealings. Psychologist Vernon Fox recounts how he tried to help his clerk avoid the tariff for a cell change but, while he was never told "no," his requests were "misplaced, misfiled or simply lost" until the tariff was paid.[37]

Inmate John Hamilton reported this experience from a job interview:

> Foreman Cline wanted me for his clerk and wrote a letter requesting me—in the meantime a fellow working for (Ray) Fox forged Cline's signature and recommended another clerk—so Fox kept the letter recommending me and the other guy got the job. Cline told me 'I don't know what happened.' I went to work as an electrician.[38]

---

[35] *Ibid.* File 11.

[36] *Ibid.* File 1, Dennis statement.

[37] Fox, Vernon, *Violence Behind Bars*, 1956, p76.

[38] John Hamilton, Attorney General, Investigation of Jackson Prison, 1945-47, 8-13-1945, File 2, 127

Whatever profit sharing arrangement existed between Pettit and Fox will forever remain secret since only they knew about it and they were not talking, but the cash flow must have been considerable. All understood that Raymond Fox was not to be taken lightly by either inmates or staff.

Another of the privileged elite, through having influence within the Purple Gang, was Mike Selik. Selik, who was dapper, cocky, and small in stature, and who had an eye for the ladies, one day spotted an attractive young woman waiting in the prison lobby to visit her husband. It was a simple matter to learn that her name was Naomi and her husband was inmate Rupport. As the Warden's houseboy, Mike had the run of the prison and considerable free time so somehow he charmed Naomi—but how to consummate that passion? Well, the Warden's office was handy and when not in use he, his fellow Purple Gang inmates, and their free-world cronies, had met there from time to time for the simple fee of $50.[39] Therefore, that took care of that. For a time Naomi and Selik trysted in either the Warden's or Deputy's office after she visited her husband. Seeking an even more accommodating arrangement, Selik obtained assignment as Pettit's houseboy, bartender, and whatever else, and Naomi moved right in as Mrs. Pettit's guest.[40] She may even have divorced her husband and married Selik but that remains unknown since neither party put much stock in legal niceties. They separated years later. Selik disappeared after completing his parole in 1969 and Naomi returned to her parent's home in Kansas.[41] This episode probably brought the position of "special privileged inmate" to a level never before or since surpassed.

These are but three examples. There were hundreds more inmates in key positions whose power arose from their roles in accessing prison files and records; or working as clerk-typists processing the paperwork that drove the bureaucracy; or in providing medical care. Others "on the in" were skilled tradesmen and straw bosses, and servants/drivers

---

[39] *Detroit Free Press*, July 24-25, 1945.

[40] Attorney General--Criminal Division Files, *Special Investigations of SPSM*, Box 1, File 1, page 28, Guard Robert Renkert.

[41] Ziewacz, Lawrence E. and Bruce A. Rubenstein, *Three Bullets Sealed His Lips*, East Lansing, Michigan: Michigan State University Press, 1987, 206.

for the Warden and Deputy Warden. All of these were granted special dispensations or privileges and had the means to help or harm prisoners of lesser status—the laborers and factory workers. They comprised a shadow prison staff more numerous than the salaried personnel.

The task force reported that, as a result:

> . . . practically anything which may occur in the front office passes through the prison grapevine . . . it is known to all inmates . . . that these positions assert strong influence on prison affairs and have asserted direct influence on the (prison) administration . . . It is the opinion of many guards that it is almost useless to try to enforce discipline because of the connections . . .between certain inmates and the leading officials of the prison [42]

This reliance on inmate staffing dated from Warden Hulbert's time, and was to a lesser degree present before that, but Warden Grey's massive depression-era cuts in salaried personnel that continued during World War II aggravated the problem. But, the most egregious corruption between staff and inmate aristocrats almost certainly occurred during D.C. Pettit's 11-year reign as de-facto Deputy Warden with the support of Warden Jackson.

On July 24, 1945 the *Jackson Citizen Patriot* headlines blared, "Dethmers says Inmate Ring Rules the Prison", and the article included a litany of tittilating accounts of sexual escapades gleaned from the task force report which Dethmers sent to Governor Kelly, the Corrections Commission, and the press.[43]

The report charged that privileged inmates attended "bawdy houses" in Jackson while others faked illness to arrange for wives or girl friends to meet for sex in the prison hospital, and claimed that rampant sexual perversion went undeterred within the walls.[44]

---

[42] Attorney General, Investigation of Jackson Prison, 1945-47, Box 11, file 3, Harry W. Jackson 6-19-1945,

[43] Guy Jenkins, *Jackson Citizen Patriot*, July 24, 1945.

[44] Jackson, Harry W. Attorney General, *Investigation of Jackson Prison*, 1945-47, Box 11, File 3, 6-19-1945.

Furthermore, officials allowed Purple Gangsters from Detroit—for a price—to meet and carry on gang business with their imprisoned leaders in the private offices of prison officials. Dethmers' report said "the worst instance of this appears to have occurred shortly before the Hooper murder, and some of the parties now under arrest in connection with the Hooper case are involved.[45]

Even Marquette County Prosecutor John Volker, later to achieve fame as author of *Anatomy of a Murder*, piled on. According to Volker, the County Social Welfare Department paid for one Riza Burns' "still birth" and reported that she said she *"got pregnant from her inmate husband at the Jackson Prison hospital. The Welfare Department wonders how,"* Volker remarked, and added, *"I cannot help but share their wonder."[46]*

Cleaning House

On July 25, 1945, the Corrections Commission had heard enough and dismissed the Warden, Deputy Warden, Assistant Deputy Warden, Inspector, director of records and classification, supervisor of inmate accounts, and the director of athletics, all to be effective on August 17, 1945. Their immediate replacements were the Warden from Marquette, the Jackson State Police Post Commander and the superintendent of the Cassidy Lake correctional facility. Warden Jackson immediately disavowed any knowledge of the things charged in Dethmers' report, including an inmates' picnic at a Lake cottage with Pettit, or of the Purple Gang's visiting in prison offices. The remaining fired staff demanded hearings without result. In addition, twelve of the most notorious inmate "aristocrats" were shipped 400 miles north to Marquette. Losing their privileged status must truly have been a culture shock. At least one, Big Moe Jurcyzyn, petitioned the Michigan Supreme Court, alleging Marquette was too tough with too much discipline, which amounted to constitutionally prohibited "cruel and unusual punishment."[47] The Court was unimpressed. Therefore, in just six short months, Medley's murder spree brought the prison

---

[45] Jackson, *op. cit..* Box 11, file 3.
[46] Volkers, John, *Ibid.* Box 1, File 11, 4-29-45.
[47] *Jackson Citizen Patriot*, August 21, 11942, p2.

administration and the inmate aristocracy crashing down together. The Warden Jackson era was finally over.

Chapter Five
The Purples

MOBSTERS HAVE LONG HELD A MACABRE ATTRACTION for the public despite their brutality and the corrupting influence of their money and power. How else can one explain the overwhelming popularity of the *Godfather* movie series or why notorious mobsters such as Al Capone rated standing ovations from crowds at ballparks? Detroit's Purple Gang exerted at least some of this kind of bizarre charm and influence. As it happens, I had the opportunity to meet a few remaining members of the gang when I started out at Jackson prison.

In summer of 1955, I had just started working on "counselor's row"—a moniker hung by prisoners on our offices, which were centrally located in the prison, just a short distance from the kitchen. I soon learned not to miss lunch on Thursdays because T-bone steak and French fries, the only good meal for the week, were always on the menu. Going to lunch meant passing through a security gate to get on the elevator that deposited us at the upper floor mess hall, known as the OD for "Officer's Dining Room." A herky-jerky ride on the old-fashioned lift operated by a wizened lifer with a hilarious gift of gab lightened our day on the way. Once on the second floor we could look out to our left through a wall of prison casement windows onto the immense main kitchen with its massive cooking kettles, each big enough to scald a hog, and on the huge ovens and grills which prepared more than 12,000 meals each day. Uniformed officers, whose meals were provided, but were optional by purchase of a meal ticket for us "civilians," filled most of the dining area. Our tickets were always punched by a stocky, graying but well-groomed inmate of average height dressed in crisp, neatly pressed kitchen whites. What set him apart were his slightly cherubic, friendly, almost grandfatherly face and his confident manner, as he seemed to oversee the dining area like a maitre d'—always courteous and helpful.

After observing this routine for a few weeks my curiosity prompted me to ask my boss, Leo Schmeige, "Who is that guy? He looks like he could have been a banker in the free world." Schmeige chuckled, "That's Harry Fleisher, he's a Purple."

"OK, so what is a Purple?" Schmeige, who always enjoyed being in the know and with plenty of stories to tell, was glad to enlighten me. His account in summary was that The Purple Gang was a group of prohibition era Detroit gangsters, of whom a dozen or so ended up in Jackson prison. This bunch became a corrupting influence in the prison during Warden Jackson's regime, and this had contributed to the scandal leading to demise of that regime a decade earlier. The most salacious rumor at the time was that the Purples were able to pull off a mob-style hit on a state senator while they were serving time in Jackson Prison. Fleisher, who was in the street at the time, was convicted along with others for conspiracy to murder for that crime, but no one was ever convicted for the actual killing.

Schmeige added, "That was a dozen years ago, now Harry and the other Purples are working diligently and keeping their noses clean hoping to make a good impression to get paroled." His rumors only stoked my curiosity about Harry Fleisher and the Purples. Especially vexing was the question as to how mobsters serving long prison sentences could pull off a contract killing miles from the prison and then evade prosecution for it, and how a handful of them could contaminate an entire prison bureaucracy.

Prohibition

Prohibition became the law of the land on January 16, 1920. Sensing a business opportunity, Canada immediately began developing distilleries and breweries, and Michigan, a smuggler's dream because of its proximity, became the primary market. Historians estimate that 75% of the liquor supplied to the US during Prohibition came across the Detroit and St. Clair waterways, so smuggling and distribution of liquor became a major Detroit industry.[1] All of this traffic, which required broad participation by its consuming public, while illegal was of course very lucrative—a virtual gold rush for shady characters. Therefore, an unintended consequence of prohibition was the funding of mobs, including Detroit's Purple Gang.

The principle gang members, most of whom would serve time at Jackson Prison, were: Harry Fleisher and his brother, Sam; the Bernstein's—Abe, Joe, Ray, and Izzy; Mike Selik; and Phil and Harry Keywell. They and others grew up as delinquents in a poor Jewish neighborhood around Hastings Street in Detroit.[2] They soon became the scourge of local businesses and, as one shopkeeper exclaimed, (these boys) "are rotten, purple like the color of bad meat, they're a purple gang."[3] The name stuck. The Purple Gang would go on to become wealthy and powerful through illicit alcohol traffic.[4] They first became enforcers for mobsters Charlie Leitor and Harry Schorr.[5] The gang then graduated to taking over the illicit alcohol traffic to blind pigs and speakeasies and to bootlegging liquor from Canada.[6]

Soon they discovered that highjacking other bootleggers' booze provided more profit for less work. Their methods were brutal, often involving the murder of competing bootleggers and anyone else getting in their way.[7] They feared Harry Fleisher as a mobster who "did his own work." As one story had it, Harry would locate some bootlegger's cache, bring a truck, and hire a local street bum to load the purloined

---

[1] Engelmann, Larry, *Intemperance: The Lost War against Liquor* New York, N. Y. *The Free Press*, 1979, 125.

[2] Whitall, Susan "The Purple Gang's bloody legacy," *The Detroit News Rearview Mirror*, August 30, 2004, p1.

[3] Gribben, Mark, "The Purple Gang: Bootlegger's Paradise," www.courttv.com: 2003 Courtroom Television Network LLC 2003, p1.

[4] Nolan, Jenny, "How Prohibition made Detroit a Bootlegger's Dream Town," *The Detroit News Rearview Mirror*, Detroit, MI, 2005, p2.

[5] Kavieff, Paul R. "Detroit's Infamous Purple Gang," *The Detroit News Rearview Mirror,* 2005, p2.

[6] Kavieff, Paul R. "The Purple Gang--Organized Crime in Detroit 1910--1945," Barricade Books, New York, NY, 2000: p159.

[7] Kavieff, "Detroit's Infamous Purple Gang" *op. cit.* p1.

booze— a bullet in the head paid off the bum with his corpse left on the street.[8]   Their tactics were so vicious and brutal, even by mob standards, that Al Capone, when advised by them to stay out of Detroit, chose to buy booze from the Purples rather than risk competing with them. All told, the Purples were blamed for some 500 murders[9] during the 1920s but were never brought to trial on any of them. Other gangs however, did not grant them immunity on the Detroit streets and 18 Purples came to violent deaths by 1935.[10] Detroit Mayor Bowles' spin on this gang violence in 1931 was that the murders were just gangsters helpfully eliminating each other.

Doing so much crime with no legal consequence lent an air of invincibility to the Purple Gang and they did it the old fashioned way: through bribing officials, police and potential witnesses; intimidating or killing witnesses; jury tampering; and by hiring high-powered mob attorneys. They would rule Detroit's underworld from 1927 to 1932.[11] Harry Fleisher and his cohorts were hardly the gentle souls they appeared to be when I saw them during their later years in Jackson Prison.

The Purple's hold over the Detroit crime scene finally ended because of two of their more brazen crimes early in the 1930s. The first involved the murder of Arthur Mixon in July 1930. Arthur Mixon was delivering ice from a horse-drawn wagon on a hot July night near Hastings Street in Detroit when for some reason he stopped and looked under the doors of an old barn that just happened to be a Purple Gang cutting plant (where labeled whiskey from Ontario was cut with cheap alcohol and re-labeled with counterfeit seals.)[12] A gang member tipped Phil Keywell about the snooping and he immediately confronted Mixon and shot him fatally during an ensuing argument. Four witnesses, who would later identify Keywell as the killer, were immediately placed in protective custody to keep them alive for his trial. The shadow of the mob appeared almost immediately when $2,000 mysteriously appeared

---

[8] Kavieff, "The Purple Gang--Organized Crime in Detroit 1910— 1945," *op. cit.* p159.

[9] Whitall, Susan, *loc. cit.*

[10] Kavieff, *The Purple Gang, op. cit.* p199.

[11] Kavieff, "Detroit's Infamous Purple Gang" *op. cit.* p2.

[12] Kavieff, *The Purple Gang, op. cit,* p98.

to gain release of the witnesses on bail. Prosecutors, suspecting a mob setup to kill their witnesses, refused the offer.[13] The Mixon trial resulted in a first-degree murder conviction, and Phil Keywell became the first Purple Gangster ever convicted on a murder charge. He began his "life without parole" sentence at Marquette Branch Prison and transferred later to Jackson.

The second brazen crime causing the Purple Gang's luck to run out was the infamous Collingwood Manor Massacre in 1931. This crime was set in motion when the Purple Gang's leader, Ray Bernstein, decided during the summer of 1931 that the gang had a problem that needed elimination.[14] Five years earlier three Chicago hoodlums, Isadore Sutker, Joseph Lebowitz, and Herman Paul had received an "offer they couldn't refuse" from the Capone gang and had to leave Chicago. They were brought to Detroit by Leiter and Schorr's Oakland Sugar House Gang as "rod men" to protect the mob's lucrative alcohol supply racket, but they proved unreliable and troublesome.[15] They had hijacked Purple gangsters' stashes, disregarded mob territory, failed to pay off bets, and undercut Purple Gang prices. Now, being mob outcasts is not an easy life so the three, trusting no one, were always armed and seldom alone; getting rid of them would be a job requiring careful planning. Bernstein decided to use a bookie, Solly (Sol) Levine, as an innocent accomplice because he had been a go-between with the three and the Purples in the past.[16] Bernstein told Levine that the Purples had decided to let him and the three miscreants become agents in the liquor business with the details to be worked out at a future meeting. A person with the alias "James Regis," probably Bernstein himself, then rented a second floor apartment at the Collingwood Manor Apartments and scheduled the meeting soon after. Ray Bernstein met the four as they walked into the lobby and escorted them to the apartment where they were greeted by Harry Fleisher, Harry Keywell (Phil's brother), and Irving Milberg. Shortly afterward, Ray Bernstein left to "get the books" necessary for their business agreement and as he started his car in the alley below he raced the

---

[13] *Ibid.*, p99.

[14] *Ibid.*, p112.

[15] Gribben, *op. cit.* p2.

[16] Kavieff, *The Purple Gang, op. cit.* p114.

engine until it started backfiring. At this signal, Fleisher calmly stood up, pulled a revolver, and shot Lebowitz. Milberg and Keywell jumped up and began shooting until Sutker and Paul were also dead. Solly Levine was understandably terrified as bullets flew by him, thinking he might be next. Fleisher actually did want to kill Levine, but Ray Bernstein had given specific orders not to harm his friend.

As they fled the apartment with Levine, Keywell, Fleisher, and Milberg dropped their pistols into an open can of green paint to obliterate their fingerprints. After joining Bernstein in the get-away car, Levine dropped the three murderers a few blocks away. Later on, Bernstein dropped off the panic-stricken Levine with a few dollars for cab fare and some friendly advice. Meanwhile, a much shaken downstairs tenant reported the horrific racket from upstairs to her landlord, and returned to find blood seeping through the ceiling.[17]

The police immediately suspected Solly Levine as the finger-man. After intense questioning, he confessed to being an eyewitness to the massacre and made a formal statement naming the three shooters and identifying Raymond Bernstein as the getaway driver.[18] Police arrested Bernstein and Harry Keywell later that day, and Irving Milberg was arrested the following night trying to leave town.[19] Harry Fleisher made good his getaway. During the pretrial examination, Levine, under the baleful glare of the defendants and other Purple gangsters in the spectators' gallery, identified the four Collingwood killers. He was held at police headquarters under $500,000 bond, and heavily guarded at all times.[20] Levine's testimony, as that of the only eyewitness, was instrumental in obtaining first-degree murder convictions for Bernstein, Keywell, and Milberg.

Following the murder trial, police provided Solly Levine witness protection, including a new identity and a hideout location in Europe. However, when he got to New York he bailed out of witness protection, publicly recanted his trial testimony, and disappeared.[21] Nine months later, knowing that Levine, the lone eyewitness, had

---

[17] Kavieff, "Detroit's Infamous Purple Gang," *op. cit.* p3.

[18] *Ibid.* p1.

[19] Gribben, *op. cit.* p8.

[20] Kavieff, *The Purple Gang, op. cit.* p119.

[21] *Ibid.* p128.

changed his story and could not be found, fugitive Harry Fleisher strode jauntily into the Wayne County Prosecutor's office and surrendered on the Collingwood Massacre murder warrant.[22] Thus, Harry Fleisher escaped prosecution for his part in the murders and amazingly, Solly Levine surfaced several years later alive and well in Kansas City. Some theorized that Bernstein and cohorts, hoping to get a new trial based on Levine's revised testimony, needed him alive if they hoped to ever "beat their murder rap."[23] Solly correctly concluded that, so long as he stuck to his new story, the Purple Gang's witness protection program was safer than that offered by the police.

After evading prosecution for the Collingwood Massacre, Harry Fleisher's luck continued through several more successful scrapes with the law over the next few years, but the 'Revenuers' finally got him. The Federal Alcohol Tax agents sent him and his brother Sam to Federal prison in 1936. However, they were released from Alcatraz in 1940, and once free, joined Myron "Mike" Selik and other free Purples in the Detroit bar and grill enterprise known as O'Larry's[24].

Rumors rampant during the 1930s suggested that Michigan had, to paraphrase Will Rogers, "the best government money could buy." As the truth of this became evident, political pressure mounted, so Attorney General Herbert Rushton finally petitioned the Ingham County Circuit Court to convene a grand jury to look into these alleged wrongdoings. He selected senior judge Leland Carr to serve as a one-man grand juror and Carr appointed a flamboyant, politically ambitious

---

[22] *Ibid.*

[23] This information is based upon conversations with S. J. Gilman in 1959 some years after he served as a Special Investigator for Corrections Commissioner Brooks to look into the Purples' claims that they had been "bum rapped" for the Collingwood Manor murders by the Detroit Police Department. During these informal stories, which he told me when we worked together in the Corrections Camp Program, I recall that Gilman located Levine in Kansas City, interviewed him and was not at all impressed with Levine's revised story and he assumed that Levine was highly motivated by the desire to stay alive.

[24] Kavieff, *The Purple Gang, op. cit.* p187.

lawyer, Kim Sigler, as his prosecutor/investigator.[25] This grand jury successfully prosecuted a former lieutenant governor, 12 state senators, 11 state representatives, scores of prosecutors, police officials and lobbyists—in all generating 130 arrests, of which 62 resulted in convictions.[26] Late in 1944, as the grand jury wound down, Kim Sigler fixed his crosshairs on his biggest target of all—the state's most powerful political boss, Frank McKay. McKay, who blatantly used his political clout and patronage to become extremely wealthy, [27] had in 1931 successfully fended off a previous grand jury investigation regarding his conduct as state treasurer as well as three further allegations in 1940 charging fraud, bribery and extortion.[28] In addition, the *Detroit Free Press* had been nipping at his heels for several years. Sigler knew that bringing down McKay would be a major coup, and in late 1944 he found his opening—he was able to 'flip' a minor offender his investigation had uncovered, Senator Warren Hooper, to agree to testify against McKay for a grant of immunity.

Emboldened, and perhaps hoping to panic McKay into a plea, Sigler confronted him and his alleged co-conspirators with Hooper, but this served only to put McKay and confederates on notice that they were at risk. A terrified Hooper confided his predicament to his wife, Callienetta, who then warned him that his, "life wasn't worth a penny from then on."[29] This proved all too prophetic: on January 11, 1945, Senator Warren Hooper's body was discovered alongside a lonely stretch of highway M-99 some eighteen miles from Jackson Prison just four days before his scheduled grand jury testimony. He was shot in the head execution style. With the death of his star witness, Sigler's much publicized bribery case against Frank McKay collapsed.

Because Hooper's murder was of such obvious convenience to McKay he became Prosecutor Sigler's primary suspect—a suspicion that turned into such an obsession, it eventually obscured a logical

---

[25] Ziewacz, Lawrence E. and Bruce A. Rubenstein. *Three Bullets Sealed His Lips*, East Lansing, Michigan: Michigan State University Press, 1987: p2.

[26] *Ibid.* p1.

[27] *Ibid.*, p4.

[28] *Ibid.* p5.

[29] *Ibid*, p8.

conclusion to the criminal investigation. As in so many gangland contract executions, the killer had left few clues, but after sifting through hundreds of tips, on March 22, 1945, police arrested Sam Abramowitz, an ex-convict with ties to the Purple Gang, for the crime. Sam confessed that Harry Fleisher had hired him and three-time loser Henry Luks to kill Hooper.[30] It seems that Luks was handy with explosives and the plan was to wire Hooper's car so that dynamite would do the job. This confession led to Luks arrest and, with the promise of immunity, he also admitted to the plot.

According to Luks, he met with Harry Fleisher, Mike Selik and Harry's brother Sam at O'Larry's Bar on December 23, 1944.[31] He was supposed to get $3,000 for the job and actually went to Hooper's home with Sam Fleisher to case the operation. But when it occurred to him that his pay for the murder might be a bullet in the head instead of the money, he called off the caper claiming he was having trouble with his parole officer.[32] As the investigation continued, Sigler accumulated sufficient evidence to charge Harry and Sam Fleisher, Mike Selik, and Harry's close friend, Pete Mahoney with conspiracy to murder Senator Hooper. In his opening statement to the jury, Sigler charged that the, "State will prove that Harry Fleisher and Mike Selik received $15,000 to arrange Senator Hooper's death."[33] After a lengthy and acrimonious trial, the four were found guilty of conspiracy, and on July 30, 1945, each was sentenced to four and one half to five years at Jackson prison, but the claim of a $15,000 contract for the senator's murder remained unsubstantiated. Since the conspiracy conviction flowed from an aborted murder plot and not the actual Hooper killing, and since it did not prove any connection with Frank McKay, Sigler's hunt continued.

---

[30] Sheridan, Joseph, "Attorney General, Select Investigations" 1946, box 15, file 7. This file contains a packet of Sheridan's (Detective MSP) hand written notes of interviews with witnesses and principles regarding the Hoover and Warden Jackson scandals. The notes are unnumbered but provide a basis for much of this story.

[31] *Ibid.*

[32] *Ibid.*

[33] Ziewacz, *op. cit.* p116. (Note: Sheridan's notes indicate $25,000 was agreed to with $10,000 paid in advance but Sigler only charged the $15,000.)

During his interrogation, Sam Abramowitz inadvertently revealed involvement in a Purple Gang robbery of an illegal gambling den called the Aristocrat Club in Pontiac on December 1, 1944. Since crooks tend not to call the police on other crooks, it was an unreported crime. Seeing an opportunity to pressure Fleisher, Selik and others to turn state's evidence against McKay under the threat of long prison terms, Sigler pounced. On June 10, 1945, he charged them with armed robbery.[34] The prosecution was successful, but they would not testify on the McKay connection, so Sigler convinced the judge to hand out 25 to 50 year sentences for each one. Each immediately appealed their convictions and Fleisher, Selik, and Mahoney were freed on $25,000 appeal bonds. After the appeals were exhausted and the convictions affirmed in October 1948, to no one's surprise neither Fleisher nor Selik could be found. But 15 months later in Pompano Beach, Florida, while Fleisher was lolling in the sun as his lady friend slathered his back with suntan lotion, four FBI agents drew down on him and his vacation was over.[35] It would be another eighteen months before police located Mike Selik and arrested him in New York City on June 16, 1951, with his pockets full of stolen jewels. Thus, both Fleisher and Selik finally began serving their Michigan sentences.[36]

Prosecutor Sigler was currying a "white-knight" crusader image in pursuing McKay and prosecuting the on-the-street Purples—an image he hoped would promote his prospective campaign for the Governor's office. Meanwhile, Attorney General Dethmers, Sigler's principal opponent in the upcoming race, publicized the mischief involving the Purple Gangsters serving time inside Jackson Prison. That being the horse *he* hoped to ride to the Governor's mansion. So, in the midst of Sigler's court cases, on July 24, 1945, Dethmers released the first of four installments reporting the scandalous conditions he had uncovered.[37] The report made national news with the intimation that inmates from the prison plotted and perhaps carried out Hooper's murder.[38] Because the murder conspiracy trial was ongoing

---

[34] *Ibid.*, p109.

[35] *Ibid.*, p177.

[36] *Ibid.*, p186.

[37] Ziewacz and Rubenstein, *op. cit.* pp126-128.

[38] Kavieff, *The Purple Gang, op. cit.* p195.

at the time, the presiding judge quashed these rumors until a verdict was reached on the conspiracy crime. However, the rumors and speculations persisted and were investigated as the murder investigation continued. What follows here, based on that investigation, is what I believe to be the most plausible account of the Purples' involvement in the murder of Senator Hooper.[39]

Detective Lieutenant Joseph Sheridan, underworld specialist for the MSP, received a tip in November 1946 that a parolee, Louis Brown, was 'a person of interest' in the Hooper case. Caught between putting his parole in jeopardy with corrections officials, and his life at risk from the Purples, Brown agreed to tell his story in the presence of Sheridan and Dr. David Phillips, prison psychiatrist—but only with a promise of around-the-clock police protection.[40] Lieutenant Sheridan found Brown's preliminary statement consistent with the known facts of the case, so he arranged a meeting on January 27, 1947, in Lansing so that Sigler, who had been elected Governor in November, State Police Commissioner Leonard, Corrections Commissioner Heyns, Dr. Phillips, Attorney General Eugene Black and the Governor's legal counsel, could all hear and question Brown's story.

Governor Sigler grilled Brown for more than four hours, obtaining from him an incredible but unshakable account of the intrigue surrounding the murder.[41] According to Commissioner Leonard's papers, Governor Sigler said that he believed Brown and urged Leonard to proceed on the assumption that the testimony was truthful. Brown's testimony also led Lieutenant Sheridan to question Ernest Henry, who

---

[39] Ziewacz and Rubenstein, *op. cit.* pp126-128.

[39] Kavieff, The Purple Gang, *op. cit.* p195.

[39] For a fascinating and comprehensive analysis of the Hooper case, which goes far beyond the scope of this Jackson prison story, the reader is referred to Bruce A. Rubenstein and Lawrence E. Ziewacz, *Three Bullets Sealed His Lips,* an excellent investigative work cited in this chapter.

[40] Sheridan, Attorney General, Selected Investigations, b15-file 7, *op. cit.*

[41] Ziewacz and Rubenstein pp167-68. (The abbreviated quotations from the notes of witness Brown's testimony are from Leonard Papers, Box 19.)

at the time was another of Deputy Pettit's houseboys. Henry corroborated Brown's statements and added some detail.

Notes from the interrogation of Louis Brown and Ernest Henry are edited and abridged here for sake of brevity while preserving the essence of their testimony:

In early December 1944, a Jackson Prison inmate group, headed by Ray Bernstein was offered $15,000 to kill an unnamed prominent politician. Without asking for details, Harry Keywell told the emissary that the amount was at least $10,000 "too light," and Bernstein concurred. About a week later, Deputy Warden D.C. Pettit and Inspector Robert Wilson reassembled the clique and suggested that the ante would be raised. A few days passed, and then Pettit introduced "a Jew from Flint named Wake" to the prisoners (Wake was later identified, from photographs shown Brown, as Max Davis, a prominent Flint jeweler and reputed political ally of a former McKay assistant.).[42] Wake showed them a photograph of Hooper and promised to pay $25,000 for the murder. The deputy warden promised Bernstein and Harry Keywell guns, a state car, a bogus set of license plates, and passage from the prison if they would accept the offer. Three days later another gathering was called at which Wake removed $10,000, earnest money, from a valise and stacked it on the table. Warden Harry Jackson and Frank McKay were also present as a show of good faith for payment of the balance according to Brown. After the warden introduced McKay to the mobsters, the two men left. Pettit then placed the money in a large envelope and entrusted it to Joe Poirier, the treasurer of inmate funds.

Wake said he would discover the day the intended victim was to leave Lansing (Hooper stayed in Lansing during the week) and notify Pettit. Wake went on to stress McKay's wealth and influence, and added that he was relying on them to protect his gambling interests by silencing Senator Hooper. Furthermore, Wake assured Keywell that the job could be accomplished effortlessly on a deserted highway.

---

[42] Sheridan's interrogation notes, *op. cit.*

Of relevance, here is the fact that the state-owned houses for the Warden and Deputy were located near the intersection of Cooper Street and Parnell Road. The murderers ambushed Senator Hooper on M-99 near where Parnell Road runs straight west to intersect M-50. Some two-dozen "houseboys" and yardmen were assigned to these residences. The grounds were not fenced and prisoners on these assignments provided considerable foot traffic to and from the nearby trusty cellblock where they were carried on prison count. While on assignment, prisoners were checked out to their bosses who were expected to account for their whereabouts until they returned to the block at nighttime—a few bunked in the basement of the Warden's house to be available around the clock.[43] Therefore, it is clear that these actors would have had considerable freedom to do what Brown and Henry described. Henry stated that three days before Hooper's death, Ray Bernstein asked him to purchase a pair of gloves, which he did, and delivered them to Deputy Pettit as instructed. On the day of Hooper's death, Henry was working for Mrs. Pettit in the deputy's house and as he entered the kitchen to go downstairs, she stopped him, warning that D.C. (Pettit) and the gang were in the basement "cooking up something" and did not wish to be disturbed. In the dining room, he saw a nickel-plated revolver and the brown gloves he had gotten for Bernstein (a gun which mobster Al Kurner claimed he transported from the O'Larry's arsenal to Pettit's driver at the Regent Café in Jackson some two weeks earlier.)[44] He never saw them again but remembered finding two spent .38 shells in the back seat of Pettit's red coupe when he cleaned it a few days later.[45]

According to Brown, notification (that Hooper was on the way) came on January 11, 1945, but because Pettit was absent it was Warden Jackson who summoned Bernstein and Harry Keywell over the loudspeaker to his office. Jackson authorized Brown, Pettit's houseboy at the time, to check out civilian clothing for the two from the "dress-out shop." When the afternoon meal-line bugle blared at 3:30 p.m.,

---

[43] From my personal knowledge as the last Deputy Warden and Warden to use these state residences (1967-72).

[44] Ziewacz, *op. cit.* p171.

[45] Witness Harvey's statement, Leonard Papers, Box 19.

Bernstein and Keywell drove away in Pettit's dark red coupe. Two and a half hours later, they returned and changed into prison garb.

Sigler inquired if Brown knew how the crime had been committed, and Brown volunteered that Keywell had boasted about the smoothness of the job. Keywell explained to a band of inmates, which included Brown, that Wake followed Hooper from Lansing and, at a prearranged location, signaled to them by flashing his headlights as he passed the senator's automobile. Bernstein and Keywell pulled onto the highway, blocking Hooper, and forced his car off the road. Bernstein raced to the senator's door, opened it, shoved Hooper toward the center of the seat, grabbed him, and fired three shots into his skull. After making sure he was dead, Bernstein ran back to the maroon coupe driven by Keywell,[46] and they raced back to the prison (presumably to Pettit's garage). It was then but a simple matter to change back to prison blues and blend into their normal prison routine.

Keywell's boasting, as recalled by Brown, is at best hearsay, but the murder scene evidence developed by the state police at the time Hooper's body was discovered tends to support his boasts. Tire skid marks in the snow indicated Hooper's green Mercury had slid off the road to avoid another vehicle that scraped Hooper's left front fender leaving a trace of maroon paint.[47] The small footprints found in the snow around the Mercury were consistent with Bernstein's foot size. Police placed Hooper's time of death as between 5:15 p.m. and 5:30 p.m., which also fits the time-line. A motorist traveling by the scene at that time, one Harry Snyder, observed a person of Bernstein's size leave the green Mercury and run to a dark red coupe that then passed him at a high rate of speed heading north (toward M-50). Although police never found the murder weapon, Kurner's testimony about providing it was plausible. Thus, this testimony and evidence paint the picture of a chillingly simple execution by two mobsters with a near perfect alibi: they were convicts serving life sentences in Jackson Prison at the time.

---

[46] Ziewacz and Rubenstein, p37 (Statement of Harry Snyder).
[47] *Ibid.*, p199.

Aristocrat convicts in white pants, shirts and black ties pose with D.C.
Pettit's dark red coupe 1944. The archive photo has numbers
handwritten on the photograph identifying the convicts in the photo:
#1-Ray Fox; #2-Medley;# 3-Chester, the informant; #7-Joe Johnson,
Pettit's driver. *Photo by permission of Michigan Archives*

What is more difficult to assimilate than their being freed in order
to commit the murder is the web of collusion required among
politicians, the Purple Gang, prison officials, and prison inmates
necessary to make the scheme work. Too many knew
about pieces of the plot to keep it quiet and it was soon on
the grapevine at the prison and in the mob underworld.[48]
So the question becomes not "who done it," but rather
"why weren't they caught?"

It was clear that during the initial grand jury investigation
Prosecutor Sigler was not interested in pursuing the prison angle. This
was probably because he knew he had to force someone to turn state's

---

[48] *Ibid.*, p166.

evidence if he was ever to bag his target, Frank McKay, and close-mouthed prison mobsters whose life sentences rendered them immune to the threat of more time would be impervious to any pressure he could bring. However, his refusal to allow police interrogation of Bernstein and Keywell or to examine D.C. Pettit's automobile for scratches or missing paint,[49] and thus preserve that evidence, bordered on malfeasance. Meanwhile, Sigler's 1946 gubernatorial primary opponent, Attorney General John Dethmers, missed opportunities as well; he refused to investigate possibly illuminating connections between Harry Jackson and Frank McKay, and he didn't probe D. C. Pettit's relations with Bernstein and Keywell, despite rumors that Pettit's maroon coupe was the getaway car.[50] The two investigations, Sigler's grand jury, and Dethmers' on the prison scandal, should logically have been coordinated but were not, probably because neither one wanted to risk giving the other political advantage from some revelation that separately they would be able to suppress. At any rate, these were seriously muffed opportunities for criminal prosecution.

By September 1945, the political dynamics for Sigler began to shift with the elevation of his mentor, grand juror Leland Carr, to the Michigan Supreme Court. In March 1946, after several months of political infighting, Judge Coash, who succeeded Carr as grand juror, fired Sigler, his prima donna prosecutor. This act actually freed Sigler to run for Governor, but inexplicably, Sigler took all of the files he had amassed as prosecutor with him to the Governor's office thus keeping them from his successor and the Michigan State Police. Special Prosecutor Foster complained that he and Judge Coash "did a lot of work on that damn Hooper case and never got anywhere" because they lacked support from Governor Sigler. Captain Mulbar made similar complaints, stating that Sigler took "full and complete control," and refused to share information developed by his investigators, some of whom were state police on assignment to the grand jury.[51]

Nevertheless, after Sigler had interrogated parolee Brown on January 27, 1947, Governor Sigler gave his newly appointed MSP director, Donald Leonard, the green light to investigate the prison

---

[49] *Ibid.*, p200.

[50] Bright, *op. cit.* p186.

[51] Ziewacz and Rubenstein, *op cit.*, pp165-66.

angle. He stated that he believed Brown, and "urged the commissioner to proceed on the assumption that the account was valid."

Prompted by Governor Sigler's instructions, Donald Leonard prepared a handwritten list containing nine steps in a strategy to investigate Brown's story but he only followed up the questioning of inmate Henry.[52] Then, despite sworn affidavits of Brown and Henry and urging from Lt. Sheridan and other detectives, no one ever questioned Bernstein, the Keywells, Warden Jackson, D.C. Pettit, or Max Davis, whose photograph Brown had positively identified as the man called Wake. Leonard refused all requests by Sheridan to submit the case to a grand jury.[53] Ironically, when Leonard resigned in 1952 as Director of the Michigan State Police to oppose Democrat G. Mennen Williams, he removed all post-1947 state police records of the Hooper investigations.[54]

In short, it appears that political ambition got in the way of professional police work for all three principals in the Hooper murder investigation: Special Prosecutor—later Governor— Sigler, Attorney General Dethmers, and Michigan State Police Director Leonard. After their political ambitions were exhausted, The Hooper case just faded away in the dust of political campaigns. Sigler was defeated in his bid for re-election in 1948 by Democrat G. Mennen Williams, with more than a little help in his undoing by enemies in his own party, Frank McKay in particular. Sigler never again ran for public office and died on November 30, 1953, when he piloted his private airplane into a fog-shrouded TV tower.[55] In 1946, John Dethmers had been denied re-nomination as attorney general by the Sigler forces so he resigned to accept appointment to the state Supreme Court, where he served for 25 years. Questions that remain troublesome are raised by the fact that Frank McKay, for whom public disclosure of the Brown/Henry interrogations in Leonard's possession would have been a major political embarrassment, became prominent on the political landscape again. He vigorously backed Leonard in both 1952 and 1954 stating,

---

[52] *Ibid.*, p169.

[53] *Ibid.*, p169

[54] *Ibid.*, p187.

[55] *Ibid.*, p208.

"Leonard was the only hope for the State GOP."[56] Leonard was unsuccessful at both gubernatorial tries but served as Detroit Police Commissioner and for 10 years on Detroit Recorder's Court.

The upshot of all this was that the Senator Hooper assassins and their employers got off scot-free—assisted in no small part by bungling and inattention in an intense political environment.

Dethmers' Jackson prison investigation resulted in the firing of Warden Jackson and Deputy Warden D. C. Pettit in 1945, and consequently the loss of the Purples' trusty status and their return inside the walls. Prison grapevine versions of the ways in which the Purples were able to "beat the rap" became ingrained in the convict lore at Jackson prison, adding to both the mystique of the Purple Gang[57] and the general disrepute of the fired prison officials.

The Purples, hoping for parole, worked diligently and kept their noses clean as my boss, Leo Schmeige, predicted years later that they would continue to do. Mysteriously, the prison officials never charged those named by Dethmers in the Jackson scandal, or those identified by newspaper publicity as suspects in the Hooper murder, with any prison misconduct, so their prison records were technically spotless according to the Department of Corrections. Bernstein got his high school diploma at Jackson prison and then taught other inmates; he also had a reputation of giving financial aid to needy prisoners.[58] The Keywells worked as clerks in the prison hospital. The Purples strongly supported prison Red Cross blood drives and a citizens' volunteer rose garden project in the north yard.

These strategies for release seem to have met with considerable success: Governor Romney granted commutation to both Ray Bernstein and Harry Keywell thereby changing their "life without parole"

---

[56] *Grand Rapids Press*, October 10, 1953.

[57] Various prisoners on my caseload, and Ralph Hively, a civilian hospital supervisor of Keywell, in the late 1950s relayed stories about the Hooper case, many of them clearly apocryphal, and some probably planted by the Purples to provide confusion. These stories are too numerous and unsubstantiated to add to this account.

[58] Gribben, *op. cit.* 3.

sentences to make them parole eligible[59]. Bernstein suffered a severe stroke in 1963 and appeared before the parole board wrapped in a blanket in a wheel chair, claiming a 'bum rap' on his part in the Collingwood Massacre. He was granted a mercy parole in 1964 and died two years later in the University of Michigan Medical Center at age 61. The Governor commuted Harry Keywell's sentence the next year and he was granted a four-year parole October 21, 1965. He went to work, married and faded into obscurity after completing his parole. Irving Milberg, the third Purple convicted for the Collingwood Massacre, had died in Marquette prison in 1938.[60] Pete Mahoney, who was probably the least culpable in the Aristocrat Club case since he was not a Purple and whose biggest mistake was being a friend of Harry Fleisher, and who nevertheless, got the same 25 to 50 year sentence as the others, died in Jackson prison from a massive heart attack in June of 1959. Harry Fleisher and Mike Selik received four-year paroles in 1965, were discharged from parole in 1969, and dropped from sight. Rumor has it that Fleisher moved to Nevada and worked for the notorious Licavoli family, for whom he had done contract jobs, in early years. He died in May 1978. Fleisher's brother, Samuel died in 1960 in Florida—a model citizen at the time. His brother, Louis was found dead in his cell at Jackson April 3, 1964. In 1950, Phil Keywell, the first Purple sentenced to Jackson prison, became a trustee at the Maybury Sanitarium near Detroit. However, amid rumors of bribery for the cushy assignment, political pressure forced his return to the walls. Governor Swainson commuted his life sentence in 1962 despite protests from his victim's 72-year-old mother. He went on to marry and stayed off police blotters.[61] Frank McKay died January 12, 1965, a

---

[59] Under Michigan law a conviction for murder in the first degree, as Bernstein, the Keywells, and Milberg were sentenced, mandated life without parole. The only relief therefore must come from the Governor's constitutional authority to grant executive clemency in the form of commutation of the sentence to a number of years making the offender eligible for parole or by granting a full pardon.

[60] Gribben, Mark, *op. cit.* pp2-4.

[61] Kavieff, *The Purple Gang--Organized Crime in Detroit 1910—1945, op. cit.* p203.

wealthy man with extensive real estate holdings; he left an annuity trust to the University of Michigan.

Thus, the Purples' era at Jackson prison that started with Phil Keywell's 1930 murder conviction ended thirty-five years later with all the actors either dead or gone. That era began during the chaos surrounding the building of the "new prison" and would continue through the travails of the Great Depression, the Warden Jackson scandal and the 1952 prison riot. Now, institutional memories of the Purples fade with the passing of each generation, but the lessons taught about the ways in which avarice, unprincipled ambition and corrupt prison management can have deadly consequences are valid forever.

RALPH E. BENSON
Photo courtesy of the Michigan Department of Corrections

Chapter Six
A Gathering Storm

ON AUGUST 17, 1945, CORRECTIONS DIRECTOR Heyns notified Attorney General Dethmers that the Corrections Commission had ordered the dismissal of SPSM's Warden, Deputy Warden, Assistant Deputy Warden, inspector, director of records and classification, supervisor of inmate accounts, and director of athletics, to take effect on this date. Further, that the reasons for dismissal were based on information "furnished by the Attorney General and our belief therein ..." referring to the investigative conclusions attached to the order. Media frenzy, of course, followed. It is difficult to imagine how chaotic it was for an organization as large and complex as Jackson

Prison, with nearly 5,300 prisoners and 630 employees, to lose its entire management team in this manner.[1] It is also difficult to overestimate the demoralizing embarrassment experienced by many ordinary prison employees during the highly publicized six months of investigations alleging incompetence and widespread corruption in the prison. Unfortunately, events and missteps in reorganization and questionable management decisions during the next few years would not help matters much, tending to leave the experienced officers and staff embittered and cynical, questioning whether management knew what they were doing.

The actual last workday for the seven officials was July 25, 1945, the date they were first suspended pending dismissal. The next day Director Heyns announced a temporary management team to run Jackson comprised of himself (as acting Deputy Director of Prisons); Captain Hansen, MSP, Jackson Post; Ralph Benson, Marquette Prison Warden; and Superintendent Miles from Cassidy Lake and assigned extra state police to Jackson Prison in the event of any inmate disturbance.[2] A week later the management team was reshuffled: Ralph Benson was now the designated acting Warden; record clerk and photographer John Martin was promoted to assistant deputy Warden; Larry Gearing was made record clerk; and George Kropp was promoted from Director Heyns' staff to be an assistant deputy in the newly organized Trusty Division. Ralph Benson had served nearly four years as Marquette's Warden and as the State Supervisor of Paroles for six years prior and he was a much-decorated WWI veteran—so he seemed like a good fit for SPSM.[3] After the torrent of negative publicity and public derision arising from the Attorney General's account of lax security, special privileged inmate aristocrats, courtesy after-hour details, special meals, and, of course, the Medley escape and murder spree, it is no wonder that the new Warden would pursue a

---

[1] Perspectives from the SPSM employees' point of view are based on comments and stories I gathered from veterans of those times during my work at the prison during the 1950s and 1960s: i.e. Lee McCoy, Lilly Scott, Deputy Cahill, and others.

[2] Guy Jenkens, *Jackson Citizen Patriot*, July 26, 1945, p1.

[3] Wood, Ike, *One Hundred Years at Hard Labor*, Au Train, MI: KA-ED Publishing Company, June 1985, p254.

crackdown. Warden Benson's first act was to impose a strict 8:15 p.m. curfew for all inside prisoners. Regular shakedowns of cells and assignments were instituted to reduce the accumulation of cash money, weapons, and other contraband; and he promised, "Everyone would be treated alike," no favorites.[4] He promoted Captain Charles Cahill, a disciplinarian respected by both officers and inmates as being honest and straightforward, as chief inspector of security, and he selected George Bacon, an imposing, autocratic "spit and polish" manager, as his Deputy Warden. Prisoners, who were losing perks and favors, along with old time staff who were comfortable with their accommodation to the Warden Jackson system both resented this reversal from extreme laxity to tight discipline. Of the 350 guards at the time, more than 25% were over the age of 60. Furthermore, staff shortages continued to plague the prison, which was running some 50 under shift complement, and the wartime economy made hiring qualified replacements difficult.[5]

VJ day on August 15, 1945, signaled the end of WWII and consequently of war production by prison industries. With the loss of these productive high paying inmate jobs, and with no prospects of replacing them, the prison was plunged back into the problem of high inmate unemployment.

In addition, political storm clouds were once again forming. In the fall election, Kim Sigler, who had been the flamboyant, ruthless, and politically ambitious special prosecutor for Judge Leland Carr, defeated Democrat Murray Van Wagner for the 1947-48 gubernatorial terms. He campaigned as a "white knight" reformer. Citing his success in prosecuting 62 corruption convictions of state and local officials, he promised to "clean out the grafters, crooks, and cliques from state government."[6] Immediately after inauguration, Sigler initiated investigations of the Department of Corrections, which were later joined into by a senate committee and the Attorney General's office. Few prosecutions resulted from these probes although they found numerous instances of employee misconduct. A resulting purge dismissed Supt. Miles, calling him lazy and good for nothing;

---

[4] Eaton, Andrienne, John Knox, et al, *op. cit.*, p68.

[5] *Jackson Citizen Patriot*, July 13, 1945, p1.

[6] Eaton, Andrienne, John Knox, et al, *op. cit.*, p61.

prosecuted Chief Engineer Dan Johnson; pressured Treatment Deputy Warden Raymond to resign; fired three wardens; and the assistant director of prisons.[7] One legislator observed, "It's beginning to look as if the chief job is to go around and fire somebody."[8] The Corrections Commission resigned in a squabble over Sigler's instruction that they fire the deputy director for prisons, which they refused to do. Sigler then used this as an opening to amend the Corrections Act, abolishing the commission in favor of a single governor-appointed Commissioner of Corrections. He then proceeded to appoint Joseph Sanford, Warden of the Atlanta Federal Penitentiary, to be that commissioner, subject to senate confirmation. Commissioner designate Sanford hit the prisons like a storm with a dictatorial, abrasive style. Reformatory Warden Joel Moore was appalled at Sanford's appointment—he and Sanford had crossed swords years before in the Federal system leaving bad blood between them—while the ACLU opposed Sanford because he was a racist.[9] Wardens Benson, Moore and Bush (Marquette) joined with others to lobby the senate in opposition to Sanford's confirmation but they were unsuccessful—he subsequently succeeded in firing all three.

In firing Warden Benson, Sanford charged him with alcoholism, absenteeism, and incompetence. Sanford then appointed Julian Frisbie, commandant of the Portsmouth disciplinary barracks, as provisional Warden of Jackson Prison. That fall Sigler was defeated in his quest for reelection by G. Mennen Williams and Commissioner Sanford immediately resigned but the Williams administration retained Warden Julian Frisbie.

The three years of management chaos following the Harry Jackson debacle made working, or for that matter "doing time," at the prison difficult indeed—as staff rolled their eyes at each new revelation: "here we go again, another witch hunt!" Inmates transferred to other prisons also voiced unhappiness with the climate at Jackson.[10]

---

[7] Fox, Vernon, *Violence Behind Bars*, 1956, p78.

[8] Eaton, Andrienne, John Knox, et al, *op. cit.*, p64.

[9] Warden Kropp and Warden's Secretary Lilly Scott both painted this unfavorable picture of Sanford during reminiscences with Johnson in the 1960s.

[10] Eaton, Andrienne, John Knox, et al *op. cit.*, p66.

The continuing aura of suspicion and mutual mistrust on the part of prison staff with their Lansing Office overseers irreparably damaged staff morale, and their hostility toward the "Lansing Office" would last for years.

JULIAN N. FRISBIE

Photo courtesy of the Michigan Department of Corrections

Warden Julian Frisbie

Acting Warden Frisbie, hired by Sanford, would be retained by Sanford's successor but would remain in 'acting' or 'provisional' status for four years—just why that was is unclear because when given the exam for warden in 1952 he received the highest score given any applicant including Michigan's other wardens. Julian Frisbie was an interesting and intriguing candidate who was Commandant of the

Portsmouth Disciplinary Barracks when recruited for the SPSM Warden's job. He had risen from Private to Brigadier General in the Marine Corps, and his military record was indeed exemplary: he was awarded the Silver Star for gallantry in action at Guadalcanal in 1942, as well as the Legion of Merit for exceptional meritorious conduct in the Pacific Theater of Operation in 1945. President Truman presented the Navy Cross to Colonel Frisbie for extraordinary heroism and distinguished service while serving as Commanding Officer of the Seventh Marines during action against Japanese forces at Cape Gloucester, New Britain in 1944. After his regiment had made the initial landing and secured the beachhead, Colonel Frisbie advanced his troops steadily until the sector was entirely secured. Although his command post was constantly harassed by Japanese small-arms fire, Colonel Frisbie daily traversed the front lines within the dense and treacherous jungle and, by his brilliant and fearless leadership, inspired his command to such effort that it virtually annihilated the 141st Japanese Regiment.

Frisbie was promoted to brigadier general after VJ Day and assigned as commandant of the Portsmouth, Maine Disciplinary Barracks—tabbed "Alcatraz of the East" because it was a fortress structure surrounded by water and deliberately patterned after Alcatraz. It reached its maximum prison count of over 3,000 in 1945.

Frisbie was given little respect by local media and many SPSM staff upon his assignment to Jackson because "disciplinary barracks" suggested a holding facility for AWOL soldiers rather than a "real" prison. Actually, it was a massive and secure prison but it did have a higher class offender than was typical of the motley bunch at Jackson. Clearly, Julian Frisbie was more qualified to be Warden of SPSM than most preceding appointees, and did not deserve the disparaging claims which would be made following the 1952 riot that he was inexperienced and naïve.

One can only guess how Frisbie must have felt on the November 1947 day when he came to start on his new job in Michigan just as the newspapers were reporting that Governor Sigler had lost his bid for a second term. Immediately thereafter, Frisbie's boss, Commissioner Sanford, resigned. The new administration would opt to keep Frisbie on as SPSM's Warden, but his new boss, Commissioner Ernest Brooks, was a polar opposite to Sanford

106

Commissioner Brooks, University of Chicago educated and well to do in his own right, married into a wealthy Holland, Michigan family, where he helped manage his father-in-law's business and established an insurance agency. He served two terms as Holland's mayor. He had been elected to the state senate in 1936 where he served two terms, and while there co-authored Michigan's model Corrections Act. He also served for a time as state chairman of the Democratic Party.[11] As a favor to his close friend, Governor Williams, he left semi-retirement in 1948 to serve as Corrections Commissioner,[12] and because he considered public service an honor, he would remain a member of the Michigan Corrections Commission for the next quarter-century. Brooks was a gracious, easygoing man with liberal ideas about the care and treatment of inmates. He saw his role as a peacemaker to restore staff morale fractured by nearly a decade of investigations and bickering—he had found that some 200 employees quit during 1947 because of these issues.[13] As Commissioner he was, of course, the chief administrator of the entire corrections department, but Jackson Prison became something of a hobby; he spent a great deal of time there,[14] where he became known as "a sucker for a sob story by the inmates," with his well-intentioned interventions on their behalf becoming an annoyance to prison staff. Because, unfortunately, some of the most charming prisoners and disarming storytellers are also unrepentant career criminals or hoodlums in the free world. Experienced prison staff learned to check stories carefully before acting, but this was a lesson Brooks would learn the hard way. For example, he ordered a favorite, Mickey Maguire, transferred from SPSM to Camp Brighton over the objections of staff. Maguire, an eight-time loser serving life as a habitual criminal, stole a car and

---

[11] Martin, *Op. cit..*, pp35,36

[12] Fox, Vernon, *Violence Behind Bars*, 1956, p245, "Governor's Ex Sec. Lawrence Farrell observed that, "(Brooks) possessed a welfare heart and can't turn down a sob story. Further, his personal and financial position was such that he did not have to take abuse, and that he is on the job only as a favor to the administration."

[13] Eaton, Andrienne, John Knox, et al, *op. cit.,* p 72.

[14] *Ibid* p72, 73.

escaped two months later making for embarrassing headlines when the story was discovered by the press.[15]

Commissioner Brooks was able to establish a counselor system for Jackson in May of 1949 with the appointment of 10 counselors; the last digit of the inmate's prison number assigned caseloads. The modest goal of having a counselor interview each man on his caseload a minimum of three times a year was soon subverted by sheer numbers. Jackson Prison's population increased more than 700 from 1949 to reach 6,267 in 1952.[16] This made a counselor's caseload over 600 at any moment, but the workload amounted to much more than that in practice because of the hundreds of commitments and transfers flowing through each year.

There was also a staff morale problem: the relationship between Deputy Warden Bacon (custody) and Assistant Deputy Sidney Moskowitz (treatment) was so bitter that neither would speak to the other; the overwhelmed counselors considered themselves merely paper pushers; and the average guard thought of them as overpaid wastes of money.[17]

Commissioner Brooks recognized these problems with Jackson's treatment program and came up with a creative solution. Treatment Director Sid Moskowitz would be booted upstairs to the Parole Board and Brooks had just the man to replace him—the bright, enthusiastic, charming young treatment director at Cassidy Lake Technical School who was wrapping up his Ph.D. in social psychology at Michigan State University and was about to accept a position on the MSU faculty— Vernon Fox. Brooks was intrigued by the fact that Fox had spent four years at Starr Commonwealth (a program for wayward youth) and was one of Floyd Starr's highly publicized success stories. Brooks sweetened his offer to Fox by promising the position would be up-graded to full Deputy Warden of Treatment, matching the pay and grade of Deputy Bacon.[18] Bacon would be responsible for all custody and security matters and Fox for those involving inmate programs: counseling, academic and vocational schools, hobby craft and

---

[15] Fox, Vernon, *op. cit.,* p249.

[16] Martin, *op. cit.,* pp284-285.

[17] Fox, Vernon, *op. cit.,* pp79,80.

[18] *Ibid.,* pp83,84

recreation, as well as the print shop, library and law library. Later Brooks moved Fox from Moskowitz's cramped office to a spacious one matching Deputy Bacon's. A weakness in the plan was that it pretty much ignored Warden Frisbie. After all, those involved were the Warden's staff working in the Warden's prison. But while Fox claimed that after a chilly start he and Warden Frisbie developed a good working relationship,[19] problems beyond the control of either the Warden or his treatment director were festering inside Jackson Prison.

The magnitude and composition of the prison population was difficult to deal with by 1952. It exceeded 6,200, with 100 inmates with no cells sleeping on cots in hallways. The 6,200 prisoners were a conglomeration of old and young, long and short timers, medical misfits and the mentally ill, security risks shipped to Jackson to give relief to other Michigan prisons, and criminal sexual psychopaths (CSP) from the Ionia State Hospital for the Criminally Insane. (The prison had no psychiatrists on staff—the Ionia State Hospital had no space, so an exchange was negotiated where the prison could commit one psychotic prisoner and bring back one CSP. This resulted in 127 criminal sexual psychopaths being housed in Jackson Prison by 1952.) Commissioner Brooks inadvertently created another problem in an effort to help the Michigan Reformatory by decreeing that no inmates 21 or younger with an IQ 75 or lower could be transferred into it (because they could not benefit from Reformatory programs.) The policy was bitterly but unsuccessfully opposed by SPSM treatment staff. It resulted in housing some 300 inadequate and vulnerable teenage inmates who became the target of Jackson's homosexual wolves and extortion artists.[20] Instead of increasing staff to try to cope with all these problems, the Republican controlled legislature (FY 1950 v FY 1952) reduced the guard force by 32 positions (498 to 466.)[21] In January 1952, Governor Williams sounded an alarm that "Jackson Prison was dangerously overcrowded." It was a combustible mixture just waiting for a lighted match.

---

[19] *Ibid*, pp79,80.

[20] Fox, Vernon, *op cit*, pp253-54.

[21] Martin, John B., *op cit*, pp37,38.

A Week of Anarchy—the 1952 Jackson Prison Riot

Officer Thomas Elliot was half way into his 2 to 10 afternoon shift—it was Sunday, April 20, 1952, and it was becoming a long day. Because of staff shortages Lieutenant Louis Baldwin had assigned him two floors, four and five, in 15 Block—"the jail within a jail" at the prison—but he had the best of the lot on his floors—a mix of administrative segregation (000) and general population inmates waiting for cell assignments. While making his rounds, inmate Ray Young stopped him, saying that he would be getting off 000 tomorrow and going home and would like to give a box of personal property to an inmate down the "rock," and would the officer take it to him? Elliot agreed, but when he opened the cell Young put a nasty looking butcher knife to his throat, took his keys, and locked him in the cell.[22] Young then crept down to the cells of Earl Ward and "Crazy" Jack Hyatt—labeled homicidal psychopaths by the prison but who were just "convicts with a rep" to prisoners like Young. Their convict reputation had been built partially on their aborted 1950 attempt to kidnap Governor Williams at Marquette Prison, and more generally on their ongoing challenges to authority.

Within the hour, the three had captured the remaining three duty officers and were unlocking 15 Block's 185 prisoners. Ward assumed leadership of the kidnapping and 15 Block revolt and designated Hyatt his lieutenant, thus putting the hostages lives at the mercy of two "homicidal psychopaths." While that would seem to have been the worst possible situation, in retrospect it turned out to be fortunate because both were very bright and were ruthless enough to control and intimidate the rest of the wild and violent group and protect the hostages.

Meanwhile, Captain Harold Tucker was wrapping up his afternoon shift duties in the main hall office in the Rotunda, totally unaware of the hostage taking or that a 100 or so inmates were rampaging in 15 Block, smashing toilets, lavatories and locking devices and ripping up plumbing. When he answered his ringing phone he was told, "This is Ward talking in 15 Block." Ward went on to say that he and others controlled the block and were holding four officers hostage,

---

[22] Wood, Ike, *One Hundred Years at Hard Labor, op. cit.,* p295.

and demanded that Tucker get Deputy Bacon in the next 10 minutes or they would kill one of the guards.[23] Tucker instantly knew they had a serious problem on two counts aside from the predicament of the hostages and the fact that Ward should not be out of his cell. First, 15 Block was a reinforced concrete fortress almost impregnable for those controlling it; second, those in control were a collection of unmanageable misfits and the very dangerous (of the 185 inmates, 43 were in punishment detention, 86 were in segregation, and 56 were just awaiting cells in general population. Dr. Phillips listed 27 as psychotic, 26 as mentally defective and 44 were serving for murder in the first degree.)

Tucker immediately called Warden Frisbie and Deputy Bacon; he then ordered all sally ports and gates to stop all movement except for the Warden or Deputy. Then he alerted all gun posts and turned on the red trouble light on One Post.

Frisbie and Bacon arrived within minutes, and weekend Duty-Deputy Fox arrived back from home by 9 p.m.[24] Warden Frisbie ordered the afternoon shift held over to reinforce the incoming night shift. The Michigan State Police were notified about the hostage taking at 10:30 p.m., but assistance was not requested at that time. News media were given access to Inmate Ward in compliance with his demands for media coverage.

Tucker learned later that Ward was having his own problems with his motley mob: he had to break up grudge fights, and even locked some back in cells to control them. Becoming concerned about the safety of the hostages, he assigned Crazy Jack Hyatt (his most formidable ally) to guard them. It was still chaotic inside; some dozen or so of the mob sodomized an effeminate, mental defective teenager who was released for transport by litter carriers to the prison hospital. (This may suggest at least a bit of compassion--later in the week, one of the older guards began suffering a medical crisis and Ward released him.) Meanwhile, the noise and confusion emanating from 15 Block was beginning to cause a late night buzz in the nearest cellblocks and rumors were stirring on the prison grapevine.

---

[23] Martin, John B. *op. cit..,* pp3,4,5.

[24] Fox, Vernon, *op. cit.*, p86.

Fifteen Block circa 1950s-60s *Photo by permission Archives of Michigan*

In the midst of this chaos, time was running short on a critical decision: how to feed breakfast; Warden Frisbie had to decide whether to keep more than 4,000 men locked in their cells and bring them sandwiches, or unlock them to use the prison dining room. (Exempted from the lockdown were 1,200 in Trusty Division plus key assignments like kitchen, maintenance, and the hospital.) It was a difficult decision. If the men were locked in and fed in their cells, then by working from early morning to late at night and using all available staff and inmate kitchen help only two meals of soup and sandwiches could be served. Furthermore, the locked in inmates would soon begin chafing at the enforced idleness they did nothing to deserve. On the other hand, trying to run normal meal lines with the nearby 15 Block disturbance in full uproar might be just the lighted match to ignite a greater conflagration. The staff decided to feed in stages and see how it went (Warden Frisbie took full responsibility for the decision but there had been general agreement.) The kitchen crew would be unlocked at the usual 3 a.m. time and if food preparation went without incident the five north side blocks would be released in sequence but instead of sending those prisoners through the north yard and alongside 15 Block as usual, they were marched down the inside corridor of each block, going from 5 Block into the rotunda and then turning left up the central corridor to the main kitchen.[25] This was a parade of some 2,000 inmates—a sight never before witnessed by the hall-office. All went well and the men returned to their cells without incident. So custody then proceeded to feed the south side blocks starting with free-standing 11 and 12 Blocks which housed medical and mental 00's (unemployable inmates), again with no problems. Then came Seven Block, a group of idle ne'er-do-wells. As soon as this group was seated someone yelled, "There is salt in the coffee!" That proved to be the spark that would bring the rest of the prison into the revolt. There was instant bedlam in the mess hall, with inmates surging past the serving stations into the "big top" kitchen, smashing everything in sight. Mobs of rioters looted the commissary then set it on fire, smashed security boxes to seize butcher knives, and cleavers, as well as tools and sledge hammers from maintenance—anything which could be used as a weapon or to smash and destroy. They set fire to the laundry, quartermaster, green house, chapel/theater, and library and soon had the locks smashed in Blocks 8, 9 and 10.[26] From there they begin breaking into the north side blocks, smashing locks, toilets, and lavatories and forcing inmates out into the yard.

---

[25] Martin, John B., *op. cit.*, pp11, 12, 13.
[26] Martin, *Ibid*, pp11,12, 13.

Michigan State Police 1952 Riot
Photo by permission Archives of Michigan

Inmate James Hudson was one of the vocal early riot leaders. [27] A huge, assaultive troublemaker suffering from the advanced ravages of syphilis he was a fearful force, leading a mob, smashing cell locks, driving inmates from their cells and delivering more hostages to 15 Block at Crazy Jack Hyatt's request. The result was that the original four hostages grew to nearly a dozen. Reporters who wrote that 2,000 inmates[28] were strolling about the yard enjoying the summer sun, did not realize that many had been driven out of their cells by the roving mobs and wanted no part of the riot. Stories of blatant sexual acts abounded (the Attorney General was able to prosecute only five). On the other hand, inmates fought off rioters to protect the vocational school and the prison hospital, and there was a cadre of loyal maintenance and food service workers who, by and large, buckled down to work their assignments—preparing food and making emergency repairs throughout the riot.

---

[27] Wood, Ike, *op. cit.,* p295.
[28] Martin, *op. cit.,* pp18, 19.

Michigan State Police 1952 Riot
Photo by permission Archives of Michigan

The Department of Corrections requested assistance from the Michigan State Police as soon as the riot broke out in the mess hall during the morning breakfast—by 10:30 a.m., more than 200 troopers were available for action at the prison. About 100 state troopers (with a like number held in reserve) mustered at the south vehicle gate and formed a diagonal line to shield the fire trucks behind them and to force the inmates toward the cellblocks. The inmates immediately threw up barricades to block the fire trucks. The leader of this group, Darwin Millage, was ordered off the barricade but refused to leave and after the third warning was fatally shot—the only fatality of the riot (although police wounded 15 others). Inmates rushed 15 Block demanding the life of a hostage in reprisal—to appease them, Ward shoved out an officer who eluded the mob and, with police guns covering him, ran to the rotunda.[29]

---

[29] Martin, *op. cit.* pp88-90.

After the first police sweep, prisoners spilled back out of the cellblocks as soon as the troopers passed so it was necessary to drive the diagonal again and leave a few armed officers to keep the prisoners in their cells. Officer Lee McCoy, who was there at the time, said: "a short burst from a Thompson submachine gun by a trooper sure cleared the galleries of stragglers!"[30] Police cleared the inmates from the yard, some locks were replaced or repaired, and feeding in the cells began at 5:00 p.m. Monday evening.

There was universal praise for the performance of the State Troopers on that day—they were fully armed but absorbed verbal abuse and threats without a break in discipline that could have led to many deaths. Much less noted was the courage of several guards who tried to persuade inmates to return to their cells, working unarmed at the risk, and sometimes the fact, of being hostages themselves, before the police arrived.

Hostage Negotiation

Jackson Prison was unprepared for a riot in April 1952. There was no riot control plan (Warden Frisbie said Commissioner Brooks had his proposal for such preparation "pigeonholed,") and hence no gun squad training, so the Warden was reluctant to send untrained armed officers into the riot and instead relied on the Michigan State Police who he said, "performed admirably." Hostage negotiation training was relatively unknown until the 1960s.[31] Deputy Fox became hostage negotiator by default, forced to operate by the seat of his pants with no team partner to spell him. Initially he listened, asked questions, and sized up Ward whom he had never met before. The fundamental question, of course, was "What was being demanded in exchange for the hostages?" Ward told Fox that the guys didn't have demands because their gaining control of 15 Block was unexpected and unplanned. Standing at the 15 Block window with Ward, Fox attempted to blend the inmates' gripes and complaints into a format that

---

[30] Lee McCoy, Arsenal Lieutenant during my administration, was a guard during the 1952 riots and told of observing the State Police operation.

[31] Fox-WJIM TV, pp283, 285.

116

could serve at a basis for a negotiated solution to free the hostages. Deputy Fox then drafted the following 11 demands:[32]

(1) Remodel 15 Block to provide adequate lighting and treatment facilities.

(2) Counselors should have free access to . . . 15 Block.

(3) Revise segregation policies and place treatment staff. . . on Segregation Board.

(4) Eliminate inhuman restraint equipment and dangerous hand weapons.

(5) Guards should be chosen for 15 Block who would not be inhumane in their treatment of prisoners.

(6) Provide adequate and competent personnel for handling mental cases and an adequate screening board.

(7) A letter on prison stationery should ask the Parole Board to revise its procedures to give equal treatment to all inmates.

(8) Postoperative care should be given under the direction of the medical director.

(9) Equal opportunities for dental treatment should be established for all prisoners, with special regard to elimination of buying preference or obtaining it through friendship.

(10) Create a permanent council, elected by inmates, to confer periodically with prison officials.

(11) No reprisals should be made against any ringleader or participant in the revolt.[33]

These 11 demands proved acceptable to inmates Ward and Hyatt, and Warden Frisbie and Commissioner Brooks approved them. Later on Tuesday, Brooks and Fox took them to Governor Williams in Lansing for his approval. Still later that day and on Wednesday, they broadcast the agreement to the inmate body. Outside the prison, there

---

[32] Eaton, Andrienne, John Knox, et al, *op. cit.* , pp84, 85.

[33] Fox, *op. cit.*, pp108-113.

was much media buzz and holding of press conferences. As a show of good faith, Ward released one hostage on Tuesday and another on Wednesday leaving a total of nine.

Released Guard 1952 Riot
Photo by permission Archives of Michigan

Negotiations were rising in the political arena—with gubernatorial aspirants preparing for the fall election trying to make Governor Williams look weak, and the government ineffective. State Police Commissioner Leonard, who was looking to resign and run against Williams and wanted to appear tough, was anxious to have a "show of force." He obtained explosives from the Michigan National Guard sufficient to blast a hole in 15 Block. This concerned Fox because it appeared to him that if the inmates were not out on Thursday Leonard would move on Friday, raising the potential of significant loss of life for both inmates and hostages.[34]   Adding to the tension was a phone call from Hyatt saying he was now in control of 15 Block and was going to murder all the hostages (which proved to be a ruse he and Ward cooked up to move things along).   However, matters were brought to a conclusion by a phone call from Ward to Fox, which set in motion the acceptance of the final surrender document and led to a 'congratulatory' speech from Fox. The most controversial phrase from the speech was: "Earl Ward is the head leader, and the other boys are to be congratulated on the ability with which they have bargained. Their word has been good."

Fox then went to 15 Block and Ward surrendered to him, searching his cohorts and throwing weapons to the ground. They in turn searched the other inmates and the remaining hostages. All of the inmates from 15 Block then went to the mess hall for the steak and ice cream promised to them as an inducement for surrender.   In commenting on this outcome to the riot, a Special Study Committee wrote:

> While the Ohio Penitentiary riot involved as many prisoners as SPSM and resulted in greater property damage—Jackson must be accorded the dubious distinction of being in many ways, the most dangerous riot in American history. Never have hostages been in more danger for as long as those held in 15 Block by homicidal psychopaths . . .[35]

So, now that all of the hostages were unharmed after a harrowing and dangerous experience, would plaudits of praise and appreciation be showered upon the man who arranged to save them, Deputy Fox? Well, not exactly. The *Jackson Citizen Patriot* and *Detroit Free Press* published blistering attacks on Fox's congratulatory speech—seeming to forget that he made it while hostages' lives were still on the line. Republican gubernatorial candidate, John Martin, Jr. demanded the firing of Fox and the resignation of his superiors. Neil Oakley, vice-president of the guard union, demanded his dismissal, apparently

---

[34] Fox, *op. cit.*, pp250-253.

[35] *Ibid*, pp274-281.

oblivious to the fact that Fox was instrumental in rescuing union members, and that prior to that he had nothing to do with the safety and security of 15 Block—solely a responsibility of custody. Both Warden Frisbie and Governor Williams' Office criticized Fox's speech, which gave away nothing but was an inducement to bring the standoff to an end, while the 11 point agreement, that both had agreed to, was accepted by the inmates unchanged. As the political and media pressure mounted, and with no avenue of support, Vernon Fox resigned and subsequently closed out his career as a professor at Florida State University.

On the following Monday (April 28, 1952), Governor Williams ordered a "get tough policy" (which Commissioner Brooks broadcast the same day over the prison radio system) also threatening to bring in the Michigan National Guard and the state police.[36] The prisoners were not initially intimidated however, and the prison continued to be unsettled with periodic skirmishes for weeks afterward.

Commissioner Brooks appointed his chief staff aide, Seymour J. Gilman, as Deputy Warden on June 1, 1952, a move not supported by Warden Frisbie and opposed vigorously by the incumbent, Deputy Bacon, resulting in his two-week suspension.[37] Brooks transferred Bacon to Jackson's Trusty Division a few weeks later.

A new disturbance broke out in Nine Block on July 6, 1952, at 5:30 p.m. and within two hours cell doors were torn off, two guards were taken hostage, and rioters were demanding to see Warden Frisbie. By 8 p.m., the prison requested state police assistance, and shortly thereafter Deputy Gilman went into the block and negotiated an end to the affair, though not before an inmate was shot and killed.[38]

---

[36] Fox, *op. cit.*, p184.

[37] *Ibid.* p239.

[38] *Ibid.* p241.

Author's Note: The Jackson prison riot of 1952 was a major event in the Department's history; not only was it investigated and reported on extensively at the time, but the events of those few days have provided plot material for movies and TV shows ever since. It is because it is such a well-hoed field that I have preferred to give more coverage to matters which may not have been brought so much to light before. If the reader is interested, one book telling

A Gathering Storm

Commissioner Brooks dismissed Warden Frisbie four days later, ostensibly for not being able to maintain order after the riot. William Bannan, a Deputy Warden from the Ionia Reformatory, would become Jackson's next Warden.

---

more about the riot is *Violence Behind Bars,* by Vernon Fox.

WILLIAM H. BANNAN
1952–63
Photo courtesy of the Michigan Department of Corrections

Chapter Seven
The Warden Bannan Decade

WARDEN BANNAN WAS A SHORT, STOCKY, BALDING AND bespectacled man whose unexceptional appearance belied a powerful and effective leadership style. His fiery temper earned him the affectionate title of "Wild Bill" Bannan from staff, and his spectacles resulted in the nickname "Old Bad Eye" from prisoners. He could be funny and charming with an endless litany of stories. He was a great favorite as an entertaining local luncheon speaker. Fishing partners at their Canadian retreat told me he was the life of the party. His bluster and outbursts of temper never seemed to come at inopportune times and were never out of control, leading one to suspect that he choreographed them to make a point, enhance his image, or feed the "grapevine" he used for communication.[1] Bannan held a bachelor's degree from Western Michigan University and received the American Correctional Association's E.R. Cass Award for correctional excellence. A framed print prominently displayed in his office entitled *"The Engineer"* was one of his favorite readings. He would recite it during frustrating moments:

> Mine is not to run this train
> The whistle I can't blow
> Mine is not to say
> How far this train can go
> I'm not allowed to blow off steam
> Or even ring the bell
> But let the train go off the track
> And see who catches hell

Wild Bill served as Warden of Jackson for nearly 11 years, giving him the record for longest continuous tenure, with only Harry Jackson serving more years in total. He left an indelible mark on the prison—in some ways for the better and in some quite the opposite. His first assignment was to implement Governor Williams' "get tough" policy that aimed to restore and maintain order at Jackson Prison, "by any means necessary." Local legend has it that Governor Williams' limousine appeared at SPSM's administration building where the Warden received his instructions directly from the Governor. It was a legend Bannan did nothing to dispel—playing the "Governor's man" to the hilt so as to brook no interference from Lansing. It was a popular stance with custody staff disenchanted with Commissioner Brooks' perceived meddling with Warden Frisbie's management practices.

---

[1] Comments and observations which secretary, Lilly Scott and numerous officers made to me over several years on various assignments at SPSM from 1955 to 1968.

By Any Means Necessary

Several political forces drove the Governor's get tough message: (1) He was facing a very difficult fall election as a Democrat in a traditionally strong Republican state. (2) The media frenzy surrounding the April 1952 riot and hostage taking made his administration appear weak and inept. (3) Grandstanding by inmate riot leaders had angered the average citizen who had no patience with "uppity" convicts.

Adding fuel to this fire was a riot at the Ohio State Prison on October 30, 1952, the so-called "Halloween Riot," (which incidentally resulted in more rioters and more damage than the one six months earlier at Jackson.) This rekindled memories still fresh in the public mind and added to a general panic over prison disorder. The Republicans attempted to capitalize on this by claiming that SPSM was again a powder keg ready to explode at any minute. Williams' political advisors, fearing blood in the water, felt it was critical that he assert strong control so as not to appear wounded. Their political concern proved well founded because he won the fall election by such a close margin that for several days the Republican Party considered calling for a recount. The negative effect from even a minor last minute disorder could have cost him the election.

Luckily, for Governor Williams the new explosion of the powder keg waited until two weeks after the election. On November 19, 1952, a disturbance started in the dining room when 80 or so men protested about a spaghetti dinner. Deputy Cahill, leading seven guards, all armed with Tommy guns and shotguns, quickly quelled the uprising and the 2,000 or so other inmates unlocked at the time did not join the protesters. Guards fired twenty shots but no one was injured and total damage was less than $2,000. Warden Bannan, away deer hunting, rushed back, but it was all over before he arrived.[2]

To the guard force, the get tough policy signaled a return to the good old days and a diminution of Deputy Fox's individual treatment philosophy—that is, to a time when custody would reign supreme again. When officials hold life and death power over people's lives, as is the case with police and in prisons, firm ethical guidelines are

---

[2] Fox, *op. cit.,* p268.

essential to prevent unwarranted use of force and other abuses. Unfortunately, Governor Williams' "get tough" message contained no such safeguards. Therefore, it was not surprising when allegations of abuse and reports of beatings surfaced during the months following that policy declaration. During the summer and fall of 1952, prisoners in 15 Block began requiring medical treatment for injuries received. On November 30, Governor Williams announced that he had investigated the beating of two inmates several weeks earlier, one with a broken wrist and another severely beaten about the head. He said Warden Bannan was "having a rough time" and had sent guards in to quiet the block with fists and clubs, and the guards claimed self-defense. Commissioner Brooks said the beatings were necessary to head off another riot—"that troublemakers were ordered out of their cells and given a severe reprimand."[3] Four inmates (Jack Russell, Robert Fisher, Harrison Wilson, and Tom Gisevan) were injured on November 30 and another, Luther McCoy, was seriously injured on December 7.

The prison's Medical Director, Dr. Russell Finch, resigned in protest over what he considered brutality, observing that given the size and number of guards vs. the inmates involved it was difficult to accept a claim of self-defense against a 120-pound youngster whose limbs were broken, and added that an inmate lost an eye from a direct teargas blast. He said, "A policy of brutality has no place in a civilized and Christian community."[4] Nevertheless, incredibly, Paul Weber, the governor's press secretary, declared that Dr. Finch's resignation had nothing to do with the beatings.

By early 1953, Jackson Prison was facing a civil rights investigation by the U.S. Justice Department, and by the latter part of May, FBI agents were interviewing staff about reports of brutality.[5] Officers grumbled in later years that they felt "hung out to dry" by aggressive interrogations and a warden who claimed to know nothing about the use of force—saying, "He is the same guy (Warden Bannan) who brought us an armload of billy clubs, saying, "If you don't know

---

[3] *Ibid.*, 268-270.
[4] *Ibid*
[5] Fox, *op. cit.*, p296.

how to use them, I'll teach you!"[6] Governor Williams dispatched his most trusted aide, Phil Hart (who would later become one of the nation's longest serving Senators) to Washington to try to call off the FBI probe with the Governor's assurance that Michigan would correct the problem.[7] Apparently, the assurance was sufficient; the Justice Department took no further action.

Escape of the Sewer Rats

One of Jackson Prison's most infamous prison escapes occurred on December 19, 1953, when 13 prisoners, including four serving life for murder, used an acetylene torch to cut their way into the prison sewer system and emerge some 70 yards outside the east wall. The torch they used was stolen from a project which involved cutting up the old water tower inside the walls. It had been conveniently appropriated by an inmate working on that assignment. The escapees crossed the prison farm field to the home of a neighbor, Glen Milman, where they invaded his home, tied him and his wife up, and stole his clothes and car. They next went to the City of Jackson where they split up. Six of them continued in Milman's car, fleeing southeast toward Napoleon where they were apprehended by the State Police.[8] The other seven invaded the home of Joseph Watts at 109 Leroy Street. After eating, shaving and changing clothes they left in Watts' car taking his wife Mary and a nurse, Helen Gilbert, as hostages. Both women were released unharmed in Detroit. Five of these seven were apprehended shortly afterward while the two remaining fugitives, including the escape mastermind and first degree murder lifer, Ramon Usiondek, and Robert Dowling, were discovered four days later in Richmond, Indiana and captured in a gun to gun confrontation in a local hotel room.[9]

Prison staff then blocked any future sewer escape attempts by stacking a honeycomb of small diameter sewer pipes in the nearly five

---

[6] Comments I overheard during shop talk by officers interviewed by the FBI in 1953, such as Lee McCoy and Frank Lavoy, during shooting events in 1955 and 1956.

[7] This according to S. J. Gilman in conversation with me, ca 1961-62.

[8] *Jackson Citizen Patriot*, July 30, 1980, p 2.

[9] *Jackson Citizen Patriot, Ibid.*

foot diamater sewer drain. This creative solution would allow waste but not people to pass under the prison wall. The vast subterranean maze of tunnels for utilities, steam and sewer inside the walls was also hardened, along with more stringent custodial supervision of inmate repairmen working in them. In 1965, some eight years later, escapee Roman Usiondek succeeded in getting his life sentence overturned. Later, while on parole, Usiondek, murdered a Hamtramack fruit peddler but shot himself in the head minutes afterward as the police moved in.[10]

Guard School under Bannan—A Personal Recollection

Bannan's "guard school for all" policy was his signature program in the 1950s although it was not without controversy. The Warden argued that all "contact" employees had an underlying responsibility for safety and security, whatever their primary duties, and must pitch in during a riot or disturbance even using deadly force if necessary. He underlined his point with this colorful quote, "One of the nicest sights I have ever seen was a psychologist out in the yard with a shotgun telling an inmate he would let him have a blast of buckshot if he didn't get in line."[11] Further, he held that it was important that all non-custody staff understand the job of a corrections officer in controlling prisoners as well as in preventing escapes and the introduction of contraband. In addition, they should appreciate the mundane but essential importance of regulating the day-to-day operation of the prison (involving meals, recreation, counts, and movement). Warden Bannan stressed cooperation, and it was his belief that new staff attending guard school together would facilitate this.[12]

Some professional staff grumbled that attending guard school and taking weapons training created a barrier to establishing the inmate rapport necessary to gain the trust and confidence essential for a therapeutic relationship. However, I considered guard school an excellent learning opportunity. I came to the prison in February 1955 to do field training as a police administration student from Michigan

---

[10] *Ibid.*

[11] Fox, *op. cit.*, p302.

[12] From Warden Bannan's welcoming remarks at guard school class February 1955.

State University. A few weeks later, I was assigned to a vacant counselor's office (Counselor #6) under the guidance of Ted Koehler (Counselor #5). I found it a mutually beneficial arrangement, giving me real experience while helping the prison cover a staff vacancy they had been unable to fill. I became one of eight joining the next guard school. It consisted of two weeks in the classroom followed by a week working in a cellblock—actual guards received two additional weeks of training.

The training classroom was under the visitor's lobby of the Prison Administration Building. Our instructors were Lieutenant McNaughton (Lt. Mac) and Captain Demboski (Cpt. Joe), both with extensive prison experience and with a sensible fatherly manner of passing on their knowledge. They gave us a reasonable dose of prison regulations mixed with practical guidance. They included enough examples of actual things gone wrong when staff violated these principles to retain our interest.

We were told to be firm but fair, and to see a living breathing body in each cell when taking count—counting a dead man or a dummy not being acceptable—and both had happened. They stressed the importance of tool and key control—citing escapes and the Inspector Boucher murder as past consequences of failure in these matters. They used actual examples showing how favoring inmates with minor rule violations can lead to extortion or entrapment.

Accurately accounting for some 6,000 inmates three or so times daily takes some doing that most of us had never considered. "It's simple," Lt. Mac said, "you just take either an "out count" when the men are in or an "in count" when they are out. Got that?" he chuckled. For example, let us take an "out count" of the 500 cells in Five Block. It is taken at nighttime when most men are locked in; one officer takes the front side and the other the back, each containing 250 prisoners; checking each cell and seeing skin or breathing of a live occupant; at each empty cell with a door (occupant identification) card the officer notes the inmate name, number and cell number on his count sheet. The hall office then matches the empty cell names with night work details, hospital admissions; those out on court orders, and so forth. The 'in count' is the reverse of this—when most inmates are out working on assignments, block officers record the few that are in their cells, which are to be matched with assignment tallies. When everything matches, the hall office signals, "count is clear." If it does not, as Lt. Mack would say, "All hell breaks loose" with escape procedures mobilized.

By now, I had completed my classroom training, weapons qualification, had tasted tear gas, and had been outfitted for my uniform by an inmate tailor in the quartermaster department. On Monday of the third week, I reported to the base officer in Five Block to begin my week's cellblock assignment on the 6 a.m. to 2 p.m. shift. Memory fades after half a century but several sights and sounds remain: the bugler, playing reveille to awaken the block, the systematic clang of brake bars signaling men to "catch their doors" as brakes were thrown for mass movement, and the pungent fragrance of Pine Sol applied by hall boys perpetually mopping the floors. I also recall the awesome vast expanse of Five Block with five tiers of cells and window walls 350 feet long and 40 feet high.

Captain Penny Buchman's favorite bugler—an inmate who they claimed played in the U.S. Army Band and performed before General Eisenhower during WWII—was a special treat; his clear flawless renditions of reveille, taps and call to arms were show stoppers. Unfortunately, his life after the war had changed dramatically when he killed a man in Detroit. He was now serving 20 to 40 years—a shameful waste of talent. A few years later, someone decided that using buglers was inefficient. They were replaced by a raucous, grating public address system. As happens too often in our society, efficiency trumped class.

Warden Bannan was indeed perceptive about the value of "walking a mile in another man's moccasins" because just a week working in Five Block gave me a deep and lasting appreciation for the lot of correction officers. Five Block staff at that time consisted of three officers each on the morning and afternoon shifts and two at night. A "base" officer worked the ground floor controlling movement to and from the block, including inter-block to Four Block to the north and to the hall office-rotunda to the south, while the other two officers worked the four front and back galleries. An inmate block clerk and four hall boys completed the shift staff.

On my first day, base Officer Barton told me to learn by watching. I was to help the gallery officers until the meal lines were

130

out, then report to the kitchen sergeant while meals were in progress, and finally return to base. It sounded simple enough.

I would learn that food service was far more complicated than I imagined. Nearly 600,000 meals were prepared each month to feed the more than 4,000 men housed inside the walls and another 1,600 living in the Trusty Division, plus 300 or so shift employees who needed their meals on assignment—all prepared from an appropriation of fifty-four cents per meal.[13] Manpower to accomplish this was provided by several hundred inmates who were housed in the "Kitchen Block" (One Block). These included servers, cooks, bakers, clerks, dishwashers, and janitors all supervised by a dozen or so civilians. Reveille came at 3:30 a.m. for the early kitchen-crew to begin the early food line for themselves and others who needed to be on their jobs before the general workers. The main meal line for the general population, and a "diet line" for those with diabetes and other afflictions requiring special diets, followed. The main kitchen and dining room, known locally as the "big top" were located in the north quadrant of the core service building directly east of the infamous 15 Block. The dining room would seat nearly 2,000 at wooden tables and benches all facing the same direction and anchored to the floor (tables seating four each, restaurant style, replaced these benches by the 1960s.) The men from the north side cellblocks were fed their main meal first; then those from the south came through the sub-hall gates to the dining room. Food carts provided meals for shut-ins such as hospital patients and those in protective custody, detention, and punitive segregation. The logistics and scheduling of all this all were challenging indeed.

[13] Bacon, Ila J., *The State Prison of Southern Michigan 1837--1959*, Jackson: Unknown, April 21, 1959, p21.

The Dining Room, New Michigan State Prison, Jackson, Mich.

Prison Dining *Photo courtesy Jackson District Library*

As I stood in the block, activity was beginning with the rumble of 500 men awakened by reveille. The gallery officers were already at each end of the second tier (also called the first gallery) unlocking the "break boxes" for the inmate break-boys. (The gang-locking mechanisms for each tier were clad in ¼-inch boilerplate with a hinged access door securing the mechanism at the end of each tier—called a break-box and could only open with a large Folger Adams key.) Each cell door could be gang-unlocked by using a "break bar" to leverage an iron bar concealed in the jamb above the doors that would slide a few inches to unlock all that were not separately key locked (top locked). This gang-locking arrangement was obviously much more efficient than having to lock and unlock all cells individually.

At the officer's command, each break-boy in sequence bangs the break box, a signal to grab your door and then throws the breaks—the men step out, close their door behind them, and march down the gallery and the north stairway to base where they form an informal column awaiting release to march to the dining room for breakfast.

We all move in sequence to repeat the process on galleries three, four, and five. On the way, back down they instructed me to check for "cracked doors." The men were supposed to close their cell doors tight to latch them for locking but if one was left just slightly ajar they could slip back and open it with a piece of wire—allowing for mischief. The leading edge of the door was painted red to show if the door is ajar. To have "a cracked door" was a rule violation, which in those days could get a man five days in detention.

Inmates from north side blocks, one through five, walked from their cellblock on a service road looping around 15 Block into the dining room west entrance—in a rotating sequence determined by the yard sergeant. Five Block was first on this day and our nearly 500 men were assembled on base awaiting the command to proceed to breakfast. Officer Barton opened the door and they poured out three and four abreast swallowing up the two gallery officers supposedly escorting them, and me. I had never seen so many prisoners up close and personal before but the men were mostly cheerful; to them it was routine. That moment reminded me of the courage shown by officers in the midst of a thousand or more rioters in 1952 trying to persuade them to leave the chaos and go to their cells—with some of these officers becoming hostages themselves.

As I entered the Big Top, the Sergeant told me to go stand with my back to a post and said, "don't let them skip a row and don't you cause any trouble." He slammed a stainless steel food tray on the service counter signaling workers to be ready—I thought it was a gunshot and hoped my flinch went unnoticed. The men funneled down to a single line along the serving counter separating the kitchen from the dining area—a seemingly never-ending stream but one which rapidly and efficiently seated about 1,500 men. They filled the tables from the front to back, and about 15 minutes afterwards un-seating began—an officer backed up an aisle signaling each row to depart. It was efficient and orderly but later, I would hear some grumbling that it was unfair because the last seated were the first to go leaving little time to eat. Men with work assignments went directly to their jobs and the unemployed returned to their blocks.

I assumed that working a morning shift would involve little activity because most inmates would be out of the cellblock working. However, I soon found there was plenty to keep us busy: supervising the hallboys doing the cleaning; managing moves (inmate and their personal property) both coming in and leaving, as well as moves within the block; writing "call out" passes to send men for job classification, parole hearing, or to their counselors. An "in count" had to be taken and a cell or two searched for contraband. Further, the third officer was seldom in the block; he was out running errands, carrying messages, or conducting inmate block moves.

The inmate block clerk, who had been on the job for five years, proved invaluable to the officers—keeping track of paperwork from the hall office and preparing responses, inmate passes, count sheets, block inmate payrolls, cell move reports and top lock records. ("Top lock" is a second locking function similar to a dead bolt, and is used to secure the cell when unoccupied or keep a particular inmate in during mass movement.) The afternoon shift was even more hectic because of yard recreation and evening programs like Alcoholics Anonymous, as well as the requirement that count be cleared for the midnight shift.

Counselor's Row

In March 1955, after guard school, I began my internship on counselor's row in the main prison—there were 10 of us with inmates assigned according to their prison number's last digit. I had number six. Our offices lined the corridor between the secure sub-hall gate and the main kitchen, providing convenient access for inmates from both the north and south side but with the security of screening by the sub-hall officer. Each of us shared an inmate clerk and a small reception area. Each counselor had a caseload of about 400 which was constantly changing because of new commitments and transfers in from, or out to, other facilities. The Trusty Division with its 1,600 inmates had its own staff of four counselors located in 16 Block.

Classification Director Leo Schmeige was our immediate supervisor and an excellent boss. Next in command was Gordon Fuller, who headed the Treatment Department and provided Leo solid backing. Schmeige was also the classification committee chair and teamed with Assistant Deputy Harold Tucker, the custody/security representative who held veto power over committee decisions. The inmate's counselor and a work or school supervisor completed the classification committee membership. The counselor was the hearing recorder. Schmeige also organized an efficient and fair labor pool system operated by Alex Butkewitz to manage the thousands of inmate workers. Inmates classified for programs had their names placed in the labor pool to be drawn on a "first-in first-out" basis; exceptions for cause required Schmeige's approval.

An admission summary was required for each new commitment. The summary briefly described his crime, prior criminal history and known enemies, and included reception unit test results (IQ, grade level, and Minnesota Multiphasic Personality Inventory). An approved visiting and correspondence list had to be established along with any information helpful for prison program or work assignment. Each of us averaged six to ten such cases a week (by 1957 that responsibility was assumed by the newly organized Reception Diagonositic Center located in Seven Block.) Once on our caseload, every move, change in status, parole hearing, lifer hearing, program classification, correspondence or visitor list change required a paper trail or report. As each man approached a parole hearing date we prepared a Parole Elgibility Report containing a summary of the man's work, school and conduct record and any personal observations, for use by the parole board at his hearing—which we were invited to sit in on. A lifer report was required after 10 years for men serving life sentences and before every subsequent review date set by the parole board. The typing pool transcribed confidential reports and correspondence from wax cylinders that we recorded with 1940s-era DictaPhones. We generated a virtual paper blizzard.

One of the more enjoyable rewards of working at the prison was the inter-prison weapons contest. The four major prisons at the time, Jackson, Marquette, Michigan Training Unit and the Michigan Reformatory at Ionia, held an inter-prison weapons contest, with five-man teams shooting for a combined score of rifle, pistol and shotgun matches. The championship gave the winners a whole year's bragging rights. Ammunition was free, practice was a break from office routine, and, since it was primarily a corrections officer activity, I thought a counselor shooting with them might help our image. With most guards that was so, but a lieutenant protested that counselors were not qualified to try out. Warden Bannan settled the dispute by decreeing that since all staff were required to complete guard school and had custody responsibility in emergencies, all were eligible for the shooting team. My winning of "top gun" in that year's match, which helped the SPSM team win by the slim margin of ten points, was sweet redemption and I was a welcome team member from then on.

Jackson Prison's Championship All Weapons Team 1956
(Team Captain, Lee McCoy to second from left. Perry Johnson in white shirt and tie.) All weapons: rifle, pistol, and shotgun.
Photo courtesy the author's personal collection.

One of the top marksman on the team was Lee McCoy and, although he was an intense competitor, we got along well and entered local pistol competitions throughout southern Michigan until I transferred to the camp program in 1959. Over the years McCoy won many winner's trophies for rifle, pistol, and shotgun marksmanship and also for a short time as a semi-pro boxer, and a body builder. Both he and his brother, Clare, the prison locksmith could be very funny and practical jokers. Sadly, long after they retired both met tragic ends: Lee developed dementia late in life and at age 88 left his home to cross through a familiar swamp on the way to visit a neighbor—disoriented, he became lost and died from exposure; and home invaders murdered Clare and his wife a few years before.

The Parole Conundrum

SPSM Prisoners complained for years about the obscurity surrounding the granting of parole—clarification on that issue was one of the eleven demands arising from the 1952 riot. From the prisoner's perspective, "doing time was the price of doing the crime" with the sentencing judge setting the price (minimum sentence imposed) based on harm done and the man's prior criminal history; therefore any increased time (parole denial) should be based only on the prisoner's bad conduct while in prison. They argued that parole hearings often amounted to an unfair retrial of their crime resulting in an unjust added sentence (parole denied without cause.). (Many circuit court judges shared this view.)[14]

The parole board, on the other hand, viewed parole as a privilege granted solely at their discretion to prisoners they believed deserved parole. In arriving at their decision, the parole board rehashed everything the sentencing judge considered plus the inmate's prison conduct, and information from police, prosecutors, or victims. A. Ross Pascoe, long time parole commissioner and later parole board member, the most influential voice for the parole board for many years, claimed that their parole decisions were "scientific" and that parole was a privilege, not a right. Prosecutors supported Pascoe's view that parole was a privilege, and should only be granted where there was compelling evidence of reformation.

Prison staff, especially counselors and corrections officers who had daily contact with inmates, needed rational and fair parole board policies and decisions that could be logically explained to anxious prisoners and which would lead to logical action plans. That is "clean up your conduct, let's develop a good release plan, you need more AA, achieve your GED," something tangible and achievable.

Inmates found three parole board issues for which staff had no good answer particularly vexing: (1) Parole denial with a review three years out which was sometimes longer than the original minimum sentence already served. (2) Parole denial with no explanation for inmates with a perfect conduct and work record. (3) Inmates protesting their innocence were denied parole because they would not admit guilt—even though we had evidence that innocents are wrongly convicted more often than we want to believe.

The Corrections Commission and Department Director Gus Harrison[15] were concerned about these same issues and their potential

---

[14] Judge Skillman comments, *Detroit News,* January 30, 1945.

[15] Public Act 232, 1953, abolished the 1937 Act and established a six member bi-partisan commission (MCC). The newly created

for injustice, and they began to take action to ameliorate them. In the ensuing months, Director Harrison issued orders limiting parole continuances to 18 months; requiring the parole board to state reasons on the record for parole denial when institutional record and recommendations were favorable; and prohibiting parole denial solely because the inmate claims innocence.

In December 1954, the Commission stripped the imperious and once powerful Pascoe of his parole board chairmanship and appointed board member Roy Nelson his replacement. They softened the blow by commending Pascoe for his long and courageous service, and he would continue as a parole board member until 1960. Nelson proved to be a competent manager and much less polarizing than Pascoe.

In April of 1954, a meeting between the parole board and counselors at SPSM stressed developing a co-operative relationship in pre-parole preparation. Counselors were encouraged to make recommendations to the parole board and to attend board hearings, an invitation welcomed by the counselors and supported by the department. The Commission reviewed minutes of parole board/counselor meetings in subsequent years and further strengthened their support by suggesting that counselors help inmates prepare for their parole hearing by developing potential questions that they might be asked by the board. Following this, counselors attended their men's parole hearings to offer supplemental information as needed, and to understand what follow-up the parole board wanted.

At that time, the parole board held hearings for "inside" inmates at SPSM in the secure room located in the rotunda between the hall office and the entrance gate. (Secure hearing rooms for the parole board were mandatory following a 1939 kidnapping of the parole board at the Marquette Branch Prison.) Parole hearings were typically conducted for two or three days every month or two. Inmates with an "A" prefix (first prison sentence) were first; repeat prison cases next, and finally those previously continued by the parole board known as Passover cases. I first heard of "Passover cases" from parole board members A. Ross Pascoe and Fred Sanborn when, after a social coffee

---

MCC then appointed Gus Harrison as Director of the Department of Corrections (MDOC). Director Harrison served for 19 years, the longest and most stable time in the Department's history.

moment, Mr. Pascoe announced, "Well gentlemen, put on your butchering aprons, and let's begin the feast of the Passovers." The hearings were brutal with comments such as, "the police should have shot you" commonplace; obviously this team held distain for inmates previously denied parole, either as violators or repeat offenders. It was no wonder that many prisoners feared and hated some members of the parole board, especially Pascoe. Other board members were more congenial and, to my mind professional, in their demeanor.

What was the "science" the parole board applied to determine who should be paroled? As a greenhorn counselor, I was eager to learn from these experienced old timers—A. Ross Pascoe was working in the parole commissioner's office as a new graduate from the UM law school three years before I was born. I listened, questioned, and studied the material they seemed to favor in making their decisions. There seemed to be three principle factors—the extent and seriousness of the man's criminal history, the impression his face-to-face interview left with the parole board, and his behavior and program participation while in prison. Parole on the earliest date (minimum term) was almost certain if these factors were all favorable. Board member Leonard McConnell called them "Self oilers". On the other hand, many inmates believed that they must show "progress" during their sentence so a few misconduct reports at the beginning followed by "cleaning up their record" would gain parole board favor. The only common denominator I found was that board members were supremely confident in the analytical and persuasive value of their face-to-face interview with the inmate. As Oregon's Corrections Director Amos Reed observed years later, "soon after appointment parole board members begin to hear the rustle of silken robes, thinking they have mystical powers." A phenomenon that would stand in the way of developing an analytical systems model for parole selection— and does to this day. I found no evidence of "science" used by the parole board.

However, a decade later the department's Program Bureau (research department) developed a powerful tool to predict future violent crime using just a few variables readily available in each inmate's prison record.[16] It soon became invaluable to prison security classification but the parole board remained skeptical about "actuarial prediction" as undermining its contribution to "scientific parole decisions."

Anyway, McConnell's "self oiler" label haunted my mind at the time. Why not tell a "self oiler" that he has a parole, if he maintains good prison work and conduct? That became the germ for a "parole contract program" twenty years later. After 3500 contracts, research analysis found that the program was "not cost effective" and the Corrections Commission canceled it. This conclusion was understandable at the time because prison population pressures made it impossible for the prison to provide the program support required in the inmate's contract. I still believe that it is a good program concept for a stable prison/parole system.

Before the Civil Rights Movement

I remember Schmeige most for his strategy and courage in beginning to break down racial barriers in prison assignments nearly a decade before the 1960s Civil Rights movement. African Americans represented about one-third of the prison population in the 1950s but would balloon to nearly two-thirds by the mid-1970s. White inmates held most of the better jobs, almost all of the skilled positions, and most of the food service jobs. Blacks drew the laundry and unskilled menial jobs. This led to a mainly white "kitchen cell block" and a predominately black "laundry cell block," leading some to claim in later years that the prison had segregated cell housing which was not true— racially integrating work assignments would prove to solve this problem.

Observing Schmeige at work was enlightening—coming from an all-white rural setting and knowing only a few African Americans in college, ten years before the Selma marches I had no idea about the depth of racism in the prison—among both prisoners and many of the staff. Schmeige knew all of their excuses. "I can't have him clerking in the store; those blacks will steal us blind" or "they were raised on the

---

[16] *"Information on Michigan Department of Corrections' Risk Screening,"* a publication of Michigan Department of Corrections August 15, 1978.

streets and cannot handle machinery." Staff would try to fire blacks on flimsy excuses or minor misconduct reports. Schmeige dealt with this on several fronts; he controlled the labor pool and Deputy Tucker could mediate phony tickets. He could pave the way for placement of a skilled black inmate with the more reasonable supervisors, and he handpicked well-qualified black inmates and coached them on how to deal with sabotage from white fellow workers or their bosses.

One example: No black inmate had ever been assigned to food service in the officer's dining room so Schmeige recruited an over-qualified candidate, coached him and had the kitchen steward briefed. Does that sound overly cautious? Well, the next week, when a 35-year-old black man, neatly dressed in pressed kitchen whites, began serving our food, a number of officers, including a shift captain, boycotted the officer's dining room and brought sack lunches. The captain was overheard saying, "ain't no nigger going to touch my food". Within a few weeks though, another black man joined the first and that assignment was integrated from then on. Several officers continued bringing sack lunches for a couple of years. Schmeige continued to chip away at segregated assignments at SPSM until he accepted a job at the Washington State Penitentiary in Walla Walla a few years later.

VIEW FROM TOP OF "ROTUNDA" OF THE NEW MICHIGAN STATE PRISON, JACKSON, MICH.

15 Block and the walkway goes around the end of 15 block to the dining room. *Photo courtesy Jackson District Library*

Finally, Counselors for 15 Block

When I finished my degree at Michgan State I joined the department as a full-time employee, working as a counselor at Jackson. Then, in 1957, Fuller and Schmiege obtained an added position to provide counseling services for inmates who required protection, those who posed a danger to themselves or others, who were escape or management problems, or who were mentally or medically incapacitated. 15 Block, held the most dangerous and disruptive in "segregation 000,' or detention, while the potential victims and more needy were housed in lower Six Block and on "blue hold card" status or as "unemployable 00."

It was decided that counselor Charles Egeler and I would split my number six caseload and the new counselor, DeVere Parker, would take over Egeler's number four caseload. We also divided the "special needs" caseload with Egeler, taking numbers one through five and me six through zero. We agreed to visit both Six Block and 15 Block every week to handle any inmate issues, regardless of caseload ID number coming to our attention. Because these inmates were shut ins, this required custody clearance and Charles Egeler and I became the first counselors authorized access to 15 Block—five years after Governor Williams had agreed to hostage takers' demands that counselors have regular access there. It was a grim assignment. First, the physical plant was oppressive: opposing cells across a hall on each floor with low concrete and steel ceilings and little natural light made for a tunnel-like effect. To get to each floor we had to climb undersized stairways with low overheads (both of us were over six foot tall and constantly bumped our heads.) Many inmates were hostile and uncommunicative, though thankfully not abusive. We found enough need to make our time worthwhile—even if it involved nothing more than writing a letter home to a mother for some poor illiterate soul. Door cards labeled the cell occupant's status: a '000' red card meant high security segregation while a '00' white card indicated an unemployed inmate awaiting a general population cell. The first floor housed punitive segregation—it was in inmate parlance, "the hole" but was called "detention" by the prison administration. Rule violators were sentenced to detention by the disciplinary court for up to 30 days—later to be restricted to 10 days by order from Director Gus

Harrison—with a "bread and water" diet for the first three days. Detention cells had no windows; only a ventilation louver at the top of the exterior wall allowed a glimmer of daylight. A wall mounted bench made from maple planks served as a bed; a water faucet, an oriental toilet and one blanket (two in the winter) were provided.

Egeler and I worked together with the 15 Block—Six Block caseload for two years, ending when I accepted a promotion to become Supervisor of Camp Waterloo.

From maximum to minimum security—a culture shock

In 1935, the Federal Government built a barracks type CCC (Civilian Conservation Corps) work camp near the little town of Waterloo, some 16 miles east of SPSM. "Camp Waterloo" for a time served as a POW camp for some of Rommel's Afrika Korps, but in 1948 became a prison camp as part of SPSM's Trusty Division. It became one of the Corrections Conservation Program's 13 camps under S. J. Gilman in 1952. I became superintendent of the camp in 1959 when it housed over 200 minimum-security felony prisoners. I found this a welcome relief from SPSM's prison hardware and mass of humanity. Here there were no fences or guns, and I soon knew every prisoner on sight and by name. Several men I knew from my caseload at SPSM and even two who had been in segregation in 15 Block. I was amazed at how differently they conducted themselves in camp.

One evening as I worked late I dropped by the camp dining room for a cup of coffee and one of the sumptuous cinnamon rolls the baker always seemed to have on hand. One of the former 15 block residents, this man had proved to be an excellent baker, cheerful and cooperative, earning a handsome dollar a day—twice the camp average. He sat down at the table with me and our conversation went something like this, "Bill, when you were in 15 Block you were cranky and would hardly talk to me—now you are one of our best bakers and a pleasant surprise. How come?" Bill replied, "Mr. Johnson, you don't understand. I had a reputation to keep in 15 Block. I could not be seen talking with you. Here there aren't any hard asses that matter." Bill met his Waterloo in Illinois a few years later where they executed him for a hired killing, but for now he had taught me something about the affects of prison environment on human behavior.

Another personal encounter at Camp Waterloo left an indelible mark on my mind. On a cold March day, the transfer-bus unloaded a half dozen prisoners at the camp office. As I reviewed their terse half-sheet transfer orders, I saw one was serving "natural life" for first-degree murder—somewhat unusual for a minimum-security placement. His name was Lloyd Cowell and the order said he was being moved to the Camp Program for decompression from the pressure of having lived his entire adult life behind the stonewalls of Marquette Branch Prison—the state's most secure institution. There was casual mention that some 25 years before he was labeled a psychopath by the prison psychiatrist—meaning he had no conscience or sense of remorse—a constitutional defect of personality, indelibly imprinted in his genes. He was not to be trusted. Apparently a man to be watched. It might be well to learn more about him, to take a look at his file.

Police reports about the offense bringing him to prison were skimpy but a yellowed newspaper editorial expressing community outrage over the crime told more of the story. Here are excerpts from that clipping:

> ...there is widespread grief over the tragic death of an estimable character, whose body was discovered ten days after he had been shot and instantly killed by an ingrate 18 year old grandson. . .
>
> ...When a lad of two, his parents became estranged and the grandfather took him into his own home where he gave him the best there was, lavishing his affections upon the grandson without stint...
>
> ...When the aged man had retired, the grandson took a revolver placing it near the old man's temple...Mercifully death was instantaneous and the old man never knew the lengths to which ingratitude can go...

It was a description that undoubtedly influenced application of the psychopath label—as newspaper accounts influence our view of crime and punishment to this day.

So Lloyd was apparently a psychopath serving life so his only hope for freedom was gubernatorial clemency or escape. Clemency was rarely granted but a work camp with no fences and one duty officer for 232 inmates housed in open barracks hardly provided a deterrent for a "bush parole," prison parlance for escape. Since park conservation crews, the camp's primary work assignment, provided even greater freedom, and hence temptation for escape, I decided to work Lloyd in camp where I could keep him under a watchful eye.

To my surprise, I came away from our first meeting favorably impressed—he was courteous and well spoken, neatly dressed in prison blues, of slender build and average height. Best of all, he was a prison-trained mechanic. So it made sense to assign him to camp maintenance where, as soon as the sergeant taught him to drive the camp truck, he would also be fire chief—in charge of the camp's antiquated pumper-tanker—the only response available for miles around should fire break out among the highly combustible barracks. He proved to be a competent and reliable worker who pampered the fire truck.

A couple of weeks after his arrival, Lloyd requested permission to transfer money from his prison account to his wife. His wife? He had been in prison his entire adult life—how could he have a wife? He explained that a pen-pal relationship blossomed into romance, and then into a prison wedding at Marquette. She was mother to two school-age children, and Lloyd claimed her former husband had badly abused her. But why Lloyd? Perversely, given his designation as a psychopath, or perhaps the attraction of his gentle manner, or possibly the security his confinement offered.

Within weeks, there were more requests to transfer money to his wife so I decided to check a little further. He had a $3,000 balance in his account—not bad on 50 cents a day prison pay. However, there was more—inmate accounting revealed that while at Marquette he had transferred nearly $10,000 to this woman. Where did this money come from? I learned from Marquette Warden Buchkoe that Lloyd had become a master leather-craftsman and great demand developed for his products at the prison's Hobbycraft store—that he had even subcontracted leather carving and lacing to other prisoners. For years, he worked on prison work assignments by day and made leather goods in his cell in evenings. He frugally saved his earnings. Armed with this information my next meeting with Lloyd went something like this:

"Lloyd, this is your third money transfer request since you came to camp—at this rate you won't have any savings when it comes time to go home. What's going on?"

"She's having a tough time. The kids have had a lot of sickness. She needs to outfit them for school. When she tells me her troubles what can I do? I'm just a convict in prison!"

"Well for one thing, you can tell her that I have frozen your account."

Lloyd actually seemed relieved and said, "I wish I'd talked to you earlier," and added as an afterthought, "I'd have more in my account now."

I then asked him what his release plans were—how would he use this money? His answer seemed realistic given his mechanical skill, "I want to buy into a gas station where I can also work on cars."

"Is there anyone to help you back home?"

"Just my wife."

"No friends or family?"

"No one. My wife is the only one who ever visited me."

"Are your mother or father alive?"

"I don't know."

"Do you want me to try to locate them?"

"No, they know where to find me."

Then came judgment day—the day that I must write his "lifer report" for the Parole Board. A favorable report would not assure his freedom, but continued confinement was likely to result from a bad one. My task was especially troubling because of unanswered questions about Lloyd and because I had grown to genuinely like him.

I recall reflecting on Lloyd's camp performance while reviewing his master file with great care—usually I merely screened them for key documents and recent reports. Prison files are often not worth reading thoroughly, so much is merely a rehash of reports written hastily to meet some deadline long past. Nevertheless, I looked for some missing piece, something that would help me understand both the crime and the man; I wanted to resolve the contradiction between the Lloyd I knew and the murderer described in his prison file.

His tattered file, about three inches thick, contained the chronicle of his entire adult life. Somewhat the equivalent of St. Peter's Book of Life, his sins were all neatly recorded in prison reports and criminal rap sheets. As I dug through the old correspondence and reports I found a small blue envelope tucked away unopened. It was from Lloyd's mother, addressed to Warden Coons at the Ionia Reformatory where Lloyd began his sentence at age 18. Whether through negligence or indifference it had never been read. I opened it, and though poor penmanship and time-faded ink rendered it barely legible, I was able to read it:

> Dear Warden,
> To give boy's history would start back from my girlhood, as he was brought and reared by my father who is now dead.
> My mother died leaving three children . . . I was not quite four... My brother and I managed to stay alive somehow. Before I was five we had a stepmother...I don't remember her ever punishing us but she would tell dad and we got terrible whippings from him ...
> Once I was taken from school by a family and was kept three days. They wanted to send my dad away, I wouldn't let them. I was all black and blue and had large welts on me that were laid open from whip, he wanted to rub salt in them to make them hurt more...
> ...I was 15, the following May I met and ran away with the boy's father. It was an escape but a bad mistake. We never loved... Lloyd was born from a worried, distracted mother. His father was in jail...and baby and father never met. We, the baby and I, got work almost as soon as I was up and around... Then we were quarantined for small-pox. I was bad enough, but the boy nearly died. When we were well enough took baby home to dad and step-mother. We were never welcome, mostly because I ran away and married a good-for-nothing, as Dad would say! Well, he took boy for keeps at 1 ½ years. Then I met and married the father of my three children of which all have the attentions that Lloyd should have had. But Dad wouldn't give him up, said I have to pay for all the years he stayed there

room and board and clothing. He kicked my husband
and I out when we went to visit him and the baby...
So how little Lloyd managed to grow up, sometimes I
wonder. No mother, step-mother's health gone, so
absentminded and so filthy, couldn't eat there, such a
change, boiled potatoes in jackets, no gravy, a piece
of fat pork and the fat grease from it, homemade
bread so hard and old...
We went there very seldom, if we did, we took our
lunch, boy thought we didn't care for him, he would
evade me and bite his fingernails, he looked like a
tramp, no clean clothes, hair long, we cut it there
because we were ashamed of him, terrible, he never
had any spending money, yet Dad worked him hard,
even hired him out...
Somehow I couldn't cry I felt like a sledge hammer
knocked me senseless. My father dead by my own
son's hand not even for freedom--I felt like a
murderer myself...

The letter did nothing to explain why she never came to visit her
son in prison, but her account of his childhood made it clear that
whoever wrote the newspaper report of the crime had no inkling of the
situation and events which probably gave rise to it.

I last saw Lloyd as he loaded a cardboard box and duffle bag
containing his worldly possessions onto the transfer bus. Governor
Romney had granted him clemency and he was going home. He
hunched against the raw December wind as we said goodbye; a small
man in prison blues, looking so forlorn one could imagine that was how
he looked when he came to prison as a teenager.

I asked, "Well how does it feel?"

"Truthfully, I'm scared," He said. "Suppose they screw
something up and I really don't get my parole? What's it really like out
there? Hell," he laughed self-consciously, "The only restaurant I ever
been in was when Lt. Robbie let me drive on transfer. Will the kids
accept me? I got a million worries—crazy huh?"

Lloyd went on to complete his mandatory four-year parole
without incident. He became a service station owner in the Flint area

and on one occasion was cited by the *Flint Journal* as a "good Samaritan" for aiding a crime victim. There was no mention of his past record. Many years later Lloyd—after helping raise his stepchildren—retired to Florida with his wife. If still alive, he would be in his 90s now and, I hope that if he feels any need for redemption for his youthful crime, he has found it in a life well lived.

Lloyd's story reaffirmed my belief that we should never think we know the whole story about anyone, and also that redemption must come from within; others cannot impose it.

Some people seem to believe that if a prisoner is not locked up behind concrete and steel, justice is not being served. However, the Camp Program was truly a bargain for the citizens of Michigan. We built new camps with inmate labor at a fraction of the cost of even medium security prisons. They also operated at less than a third of prison per diem cost, and the camp inmates performed valuable cleanup, maintenance, and repair work in Michigan's many parks and forests. With few exceptions, camp inmate behavior was exemplary. My four years at Camp Waterloo left me with a deep appreciation of the importance of treating inmates with respect and a recognition that making their surroundings more oppressive than necessary is not the way to elicit positive change and responsible behavior.

GEORGE A. KROPP
1963—70
Photo courtesy of the Michigan Department of Corrections

Chapter Eight
The Warden Kropp Era

IN JANUARY 1963, WARDEN BANNAN RETIRED and accepted appointment as the superintendent of the Detroit House of Correction. George Kropp, Warden at the Michigan Reformatory in Ionia, became acting Warden of Jackson Prison effective February 1, 1963. He would find his seven-year tenure a continuous adventure.

Eight Block Escape

Warden Kropp was unaware that four tough desperadoes serving long prison sentences had been planning a complicated and cunning escape from inside Jackson for many months. They were now waiting for the ideal foggy and rainy night to conceal their flight from the prison gun towers. That night came on April 23, 1963. Shortly after midnight, they removed bars, previously cut and puttied, to enter the plumbing chase behind their cells in Eight Block. This gave them access to an exterior window with bars also cut and puttied. From there they slipped directly under a gun tower and cut through the security fence at a blind spot and were free.

But on foot and without a further get-away plan, the gang had the good fortune to stumble onto the recently abandoned County Home a few miles southwest of the prison. Conveniently, the electricity was still on and clothing left by former residents was available to replace their prison garb. There was also a radio for listening to news broadcasts and some food in the kitchen. Further good luck came from the prison's delay in discovering them missing; one of the four, lifer James Hall, was discovered missing nearly three hours later and the absence of the other three only after 6 a.m. when Cpt. Penny Buchman, the morning shift commander, ordered a full prisoner count.

Besides inmate Hall, the other escapees were Richard Mauch, serving life for the attempted murder of a sheriff's deputy; Elmer Crachy, a professional safecracker serving 20 to 30 years as a habitual criminal; and Robert Gipson serving 13 to 25 years for second-degree murder. After the 6 a.m. prisoner count, the serious potential for further depredations by the escapees triggered a massive manhunt. Roadblocks were set up throughout Jackson County. The FBI, 200 police and prison officers, planes, helicopters and dogs hunted them for four days—but no one thought to thoroughly search the abandoned County Home. Figuring that the police heat had cooled after four days, on Saturday they stole a panel truck and fled west. In Oshkosh, Wisconsin Crachy cracked a supermarket safe and the gang split up its $10,000 contents. Police arrested Hall two weeks later in Carthage, Missouri, after he was involved in two auto accidents. A gunfight at the Frontier Bar in Madison, Wisconsin, resulted in the arrests of Mauch and Gipson. Crachy was located that same night at a cottage at Lake Waubesa, some two miles south of Madison, where the three had holed up.[1]

---

[1] Leanne Smith, *Peek through Time:* In 1963, four Southern Michigan Prison inmates stage a daring escape, published, September 23, 2011.

These four were the first inmates ever to cut their way to freedom through the bars in their cells as well as through the perimeter of the Jackson Prison. How they pulled that off was a question Warden Kropp and his staff had to answer quickly lest it happen again—and, of course, to quiet the political and public uproar.[2] The postmortem of the escape was not pretty! The Q and A went something like this:

Q. Metal cutting blades are tightly controlled critical tools to be accounted for every day and locked in a safe by the civilian supervisor as he goes off shift, so how did the inmates get them?

A. Most likely, Mauch purloined the blades from the prison's maintenance shop but they could possibly have been smuggled in by corrupt staff—inventory and log records were inconclusive.

Q. How did four high-risk long timers get cells on the outside perimeter of Eight Block—a known structurally weak south side cell block?

A. Undetermined; they possibly bribed the hall office cell-move inmate clerk, one at a time.

Q. How were the inmates able to pass through a high security, locked passage door in the cellblock plumbing chase to get to the exterior window they cut out?

A. Mauch fashioned keys to the door locks, probably from a mold made from putty or soap, copying the real keys during supervised plumbing or maintenance repairs.

Q. Why weren't the missing inmates discovered during regular rounds?

A. Each prisoner left a dummy in his bed, fashioned from winter underwear stuffed with rags and clothing, with heads made from wrapped rolls of toilet paper—Crachy even used hair swept from the prison barbershop to make the head look more

---

[2] Gathered during discussions between Warden Kropp and me when I was his Administrative Assistant during summer of 1963.

lifelike. The rule of "seeing skin, or seeing a live body" during counts was not followed.

Q. How could four men traverse 20 yards to the security fence and cut a hole to escape just 50 feet under the gun tower guard? (Warden Kropp was livid and was of a mind to fire the officer.)

A. The officer pleaded, "Warden, I couldn't even see the ground that night." Kropp went up on the tower at midnight and concurred that he had a point—so from then on during heavy fog he ordered foot patrol inside the fence.

Q. How could such an elaborate escape plan hatched over a period of nearly a year go undetected?

A. The prison grapevine had rumors that these inmates had something going on, because Deputy Warden Cahill had the security deputy cards for each of the four pulled and on his desk. Therefore, there must have been some sort of tip, but he had gone home the previous day without following up, a damning circumstance that contributed to his being encouraged to retire shortly thereafter.

This whole escape affair provided rich training material for guard school from that day on and caused a total review of security policy and procedure at the prison. It also resulted in staff changes, including one that involved my transfer back from the Camp Program.

On July 1, 1963, Warden Kropp appointed me his Administrative Assistant, replacing Louis Utess who became an Assistant Deputy Warden. I viewed working directly for such a respected warden as a career opportunity and was in no way disappointed by the move. Kropp's guiding principles are as valid today as they were then: To treat people with dignity and respect whether they are inmates or staff; to be firm but fair with the power of the warden's office; and to give a full measure of honest work and require the same from the staff.

One example that stands out in my mind was the way he handled the granting of "good time" and recommendations to the parole board for prisoners eligible for hearings each month. I would pre-screen the inmate files and we would work together, often late into the evening because this task came on top of the many demands on the Warden's time each day. After one particularly long evening, I remember Warden Kropp looking over at me with a sly smile and saying, "Perry, we're very generous here. You can take all the time you want to do your eight hours of work."

George was meticulous about granting or denying good time—he wanted each case to be determined on what the prisoner actually deserved. His reasoning would prove prophetic. "If Wardens don't use good time to reward good behavior, which also means taking away good time for bad behavior, the legislature will repeal the good time statute," he said. And in 1998, it was repealed. Meanwhile, of course, some prisoners complained that even though they had been granted parole they could not go home because the Warden took away good time for misconduct. George's response was, "That is good advertising, because every inmate with a clean record hears them and thinks it's fair."

There were some memorable moments in those years. I vividly recall November 22, 1963. The Warden was escorting the Corrections Commission and Director Harrison on a tour of the prison when we got word of President Kennedy's assassination, and I ended up delivering the message.

Then there was the Saturday that the Warden's houseboy stole his state car and escaped wearing one of Kropp's favorite sport jackets—I think he was more irritated about the jacket than the car.

One of Kropp's special gifts was an exceptional memory. He began his career as a 19-year-old record clerk at the Marquette Branch Prison in 1926 and nearly 40 years later could recite prisoners' names and serial numbers from that time. So he was a wonderful source for department history. He once told me that he took minutes in 1933 for a special committee the Governor appointed to study ways to subdivide Jackson Prison—because immediately after it was built many recognized that it was too large to be administered properly. Which problem was, of course, still unresolved thirty years later.

Even years after his retirement, I would call Kropp at his home to get the background on a policy or practice, or the history of some person long gone and forgotten.

In early 1964, the department made several staff moves including bringing John Elmquist from Marquette to be the Deputy Warden at

SPSM; I replaced him at Marquette, and it would be some years before I returned to Jackson. Therefore, the following event occurred after I left.

Inspector Dembosky Taken Hostage

One Monday morning, October 18, 1965, a number of inmates in SPSM's North Yard, intoxicated to varying degrees on alcohol and barbiturates, began griping about grievances—real or imagined—which they held against the prison administration. Two of them, inmates Otis Adams and Edward Whitehead, left and went to the main dining room about 11 a.m. Adams cut into the serving line whereupon an officer ordered him back to the end of the line. Adams heaped verbal abuse on the officer and left for Four Block with Whitehead. His conduct drew the attention of two yard-officers who followed him into the block. Once in Four Block the officers faced three highly agitated inmates, Adams, Whitehead, and now, Shaw, in the midst of hundreds of milling inmates in the block and adjoining yard area. The disturbance looked ominous so the gun tower notified Inspector Joseph Dembosky (commanding duty officer) in the hall office—who responded immediately. Inmate Whitehead seized Dembosky and held a knife at his throat before the inspector could take any action. Since there were approximately 1,000 inmates in the yard as they left Four Block, Dembosky felt there was danger of a riot if he and his captors remained in the yard. Therefore, he suggested that they drop into the gymnasium to talk things over. Instead, the inmates forced him to accompany them to the hospital—en route, they repeatedly shouted warnings to the tower guards that they would kill Dembosky if the guards fired. Milton Thomas, a fourth armed inmate, joined them as they entered the hospital where they seized two guards, a prison doctor, and an inmate elevator operator named Hubbard. Adams severely beat inmate Hubbard and then he and his cohorts moved their captives to the fifth floor physician's lounge, which they quickly barricaded.

Hostage negotiations followed for more than five hours and included various prison officials and a newspaper reporter, who recorded their many grievances. Adams voiced persistent fear that tower guards would shoot him when he left the floor and he demanded the department's assurance that would not happen. Director Harrison, who came to the scene from Lansing, told the hostage-takers that they had his assurance but that they would be accountable for their actions and prosecuted for the crimes they had committed. With this assurance from the Director, they released their captives and surrendered their weapons.

Demolition of 15-Block

Warden Kropp hoped to abolish the infamous 15 Block on his watch. With the blessing of Director Harrison and the legislature, planning for the demolition of 15 Block began, with Deputy Elmquist assigned to lead the project. But first, alternative housing had to be found for the segregation and detention inmates from 15 Block. The west side of Five Block was selected because of its proximity to the main hall office command center, and the advantage that gun turrets added after the 1952 riot provided armed coverage. Also, the cell fronts and locking devices in Five Block were much more secure than in any south side cellblocks, and only modest remodeling was required to divide the block's east side from the west and to provide necessary office space. Therefore, as soon as Five West was ready the demolition of 15 Block could begin.

This project was well along by February 1967, when I received a call from Director Harrison asking me to report to SPSM as Deputy Warden. He had removed the former deputy, John Elmquist, for insubordination and issued a "stop order" for him at the prison gate. I took the next plane from Marquette to Jackson. I would be a guest of George and Betty Kropp at the Warden's house until our children completed the school year in Marquette and could move down to the Deputy Warden's house next to the Jackson Michigan State Police Post.

My first hours on my new job were unusual to say the least because I noted that the prison employees were busy circulating a petition protesting the removal of Elmquist. They hastily assured me that I was not their target, but I suspected they were just hedging their bets.

Prison Arsenal Explosion

A few weeks after my arrival, I was eating lunch in town when I heard the wail of sirens. Not connecting this with the prison, I was calmly driving back toward the Warden's house when a prison lieutenant flagged me down and said, "Deputy you better get to the prison; the arsenal has blown up." I drove to the administration building with pedal to the metal, noting that the emergency vehicles with lights flashing included police, fire trucks and ambulances. Smoke was billowing out into the lobby and there was a stretcher with an obviously dead body on it. I learned that there had been a massive explosion. The officer on One Post, some 100 feet above the prison rotunda, said a nuclear-type mushroom cloud came out of the arsenal and fanned out over him. This explosion had destroyed the arsenal, which was located behind the main entrance sally port, as well as, the security gate control, and it had killed the two officers on duty there. With no electrical controls, the main prison control center could not open the gates to assist the officers or let in emergency personnel. They called Warden Kropp at home. He had a mechanical emergency override key for the gates and crawled under the smoke to release them with it.

The cause of the blast was at first a mystery, but we were able to reconstruct it. A charred Winchester 30-30 was found in a vise on a workbench in the arsenal. It had a spent cartridge in the chamber, and the muzzle was pointed toward the wall where many canisters of gunpowder and magnesium flares had been stored. The serial number identified it as a rifle that had been accidentally dropped from a guard post earlier that day. The arsenal officer was something of a gunsmith, and it is believed that he was repairing the weapon and checking its function with ammunition when it fired, detonating the magnesium flares and the gunpowder. In the follow up we learned a lot about safe storage of flares and gunpowder, especially from the Michigan National Guard munitions experts.

Attending funerals for fallen officers is always grim, but this one was particularly sad. Because we had learned that one of the officers had a secret life—he had left but not divorced a wife many years before, and had not officially married his current wife nor had he designated beneficiaries in his personnel records. So as his current wife and children sat grieving at his funeral, we knew they would get none of his benefits. They would all go to his "legal wife of record." A somber reminder to keep beneficiaries current because none of us knows what our future holds.

With 80% of the arsenal equipment destroyed, and reconstruction of the arsenal and gate area months away, the Warden and I had plenty to keep us busy.

Playing a Gambler's Game

Card sharking and gambling on the big yard seemed to be flourishing in the late 1960s, despite prison rules to the contrary. That increasing numbers of prisoners were seeking the safe haven of protective custody to escape assault for unpaid gambling debts gave evidence of the problem. Serious gambling required a bit of cunning by the players because non-negotiable paper scrip, the only legal currency for inmates, was useless on the gambling table. U.S. Currency was highly valued but subject to confiscation as contraband. There was also an informal economy based on services and goods, primarily cigarettes. Since written records of winnings and losses were prima-facie evidence of illegal gambling, they were carefully coded to fool corrections staff.

For practical reasons, a casino system of dealers at improvised card tables had been set up to provide order, settle minor disputes and see that winners were paid—and that losers paid up. In addition, big winners or losers needed an underground means of moving contraband currency. Ironically, while this was an illegal enterprise, it needed a credible legitimate structure and a reliable means of compensation for winners in order to instill player confidence. Otherwise, big-yard poker would be only penny-ante, unsatisfactory to the serious gamblers. Therefore, an inmate with the smarts and toughness to organize and operate such a big concession was needed. Informally we staff called the organizer/operators of such enterprises "racketeers."

However, a racketeer also needed outside connections to move the cash required—a "money man," an employee willing to smuggle money through the security gates for a 20% fee. In early 1968, the afternoon shift commander, Captain Baldwin, commented that he was "pretty sure that inmate Jack Harte was one of these racketeers," but was so clever that no concrete evidence had yet turned up. As we talked about this, we came up with a simple and, we thought, ingenious strategy that would focus attention on Jack to worry his "underworld cronies" if he were in fact a "racketeer," yet be perfectly harmless if he were innocent.

This plan was set into motion on the following Thursday: the yard loud speaker blared, "Jack Harte report to Deputy Johnson's Office," and soon Harte, a somewhat nervous young man in his mid-twenties—neatly groomed with the athletic build of a linebacker—checked in with my secretary, George Graham. "Deputy Johnson, sir, what do you want with me?" "Just to get to know you," I said, and then proceeded with a brief, casual, get acquainted conversation. After about the third such meeting Jack pleaded, "Deputy I'm having a bad time explaining to the boys why I keep coming up to your office." I wondered whether our plan was working or Harte was an innocent target of rumors? If innocent, then getting him unjustly labeled the deputy's snitch was wrong, so I abandoned our plan—there would be no more call-outs.

However, a few days later, a visibly agitated Jack Harte appeared at my secretary's desk pleading, "I've got to see the deputy!" He came in claiming that he had seen a loaded pistol in the yard that he thought he could get for $500—I agreed that a loaded pistol in a prison yard was not a good thing, but said I did not have $500 at my disposal. (Actually, if I were sure we could get the pistol off the yard, Warden Kropp would arrange the payout, but this smelled like a scam.) Harte was disappointed but said he would work on it. To my surprise, he dropped in a day later on a pass from his cellblock officer, saying, "I have the gun stashed and will bring it to you tomorrow."

"Do you need me to clear you through the sub-hall security gate?" I asked (this being his only access to my office from the yard or cellblocks.) "No, not a problem," he replied. I thought that was interesting, but let it pass, and the next day Jack came to my office with an object wrapped in a hand-towel—a fully loaded large frame revolver—a .38-caliber Smith and Wesson, military and police model. Underworld style, its serial number had been obliterated, but while restoring this was proved to be a mere technical inconvenience for the State Police lab, it traced back to WW II in Great Britain and was untraceable after that.

Harte then said he now had a problem because as soon as the word was out that he turned in a gun he became a "snitch." His solution was to transfer to Camp Waterloo. This was an easy request to grant because he fully met the classification requirements for the camp; he had but two years remaining on a 10-year minimum sentence and a spotless prison record. Therefore, by nightfall he was ensconced bag-

160

and-baggage in Camp Waterloo. Unfortunately, this apparently satisfactory resolution of the matter was not the end of the story. He escaped the following night. It turns out that he had some criminal cronies pick him up and left our obliging custody to return to his criminal enterprises, but this fact we would only learn a year or two later following their arrest trying to smuggle a truckload of hash from Mexico into Texas.

But I had already found out, a few weeks after Harte's escape, that there was more to the contraband gun story than I knew. This was when an inmate I had known since my counselor days, Stan K. dropped in from his hall-office job to visit, wearing a mischievous grin:

"Hey Deputy, so Jack got you, huh?"

"How is that?" I asked.

"Deputy, that gun was never in the yard," Stan chortled, "Hell, he couldn't get a hog leg like that past the sub hall officer. That gun only came 50 feet across the hall from the screws' locker room to your office."

"From the officers' locker room—really?"

I was skeptical. But Stan was fully enjoying himself by now:

"Corporal Thompson[3] was Jack's "money man" for years. All Jack had to do was get his guys out there to drop off a gun at Thompson's house and for $500 he brings it in to his locker and leaves it unlocked. Jack gets a pass, comes through Sub Hall, slips into the locker room, grabs the gun and walks it across the hallway into your office."

(We quickly checked and discovered that Corporal Thompson had resigned to accept employment at the Goodyear plant in Jackson about the same time Harte went to Camp.)

"But why go to all that to get to camp when all he had to do was get reclassified?" I asked.

"Why then there wouldn't be no 'sting'—you see this way he got the Deputy Warden," he replied.

Secretly, I had to admit that Stan's prison grapevine version of the event was more plausible, and in Stan's world, his telling me this was not "snitching" because Jack was safely on the lam and the corporal

---

[3] Name changed to protect innocent since the employee was not prosecuted.

was now insulated from administrative sanctions by taking new employment.

Now it may seem far-fetched that Harte would have gone to so much trouble just to play a game at my expense. Moreover, I am not sure that the relationship between the kept and the keeper, which led to this scam, still persists as strongly today as part of the inmate code, but it did then, at least among some career inmates. Let me give another example, which did not occur at Jackson but clearly illustrates this point:

While I was on assignment earlier at Marquette Branch Prison, a prisoner named Butch Elmore came to my attention as the principle in a sophisticated escape plot from maximum security. Based on a solid tip, I dispatched a shakedown crew and the rumors checked out. Bars in an outside window had been cut through enough to be popped out, the outside bars gave a dull thud when hammered, and hacksaw blades necessary for the final move were found secreted in sterile surgical kits. I conducted an interrogation of Butch, the plot's mastermind. He was serving about his fourth sentence—pretty much doing life on the installment plan. And now he would be serving even more time. I asked him about that.

"Butch, you have done all this time, and had only three more years to go. Why on earth get involved in an escape attempt now which will bring you a lot more time?"

"Deputy, you don't understand. Your job is "jailing" and my job is "crooking," and your bars are your statement and beating your bars is mine. If it was the last day of my sentence and I could beat you, I would."

Both Butch and Jack were dedicated career criminals, and, as another inmate once observed, "so crooked they have to screw their socks on." But they had their own code, however warped, and they lived by it. It is perhaps too bad that I hadn't recalled Butch's story when dealing with Harte, but a really good conman can be hard to beat.

Riot Control Planning

Each spring following the 1952 riot, custody reviewed the prison riot control plan and mobilized staff for training purposes. By the mid-1960s, the Selma marches and police brutality common throughout the South during the civil rights protests were fresh in everyone's minds so the emphasis was on "non-lethal" force. So now, batons (42-inch long, two-handed billy clubs) replaced the firearms used in traditional gun squads. Corrections and police officers were trained to jab, block, and use other maneuvers to control adversaries. In 1967, Warden Kropp and I decided to add a bit of realism by mustering three or four dozen civilians to act as motley uncooperative inmate rioters out on the prison gun range where the officers were drilling. It was a spirited and good-natured exercise, but all parties quickly agreed that the superior numbers of inmates they would face in most scenarios would overpower corrections officers. I assured Kropp that Arsenal Lieutenant Lee McCoy and I would come up with a solution.

We knew that we had many trusty 870 Remington pump action 12-gauge shot guns in the arsenal. Loaded with "00" buckshot they were both psychologically intimidating and extremely lethal. Even target skeet or trap loads would be more lethal than we wanted, so we knew our answer lay with a custom load that McCoy would have to invent. We agreed that a low powered charge using fine shot would function well in the 870s; it should be effective and yet meet the spirit of Deputy Director Spencer's concern.

Two weeks later, McCoy called me to the gun range. He had several cartridge boxes of custom loaded rounds—in new black casings to avoid error in loading because no commercial ammo is black. Always with a flair for the dramatic, McCoy then stood at the target line with his back to us, pulled up his pea coat over the back of his head and ordered the range officer to shoot him from the 25 yard line. The order was carried out and McCoy was not harmed. He then put up a piece of ¾" plywood and from six feet shot a hole in it. According to McCoy the #9 shot loses energy so rapidly that it soon becomes harmless, but at six feet would stop any charging inmate in his tracks. The shells were loaded with about half a normal powder load. We adopted it for gun squads and it served us well over the years in a number of incidents where we had to clear the yard. Prisoners never challenged the Remington 870s.

Riots and Rioters—a week to remember

The week of July 23, 1967, will be forever imprinted in my mind; the Detroit race riots exploded and spread like a forest fire through the ghettos of our cities and unsettled our prisons. I knew it would be a bad week when I saw looting and buildings burning on TV, and when the Sunday evening news about the rioting on Twelfth Street in Detroit reported that people had been killed.[4] Fortunately, most of the afternoon shift and much of the prison population remained in blessed ignorance about these events until the 11p.m. reports. By then, the prison was locked down and we had time to plan for Monday. Many African American inmates came from inner city Detroit, and we knew they would be worried about home and family and agitated about the killings. Monday was spent listening and talking with knots of worried inmates—supervisors, experienced officers and I went everywhere in the prison. It was a long day. We found great concern for the safety and welfare of loved ones but mixed emotions otherwise on the part of inmates. Some said the violence was expected and necessary, while others shook their heads at its futility. The Detroit Police Department and black militant organizations received about equal blame, but nowhere, as yet, did we detect any hostility projected toward us.

Since the greatest prisoner concern seemed to be about family welfare, we sent wires and attempted phone calls but had little success. Phone lines were overloaded and there was no phone service in much of Detroit. Eventually we enlisted the aid of a Detroit radio personality, Martha Jean the Queen, who had a large black listening audience. She broadcast information both to the public and to the prisoners. She instructed families to call the prison and we set up phone banks to take messages to deliver to the inmates—hundreds of such messages were delivered.

Early Monday evening, July 24, 1967, we learned that Governor Romney had declared a state of emergency and also established a sort of martial law that would allow rioters to be housed at Jackson Prison without the niceties of a criminal convictions and sentences. And by the way, we were told, the first two busloads were enroute. These busses pulled on to prison grounds at 1 a.m. with 73 alleged rioters, a dozen or so National Guardsmen and Detroit Police Officers, and two Michigan State Police trail cars. The miscreants were subdued, dirty, and more than a little relieved—which was understandable. I know I

---

[4] From Deputy Johnson's report to Warden Kropp titled "The Week that Was."

164

wouldn't want to be guarded by teenage soldiers with M-16 rifles who hadn't slept in 30 hours or eaten in 12.[5]

Some of the detainees had been held in police precinct parking garages for more than 48 hours. The relative comfort of a prison cell and food undoubtedly looked good right then. And so they came, and came, and came. By Wednesday we had filled Cellblocks Five (east), and most of Eight, Ten, and Eleven, all of which were inside the walls. We had already used all vacant space in minimum security. By Thursday we housed 1,186 people from the streets of Detroit.

But numbers do not begin to tell the story of that week. The problems surrounding security, sanitation, identification, communicable diseases, dangerous contraband, feeding and clothing, and health care for the rioters were profound. They came in their own clothing, often nothing more than a pair of dirty shorts, with some personal property and with no medical screening or positive identification. As they came though the gates they were searched for weapons and drugs, then assigned to cells and locked in. Later, teams of officers brought the men out, searched them more thoroughly, and listed and packaged personal property.

We scheduled meals for the rioters to be fed in the blocks twice a day using paper plates, and issued steel bowls to be kept in their cells to avoid contaminating the main kitchen. The men were allowed to launder their own clothing in their cells because they were in such filthy condition that an overpowering stench was beginning to fill the blocks. We issued coveralls and scratch work clothing as soon as possible. Medical staff made rounds in each block checking for medical problems such as active venereal disease, diabetes, and epilepsy, and looked for addicts suffering from withdrawal. All of these conditions were found, and one psychotic man was re-transferred

---

[5] Author's Note: Michigan was fortunate to have surplus of empty cells at Jackson as the result of the opening of a 500-bed prison near Ionia and a temporary downturn in new prison commitments. This demographic anomaly caused by WWII and the Baby Boom that followed resulted in a sag and then a surge in the most crime prone age group headed for prison (18 to 25 year old males). The low point for Michigan's prison population occurred in 1967 but soon rebounded to consume all available bed space and begin the Department's most serious period of prison overcrowding—ever.

directly to the Ionia State Hospital. Some obvious skid-row winos got caught in the net and appeared a bit dazed by it all. There was a rumor that one was a twelve year old child. It turned out he was twenty, but looked like a child. There were about six obvious transvestites; one had so many feminine characteristics that our officers told me there must be a mistake and asked me what we should do? I told them, "We don't want to know. Just process all of them out with the rest."

Dealing with these problems while at the same time managing 3,300 regular prisoners under very tense circumstances was indeed a challenge. By Tuesday, tensions had begun to build within our regular population. Rumors began to circulate that naphtha to be used in firebombs had been stolen from the license plate factory. We found no evidence to support that, but we knew it was possible. While these rumors were flying, inmates on the gym assignment decided they needed five gallons of lawnmower gasoline to cut grass that didn't need cutting. We killed that request.

On Wednesday morning, July 26, 1967, Captain O'Rourke interrupted my segregation review court to tell me that he had received several calls telling him there were specific plans to burn the textile, license plate, and garment factories. The word was that this was a strategy to distract us with fires so that sympathetic inmates could overrun 11 Block and liberate its 352 riot suspects. We knew that if there was such a plan, time was drawing short, and I held an emergency strategy meeting with our top security people. We agreed that we needed better intelligence and fast.

While we were getting that, we took precautionary moves by mobilizing gun squads and quietly assembling them at designated points outside the walls. One gun squad was designated to secure 11 Block the instant trouble developed anywhere in the prison; there were gun squads for each of the factories, to be deployed through the closest security gate; and one squad on standby at the south gate to escort and protect firefighters if they were needed. We held the morning shift over to provide double manpower in the afternoon and until the factory workers went to their cells at quitting time and the three busloads of rioters now on the way were safely locked in Eight Block. But up to this point, the inmate general population had been well behaved and working—there was no sign of unrest despite the worrisome rumors.

166

By early Wednesday afternoon, reports were circulating throughout the prison that we were about to have serious trouble. Inmates contacted me and pleaded that we bugle the population in and lock them up until tempers cool. And there were calls from officers at various locations reporting knots of inmates talking belligerently. Some of the more reliable inmates told me of rumors being circulated by agitators: we were going to displace regular inmates for house rioters; we were going to cancel night yard; and we were abusing the rioters—starving them, segregating them, not allowing them clean clothing—all aimed at generating sympathy to justify a major disturbance to attract attention.

Since work assignments, prison industries, and education programs were almost done for the day, and the men would be going to their cells within an hour or so anyway, sounding a general alarm did not seem wise or necessary. However, as soon as the inmates were in for the five o'clock count, I spoke over the prison radio system and explained as clearly as I could what we were doing and why we were doing it. I told them that the rioters would probably be moved back to courts within a matter of days and that we were trying to maintain normal work, recreation, and living conditions for the general population in the meantime. I said that if they wanted to do something for the visitors they would be allowed to donate cigarettes and magazines later in the evening. I think it helped; afterwards, we ran the dinner lines without incident.

After the meal lines, we brought a busload of rioters to the north door of Eight Block guarded by National Guard and police. That was a mistake! The sight of the Detroit city buses agitated about 80 or 90 inmates who had gathered on the roadway by 11 Block with a good view of the Eight Block operation. They refused to disperse for the inspectors and talked openly of overrunning the block and letting the rioters out. We knew and they knew that any move like that would result in bloodshed—their blood—because the National Guard and police were armed to the teeth, and they could plainly see the M-16s. We were already into it so we finished unloading and sent the buses out. After securing the block, the officers and I moved toward 11 Block and the rebellious inmates disbanded and went into the north yard and were bugled in without incident.

Thursday was the most critical day of the entire period—Warden Kropp and I were very close to locking the prison down. However, our intelligence was getting better information. It was clear that there was a small group of militant black inmates trying to trigger a major disturbance for the sole purpose of destruction, but that the bulk of the population wanted no part of it. Concerned and apprehensive black inmates told me that they and their fellow inmates were as fearful of these characters as we were. For the first time, white inmates were giving almost identical stories. Some men claimed they were stocking their cells with food so that they could stay out of trouble. As we had on Wednesday, we mobilized and waited out a storm that never came.

Friday morning I received a call shortly before 6 a.m. reporting a fire bombing in the textile factory, and I thought, "This is it!" Lt. LaVoy told me that a post officer adjacent to the factory heard an explosion, saw a flash in the cotton room, and immediately summoned the fire department. The firefighters brought the fire under control without damage to the building. The arsonists had miscalculated big time—they were sure the fire would soon be out of control and that we would be desperately fighting fire during the breakfast line. They counted on support from the population for a riot. Instead, the fire was quickly out and they were snitched out immediately by the older hands in the textile factory who wanted no part of a prison riot. The inmates implicated in the arson found themselves locked in segregation before the coals were out.

Inspector Dembosky told me that the breakfast lines ran without incident, and the inmates seemed to be in a more relaxed mood than at any time during the previous three days. As if by magic, tension was dispelled on Friday before the first busload of rioters departed for Wayne County. Obviously, we finally had the right characters locked up in segregation. Prisoners knew about the agitation but were not sure how many would join in. After it was over an old timer told me, "There weren't so many fools in this place after all."

The final farewell to the rioters went according to Detroit Recorder's Court procedures for certifying bond or returning individuals by bus. In each case we had to find the man in the institution, confirm his warrant number, find his property, and then turn him over to the sheriff's department officers or the bondsman. By Sunday, only 739 remained and by August 8 all were gone. Thus, one of the most unusual events in the history of Jackson Prison came to conclusion—I called it "the week that was." After it was over, Warden Kropp joined his wife, Betty at their Gunn Lake cottage for some R and R, and I spent some make-up time with my family.

The Honor Block

Now that 11 Block was vacant again, I thought it was a good time to develop an honor block—an idea I had been toying with for some time. SPSM had a core or cadre of prisoners who were well behaved and excellent workers but because of their long sentences would not be elgible for minimum security housing for several years. Superintendents from the textile factory and stamp plant told me they had key mechanics and lead workers who had been on the job more than ten years and never had a misconduct report. There were similar cases working on key institutional assignments. The Federal Bureau of Prisons and some progressive states were already identifying men suitable and deserving for an "open day room but lock in at night" setting in modern secure prisons. Now, while the 40 year old, five-tiered 11 Block was very different from a modern structure, it had possibilities: First, it and its twin, 12 Block, were free standing in the south yard and not a part of the prison's secure perimeter, as were cellblocks 1 through 10, so there would be little escape risk. Second, the cells faced across a common area (which we arranged to provide day room space.)

I obtained Warden Kropp's approval. The rules would be uncomplicated: only working inmates with no misconduct for at least a year could apply—seniority given preference and racial balance maintained—"lose your job or get a misconduct report and you are out." I instructed George Graham, who handled cell moves, "to treat the Honor Block like Noah's Ark,—bring them in two-by-two, one white, and one black." (SPSM was about 50% African American at the time.) Honor block status allowed inmates televisions and musical instruments, a washer and dryer for personal clothes, a hot water tap for coffee and unlocked cell doors during leisure time (single cells only.) The honor block was immensely popular and men jealously protected the privilege. Warden Egeler continued the program during his administration.

The Snitch System - A Solution

Old timer inmates often provided us with accurate information that allowed us to make rational and helpful decisions. However, according to a few hard rock career criminals, they were snitches to be despised for breaking the convict code by providing the prison administration any information. The dichotomy of those views caused me to focus on the whole issue of information gathering at the prison.

Accurate information is essential to solving crimes, obtaining convictions, breaking up criminal enterprises, and incidentally, managing the prisons where these convicted criminals end up. One of the most fertile sources of this information is from those with inside knowledge such as co-conspirators, co-defendants, and fellow inmates. Primarily because they are often opportunistic turncoats, inmates derisively called these informants "snitches." Government has the power to protect, free, or compensate the snitch for valuable information, all compelling incentives to the confined. However, these powerful incentives often result in lies and sometimes stories elaborately concocted to sound plausible and believable. We know that false testimony convicts innocent people because some have been proven innocent after sentencing. In fact, snitch testimony is the leading cause of wrongful conviction in capital cases where the worst injustices occur because the innocent may be executed or at least held for years on death row.[6] It is no wonder that prisoners fear snitches, hold them in contempt, and target them for violence.

The snitch system at Jackson Prison operated at a much less lethal level because the stakes were not as high; Michigan has no death penalty. It was a network of information and disinformation organized at its apex under Deputy D.C. Pettit and credited by some as keeping the lid on the prison during the severely understaffed war years. Even Warden Kropp concurred with this assessment. Pettit had key inmates loyal to him strategically assigned to maximize his corrupt shakedown system and they operated as an internal spy network keeping the deputy on top of schemes, escape plots, inmate discontent and his competition. Pettit's loyal snitches also profited through immunity from being

---

[6] Report from the Center on Wrongful Convictions Survey 2004-2005, Northwestern University School of Law.

'busted' in their own rackets, getting premium work assignment and numerous special favors. Although dismantled because of Attorney General Dethmers' 1945 investigation, fragments remained in the 1960s. Both staff and inmates told me that Deputy Cahill's men were in key assignments and were untouchable for minor discipline.

I found two major problems with snitch information. First, it was almost impossible to determine the truth because many were skilled at spinning plausible webs of lies, and second, others played the role of double agent claiming to be helpful to the administration while feeding information, or misinformation, to the inmate body on the prison grapevine. Therefore, we developed two helpful strategies. When investigating serious crimes or security threats, we interviewed all parties of interest in normal police fashion. Snitch information would be used to discover facts but not as evidence by itself. Secondly, we would by-pass the prison grapevine with a "resident representative" program.

Under this system, inmates in each general population cellblock would elect a representative to bring their complaints and questions to a forum with me. We broadcast the meetings live over the prison's three-channel radio system during a time when most inmates were in their cells. Thus, the inmates heard both their questions and my answers without distortion, malicious or otherwise. Questions brought to the forum were substantive, reasonable, and generally focused on practices, prison conditions, and the parole board. We were able to head off problems and solve glitches in operations on a regular weekly basis because of information brought by the inmates—even a few cellblock officers told me they plugged in a headphone to listen in and be ahead of the changes. Inmates loved the representative idea, but allowing their election was a nuisance to cellblock officers. That nuisance, plus population pressures in future years, resulted in the program's demise.

"What the Hell is a Black Muslim"

In early 1956, Deputy Cahill looked out his office window, saw a half dozen black inmates standing at military attention at the entrance to 15 Block, and ordered the Hallmaster to have it checked out. Officers reported that they were "the Fruit of Islam" members of the Black Muslim movement, and they were peacefully protesting in support of their brothers segregated in 15 Block. Cahill looking flabbergasted asked, "What the hell is a Black Muslim?" His solution was an offer to lock the protesters in 15 Block with their brothers. The prison staff shared his ignorance of the Black Muslim (officially, The Nation of Islam) movement but his dramatic question, retold many times, focused everyone's attention. Ironically, the movement was founded close by in Detroit during the 1930s and one of its most powerful leaders, Malcolm X (Little), was raised a few miles north of the prison in Mason, Michigan.

Religious tracts, publications and correspondence coming to the prison from the Nation of Islam or its leader, Elijah Muhammad, provided a confusing picture of the movement during the late 1950s and early 1960s. On one hand, Muhammad preached a militant black separatist litany referring to white folks as "blue eyed devils" and ridiculed Martin Luther King's non-violent movement as hopeless. On the other hand, the movement advocated adherence to tenants of Islam and railed against using drugs, alcohol or committing crime. Warden Bannan, believing them to be a violent threat, tried to suppress the Black Muslim inmates and denied their request for recognition as a religion until Federal Judge Wade McCree issued a consent decree on February 11, 1963 reversing him. In their April 10, 1963 meeting, the Corrections Commission officially recognized the Black Muslims as a religion and authorized a contract with Wilfred Little, Muslim Minister of Temple Number 1, to provide chaplaincy counseling at SPSM for them. (Wilfred, Malcolm X's elder brother, joined the Nation of Islam in 1947. He was the equivalent of an Islamic imam and CEO of the Nation of Islam enterprises in Detroit.)[7] Despite worries that Wilfred might be a fiery rabble-rouser like his brother Malcolm (who was assassinated in 1965); he was a calming stabilizing influence on the inmate body. Some inmates complained that he was too strict—advocating total abstinence from alcohol, drugs, any return to crime, and preaching respectful treatment of women. Further, to join the Nation of Islam they must also prostrate themselves in prayer five times each day and refrain from eating any swine products. Now it became

---

[7] The Nation of Islam enterprises were impressive: bakeries, barber shops, grocery stores, laundromats and schools—some operated as co-ops, all clean neat and professional appearing. I toured as Wilfred Little's guest at the invitation of Elijah Muhammad.

our responsibility to re-arrange the prison's All Faiths Chapel to move the pews to allow prostrate prayers to face the east and to label the food menu to identify items containing pork. By the late 1960s, more Jackson Prison inmates identified themselves as Black Muslims than as members of any other faith.

Unexpected Consequences of Good Intentions

President Lyndon B. Johnson's "Elementary and Secondary Education Act" even trickled into Jackson Prison during the mid-1960s. Its emphasis on equal access to education and funding for primary and secondary education flushed money into colleges and public schools—even into adult education for prisoners. These resources, coupled with the discovery that Michigan's Adult Education Act permitted the incorporation of Jackson's academic school in the local Union School District, brought the inmates under the State's school aide formula. Based on student count, this provided a funding bonanza. Certified teachers, a first in the history of the prison, would teach all classes, although former inmate instructors would become teacher's aides. A grant from the McGregor Foundation funded a closed circuit education program transmitting lessons to some two dozen locations at the prison. Jackson Community College provided an extensive two-year academic postgraduate program at the prison and even a "study release" vocational training program for trusty inmates bussed to the school. Both Michigan State University and Eastern Michigan University provided special programs at the prison. Warden Kropp was proud and pleased that this occurred on his watch.

Following the reorganization, inmates enrolled in classes with coursework aimed at achieving a high school diploma equivalent to that available from public K-12 schools. The teachers were comfortable with that, so problem solved. Well, maybe not! Wilburt (Will) Laubach, prison school administrator, discovered that a starting class of some 25 in September contained only a half-dozen students by December. The prisoners could hardly be playing hooky, so he checked further and found that loss of students during the school year was to be expected. Inmate transfers to Jackson's Trusty Division and to the camp program or medium security prisons, as well as, release on court order or to parole, all took their toll on school count. New students were required to wait for the start of the next semester's class, thus preventing repair of this attrition.

Laubach's solution to this unexpected consequence was ahead of its time—Jackson's Academic School would convert to "Competency-Based Education." This would become the standard, department wide.

Prisoners would now start at their knowledge level and learn at their own pace—teachers would no longer serve as lecturers in scheduled classes but would work individually to guide students' learning. As Dr. Mendenhall[8] observed in later years: "We know two things about adult learners—they come to higher education knowing different things, and they learn at different rates. . . They can move quickly through material they already know and focus on what they still need to learn." The goal of K-12 would no longer be a diploma but successful completion of a GED—a more broadly accepted measure of achievement in the work world. Thus, the new system measured learning and not time spent, which allowed inmates to enter school immediately and leave without disruption to others. Nevertheless, Laubach found this was a hard sell. Traditional teachers saw it as much more work, and felt it failed to use their lecturing, and classroom talents. Nevertheless, while some bitterly resisted competency-based education in its early years, it was the right course of action in that prison environment and became department-wide policy in force to this day.

The Braille Transcribing Program

In 1962, an SPSM inmate volunteer began transcribing English to Braille on one of the Braille typewriters supplied by local Lions Clubs in order to provide material for blind children and adults. Although the "Brailler" was a bulky strange looking typing machine that required rolls of the stiff paper upon which Braille is embossed, Deputy Cahill approved the inmate's request to keep it in his cell so that he could work on it at all hours. Soon, other prisoners volunteered for braille transcriber training and began producing brailled material from their cells also. Lions clubs from Jackson and Lansing provided the inspiration, initial funding, and training for the program, but it became

---

[8] Dr. Robert Mendenhall is President of Western Governors University, a competency-based university.

part of the prison school system and administered by the Jackson County Intermediate School District. The following year, Warden Kropp decided to move the Braille clutter out of individual cells to an improvised production area for 20 some transcribers located on the mezzanine of the prison rotunda, where it remained for many years.

The program morphed from a volunteer effort by a few prisoners to a non-profit corporation known as the Michigan Braille Transcribing Fund, paying inmates prison-industry scaled wages. In 1998, the program moved to facilities specially designed for Braille production in a new medium security facility a few hundred yards from SPSM. It is now the largest Braille production facility in the nation, ". . . producing up to 5 million pages of Braille a year—all at an affordable rate."[9] Braille transcription trainees now undergo rigorous certification prescribed by the U.S. Library of Congress, with several graduates employed in related fields after release from prison. So, after 50 years, Jackson Prison's inmate Braille transcribing program remains hugely successful, providing an important service to the blind worldwide.

---

[9] Ingrid Jacques, *Jackson Citizen Patriot,* May 31, 2010.

PERRY M. JOHNSON

Photo courtesy of the Michigan Department of Corrections

Chapter Nine
Changing of the Guard--Johnson Moves Again

THE YEARS FOLLOWING THE 1952 RIOT WERE RELATIVELY stable at Jackson Prison, but events beginning in 1968 would lead to a rapid restructuring of the department that would affect the prison. First, John Spencer, Deputy Director of the Bureau of Correctional Facilities, died in office and Director Gus Harrison selected me to replace him. Charles Egeler then replaced me as Jackson's Deputy Warden. Now I would be working in the Lansing Office; we moved to a home in East Lansing; and the children would be going to the East Lansing schools. It provided a welcome respite from prison housing for the family, but would only last for two years. Warden Kropp decided to retire in February 1970 and, since I had become unhappy with the bureaucratic nature of the Deputy Director position, I applied for the Warden's job and Director Harrison appointed me April 1, 1970 and appointed Robert Brown Jr. my replacement as Deputy Director, Bureau of Corrections Facilities.

Egeler and I would team as warden and deputy for the next 30 months. We continued Warden Kropp's policy regarding "duty deputy" and "duty warden" that went like this: The duty warden could only be Egeler or myself and must remain in the general Jackson city area when not at the prison. The duty deputy could be either of the two inside inspectors, assistant deputy warden, and the trusty division deputy warden and, of course, either Egeler or myself. A duty deputy must be on site at the prison 8 a.m. to 6 p.m. every day. Communication in the early 1970s was limited to landline phone or the police radio in our state car—quite different from today with the proliferation of mobile devices of all types.

Another move for the family

And so our family was back in prison housing; this time in the warden's mansion adjacent to the minimum security 'Trusty Division' with its nearly 1,500 or so inmates. The warden's mansion was an extravagant three-story brick residence built in the late 1920's, an era when the warden was a political patronage job. The grand rooms and, especially, the sweeping mahogany spiral staircase were things of beauty, though a bit ostentatious to be on the taxpayers dime. Our five children, ages 8 to 19 at the time, marveled that there were seven bathrooms.

Their mother, Uyvonne, announced bad news for them, that we had decided that they were old enough to pitch in and share the routine housework and cleaning and we would forgo the traditional inmate houseboys used by past wardens—or the single one we used in the Deputy's house, so they would not have servants at their beck and call. Of course major cleaning projects like window washing and grounds maintenance on the five acre grounds would be done by staff supervised inmate work crews. But family privacy is a major casualty when living on prison grounds, and we knew from past experience that having inmate staff in the house only made that worse. So the extra work was a price we were all gladly willing to pay. Besides that, while in the Deputy's house we had two bad experiences with houseboys—

one was weird and the other was totally unreliable. A third, Stemlo, proved to be exceptional but he was a rarity; a high-rise steelworker who was loyal, trustworthy, and a good worker. Though we suspect he did contribute to little Julie's card sharking ability. He taught her card games and, to her mother's chagrin, allowed her, at age six, to paint the basement floor. After his parole from an armed robbery sentence he returned to high-rise steelwork in California and, as far as I ever knew, never returned to prison.

Though we no longer had houseboys in the Warden's house, there were so many prisoners working on the grounds and visitors coming to the prison--we thought a guard dog might offer protection for the family. So we shopped for a Doberman Pincher pup. What follows is an experience the whole family remembers well.

Hans

We found a breeder who specialized in Dobermans, and she advised us that a male would tend to be protective of Uyvonne and the girls, while a female would tend to bond with the boys and me. We said a "small" male would be fine. Well, it just happened that her prize female had recently produced a litter of thirteen, too many for the bitch to handle, so she was eager to sell the non-show pups. We picked the runt of the litter—a little guy who had been picked on by the rest of the pups. Though his AKC name was much more formal, Bel-Mar's Nobel Von Hans of Gunther, we named him 'Hans.' He was six weeks old, all puppy knees and elbows, and his ears had just recently been trimmed and taped—a less likely looking guard dog could not be imagined. We asked how we should train him to guard, and when we should training start? The breeder's instructions were simple: "Only Uyvonne should feed him; this will strengthen bonding and prevent "undesirables" from poisoning him." (It turned out that as a result Hans would only eat for Uyvonne. He would have starved in a kennel). "Oh, and by the way, hand feed him two eggs, a half-pound of ground beef and 10 calcium pills in addition to dog food every day" (Uyvonne said babies are easier to raise). "When visitors arrive take him to the door, greet them and tell Hans they are OK, but don't let them pet him. No further guard training is needed—it will come naturally."

And did she know her Dobermans! Hans went everywhere Uyvonne did. A vigorous hug from the boys or me brought a warning growl. As he grew older there was never a question but that any aggressor would have to kill him before they could touch Uyvonne—they had better be ready for war.

In his first month with us, Hans underwent an astonishing growth spurt, and when we took him back to the breeder for his checkup, he was now the biggest of the litter (I had *thought* he had awfully big feet for a pup) and was a gorgeous deep red. The breeder was quite surprised. She said it must have been getting away from the litter, as well as, Uyvonne's personal attention. So much for our "little" male! Hans grew into a hundred pound athlete who could run like the wind and had a powerful body. Even as a pup he had the deepest full-throated growl I ever heard. One day a prison maintenance man dropped by the kitchen. As he talked to Uyvonne, the half-grown Hans looked up from chewing a cow's leg bone from the butcher shop and growled ominously at the man, who stepped back and noting the bone, asked "And who was that?" This jump-started Hans' reputation in the Trusty Division. As he matured, Hans took his guard duties even more seriously. People did not enter or leave the house without his permission.

For the boys there was a fun side to Hans; they would run and romp with him and, among other things, delighted in flooding out gophers for him to catch. Then there was the evening the south gun-tower officer called Uyvonne to warn her that he saw a prowler in the bushes between the house and the Trusty Division, and that she should keep the children in until it was checked out. Upon checking she found the boys were playing hide-and-seek with Hans. One would hold him while the other laid down a convoluted trail and hid in the shrubbery; with the command, "Hans, go find Randy." Hans was off like a shot, trailing the boy everywhere and locating him in a matter of seconds. It must have looked highly suspicious to the Officer, and we terminated that game for good.

How was it that Hans was so programmed as a guard dog, I wondered? I recall Flash, my Collie on the farm, who would flunk miserably as a guard dog, but was wonderfully helpful in herding and holding livestock. Since neither had been trained, did genes alone account for such detailed and distinctive behavior? And what about humans? How much of the behavior that lands some of them in prison, and leads others of us to manage them, comes from genetic imprint?

And how many little underfed urchins, bullied on their streets and at school, would make a marvelous recovery if protected from the bullies and hand fed by a 'Uyvonne.' . . . I wonder.

In the warden's seat. *Photo courtesy of the author*

Taking the Reins as Warden

The 1967 Detroit riots and the housing of nearly 1200 rioters at Jackson, on the basis of an executive order from Governor Romney, was a watershed event at Jackson Prison because the violence and destruction involved many of these prisoners' neighborhoods, homes, and families. Then, the next April, Martin Luther King, the longtime champion of non-violence, was assassinated, leaving the numerous advocates of violent revolution able to crow, "I told you so." The newly founded Black Panthers began to develop a following in Jackson. Which, coupled with inflammatory literature coming to the prison and national publicity over their confrontational violent tactics against police, worried us about transference to our prison staff. Next we received radical literature from a "White Panther Party" (WPP)

181

located near Ann Arbor. Our first thought was that this must be some neo-Nazi white supremacist group. Not so. We began to get their literature and learned that they were a white group that supported the Black Panthers, in fact endorsing their revolutionary 10 points. And even promising to attack and assault the capitalist power structure. Then, on July 28, 1969, Judge Robert Colombo sentenced John Sinclair, one of the co-founders of the White Panther Party, to nine and a half to ten years for his third marijuana offense. His WPP went ballistic, "Ten years for possessing a joint!" they screamed. They immediately formed a "Free John Sinclair" movement. So this was the climate under which John Sinclair arrived at the Reception and Guidance Center at Jackson Prison.

Inmate Sinclair appeared mild mannered and cooperative and rumors that he was trying to organize inmates probably had more to do with the hopes of prisoners—based on the WPP goal of freeing all prisoners, than anything Sinclair might have said. However, we were concerned about potential problems with the WPP "Free John Sinclair" movement, being mindful of the Ann Arbor riots in June between the "freaks" and riot control police. So, when our officers picked up information that WPP was exploring setting up demonstrations on Cooper Street in front of the prison, I decided to move Sinclair (as Deputy Director, Bureau of Corrections Facilities it was my call). Since he was just beginning a long minimum sentence, under our classification system at the time Sinclair qualified for the Marquette Branch Prison, the Ionia Reformatory or Jackson. I ordered his transfer to Marquette where he got along famously with Warden Buchkoe. Sinclair was released in 1972 as a consequence of a unanimous Supreme Court decision that warrantless wire taps of the WPP were unconstitutional.

Meanwhile, racial tensions and rumors of trouble constantly percolated within the prison. Six months after I assumed office, there was a work stoppage, involving nearly 2000 inmates—how many were protesters and how many stayed off out of fear was not clear. I reported the situation in a memo to Deputy Director Brown summarized as follows:

> During the past month, there have been a number of
> serious incidents at SPSM indicating an organized

effort on the part of . . . self-styled "Black Panthers and Panther sympathizers." There has been a deliberate attempt to murder one of our officers. There have been rumors that militant groups were going to "Go to war with the institution," and sacrifice their lives if need be. There was a full force boycott of the Academic School on November 5. There was an organized but unsuccessful effort to call an institution-wide strike on Thursday, November 12. For several weeks, there have been organized efforts to gain general inmate support to protest food, gym facilities, conditions for classes, inmate wage levels, sanitation standards in the kitchen, alleged practices of racism, and inmate store prices. In most cases, Black Panthers and Panther sympathizers have claimed responsibility. . . There has been a significant influx of radical writing and handout material, in particular, Black Panther literature.. .[1]

It was becoming a fearful work atmosphere for staff and living environment for prisoners. My first priority as Warden was to develop sound and trusted communication with my staff and with the inmates—my greatest fear initially was that overreaction by line staff or the general prison population to bad information would trigger a conflagration with disastrous consequences. Which is what the radical hope for—that the authorities, by unreasonable repression will radicalize the crowd for them.

Therefore, my early staff meetings were aimed at setting a reasoned tone for our operation. My theme was that we had three principle priorities that are essential to a well-managed institution: fiscal control within our budget; effective custody and control; and positive helpful programs for inmates. But, we should never forget that we are in the 'people business' and how we deal with every encounter, good or bad, plants seeds for the future. For example, an inmate may

[1] A November 1970 memo from me to Deputy Director Bob Brown in archives

become a persistent pain and in frustration you may wish to send him a 'smoker' letter or note telling him off, but that letter may be deliberately misinterpreted and given wide distribution to send a damaging message. You might feel better, but don't indulge because in doing so you harm all of your fellow workers. Always treat the prisoner as a man.

I asked first-line officers and staff to select one from their group to meet with me in "front line staff meetings" to bring questions, complaints, and suggestions directly to me for resolution. (The only static I received here was from the MCO officers union, which said that was *their* function. "Not as long as we didn't deal with pay, benefits, or working conditions," I replied.) Minutes of each meeting would be posted for the information of all staff.

Resident Representatives

I established a 'Warden's Forum' comprised of two inmates from each inside cellblock, selected by interested inmates and the block officer, evenly divided by race, to meet with me each month. To avoid misunderstandings or deliberate distortions, the forum would be broadcast live over the prison's closed circuit radio system. Personal issues or individual gripes were prohibited. Early on, these meetings were productive and a number of policy and operational glitches were exposed and remedied. Almost every complaint raised in the Black Panther instigated disturbance in November was covered with the forum with reasonable equanimity—unfortunately the leaders were not able to hear that discussion from their newly assigned cell in Marquette. As time wore on and the tension of the moment passed, the idea lost its novelty and issues to correct became less frequent. Also, block officers didn't appreciate the added work involved and it was discontinued a few years later. However, it was helpful to me in getting a pulse of the prison and a number of irritating issues were quickly resolved.

One issue that inmates complained about was conflicting rules and the inconsistent application of inmate rules. The existing rule book was obviously old and outdated. So I added two inmates to the committee assigned to revise the inmate rule book. They proved very helpful and staff told me they were surprisingly conservative about the rules they believed necessary.

Duty Deputies—Where the action is:

Charles Egeler and I both knew from experience that the Duty Deputy assignment at Jackson prison was seldom boring, and was where the "action was," especially on weekends. The prison escapes resulting in the slaying of Inspector Boucher and the takeover of 15 Block setting the stage for the infamous 1952 riots, both occurred on Sunday. Warden Bannon's so called 13 "sewer rats" escaped on Saturday. Michigan State Police detectives investigating criminal conspiracies between prisoners and free world criminals or corrupt employees required their information or assistance—often on weekends during heavy visitor traffic. Often the Duty Deputy had to settle issues of safety and security within the prison or conflicts between prison functions and departments. Sometimes resolving conflicts comes at personal risk, as in the case when Duty Deputy Inspector Dembrosky was held hostage on October 18, 1965. Furthermore, the social and racial upheaval following the 1967 Detroit race riots spilled over into tensions within the prison. Therefore, it was necessary to be on top of minor incidents to keep them from escalating. Egeler and the other Duty Deputies proved to be cool and effective managers of conflict.

On occasion, critical incidents with high potential for racial conflict and violence end up leaving us with a chuckle afterwards. Such was the case on my Duty Deputy tour Sunday February 2, 1969 a day I reported to Warden Kropp, "as not exactly uneventful." This is a summary of that report:

Trouble can come from unexpected sources—for instance, a normally popular basketball game between a local city team and the prison varsity. First, as the game started, a lively fight broke out in the stands between two inmates. They were quickly subdued and moved to segregation. Moments later the coach of the visiting team became incensed over officiating and began hurling obscenities and racial insults at the inmate referee, an African American, in a crowded gym of mostly black faces. Hank Menaric, recreation director, ordered the visiting team off the floor and cancelled the game amid a din of booing from inmate spectators. Sgt.

185

Mercer herded the visitors into an improvised bullpen arranged in the weightlifting pit and bugled the inmates into the cellblocks. Menaric advised the visitors that he was banning them from coming back inside the prison, "forever." By this time, the visiting coach realized his behavior had placed many in danger and was quite subdued. Fortunately, our response was quick and effective; preventing what could have been a very nasty incident.

Shortly after this fiasco, the information desk notified the Duty Deputy that there was an emergency in the lobby. Two women were in a pitched battle in the restroom and the state police were on their way. Upon arriving at the lobby, he found Sgt. Jones and Officer Flannery now trying to keep the now several combatants separated at the women's restroom door. It was impossible to understand the situation over the din of recriminations, screaming, flailing of purses, and scattered chairs. However, two state police troopers from the post conveniently located a few hundred yards from the prison lobby, helped restore order much to the relief of prison staff. It turned out that all parties were at the prison to visit one inmate. His mother, Pearl, told us the assailant was Cathy, a niece of her son's girlfriend, Geraldine; that the visibly injured person was Pearl's 17-year-old daughter, Sibina; and the other combatant was her other daughter, 19-year-old Gwendolyn. While both mother Pearl and girlfriend Geraldine were flushed and disheveled, they claimed to be onlookers and peacemakers. Pearl stated the feud had been brewing in the streets since last summer and that both Cathy and Sibina had sworn to get each other the next time they met. As we talked, Sibina bewailed the fact that she could not lay her hands on a weapon. We advised the mother that we were suspending her son's visits until a more peaceful arrangement could be agreed to, and sent the family on their way. The girlfriend, Geraldine, said that she "knew there would be trouble when she saw the daughters—that the only reason Cathy (their opponent) was here was to provide Geraldine with transportation." The inmate was relieved to learn that it was his younger sister and Cathy because when he heard the racket from his visit waiting area, he thought it was probably his mother and Geraldine. He was calm and reasonable, given the uproar, and seemed more embarrassed than upset and promised to work out some arrangement to keep the warring parties from again arriving at the prison the same day.

On July 22, 1971, three intoxicated and very abusive men came into the administration building from the parking lot—the "front gun" held them at bay until the state police arrived to arrest them. Meanwhile, two militant "Black Panthers" were soliciting sympathizers in the lobby, so we asked the troopers to escort them off grounds. (Militant activists were calling for retaliation against the "prison industrial complex" at the time and one of their leaders, Angela Davis, had criticized Jackson Prison inmates for being too docile. Therefore, it was an uneasy time.)

The sheer volume of activities at SPSM assured that the Duty Deputy Warden would have many daily adventures requiring his intervention or refereeing. On the other hand, as Julius Hewer from Prison Industries, commented, "Working in Jackson is like going to the theater—every night a new movie."

Return to the Central Office

In the summer of 1972, Director Harrison advised me he was to become Director of the soon-to-be-established State Lottery and said, "The Corrections Commission may ask you about your interest in becoming Director, so you better make up your mind what your answer will be." It was not a position to which I had aspired, so I would rather not have faced the question. On the other hand, if the Commission thought I could best serve the Department as Director I had a duty to seriously consider it. Becoming Director would mean leaving classified Civil Service and serving at the pleasure of the Commission (I could take a leave of absence and retain my Civil Service status but without the right to my warden position.) Financially, I would take a ten percent salary reduction and future raises would be subject to the vagaries of the Legislature instead of Civil Service. A greater worry had to do with my ability to deal effectively in a budgeting process with which I had no experience. My predecessor's skill at dealing with the Legislature in such matters was legendary, yet the agency had been cash starved for years—how could I possibly get needed funds?

I knew first hand that Jackson Prison's need alone was immense; I had often likened the prison to a rusty, leaky old battleship needing dry-dock. Likewise, the old prisons at Ionia and Marquette needed major renovation; probation and parole services were understaffed; and healthcare in the prisons was abysmal. On the plus side, it would mean moving the family from prison housing to a normal neighborhood, and working for the Corrections Commissioners would be rewarding: the Commission functioned harmoniously like a board of directors, despite being from opposing political parties as required by law. I would also find it a pleasure to serve Governor Milliken, one of the finest statesmen I would ever know. So when the Commission asked me to take the job, I accepted. My twelve year tenure would prove to be the second-longest in Department history and lasted three times as long as any other job I ever held.

CHARLES E. EGELER

Photo courtesy of the Michigan Department of Corrections

Chapter Ten
Charles Egeler at The Helm—A Dream Cut Short

FINALLY, IN AUGUST 1972, GUS HARRISON DECIDED THAT 19 years as Director of Corrections was enough and was glad to be offered a new and different challenge. Michigan was moving to establish a state lottery as a source of revenue to help fund public education. Both the legislature and the Governor considered Harrison to be an excellent, incorruptible, and efficient administrator. Therefore, they urged him to take the job of establishing and running the new lottery, and he accepted. The Corrections Commission then appointed me to replace Harrison, as Corrections Director.

I then appointed Charles Egeler Warden of Jackson Prison, fulfilling his long-term dream. His career began as a counselor in 1953 and most recently, he had served three years as Deputy Warden. Two major staff changes occurred during his tenure: Charles Anderson became Egeler's Deputy Warden in August 1972, and upon Anderson's promotion to Superintendent of the Reception and Guidance Center in May 1973 Dale Foltz replaced him.

In addition to the many challenges of operating Jackson already discussed, we handed the new Warden a full plate of problems not of our making. First, we all knew that health care for SPSM inmates was never fully adequate, but now it was becoming catastrophic. Then the State was blindsided by the 1973 OPEC oil embargo, forcing budget cutbacks. And finally, an obscure "Ku Klux Klan Act" (section 1983,) which had been on the books since 1871, was at last noticed by civil rights lawyers and resulted in an avalanche of litigation. In addition, Egeler had to deal with implementation of the department's new policy of integrating women as corrections officers and nurses in formerly male-only positions. A policy bitterly opposed by many officers, some inmates, and a few Lansing politicians, so it required the Warden's strong support and judicious attention. Egeler handled it all with aplomb and loyal support.

If It Can Go Wrong, It Will

Saturday, October 13, 1973 was a bad day for me. I am a Spartan fan, and the Michigan State football team had been defeated 31 to 0 by the Michigan Wolverines in Spartan Stadium. Later I learned that police had arrested Warden Egeler while he was driving home from a post-game party, and DWI charges were pending. Some reporters immediately demanded to know whether I was considering his dismissal. I said I would make no statement until the matter was adjudicated. The following morning a chastened Warden Egeler came to my Lansing office submitting a paper. It was his resignation. I told him that he was too valuable for the department to lose but that there would be consequences. I said, "I will be back with you after I have consulted with Civil Service about an appropriate penalty." After he pleaded guilty in court to "impaired driving" I imposed two weeks suspension without pay. It was the only black mark on his career.

On Saturday, November 9, 1974, police arrested kitchen steward, Jimmy Robinson age 28, for smuggling marijuana into the prison using hollowed-out platform shoes and concealing two bags in his clothing. State police detectives and the prison's internal investigator had been watching several suspected smugglers for months.

On Friday evening, March 31, 1975, I was meeting with the Pittsfield Township board trying to convince them that the new high security prison the department wanted to build next door was a great idea. Would it be dangerous? Of course not; I pointed out that prisoners rarely escape from secure prisons. After bidding the skeptical crowd adieu, I started up my state vehicle and its police radio came on with a lot of chatter. Kenneth Oliver, an infamous cop killer serving natural life at Jackson for the murder of a state trooper, was missing. The timing could not have been worse! Officers were thoroughly searching the prison now to rule out the possibility that Oliver was hidden out somewhere in the massive facility since there was no physical evidence of escape.

However, there had been an escape, and prison and police investigators finally pieced together how it had been done. Oliver had faked an illness to gain admission to the infirmary; he then concealed himself in a laundry cart used to remove old medical records, and covered by medical files, was able to avoid detection by the traffic gate officers. It was apparent that he could not have done this without help. Prison investigators immediately suspected Oscar Rodriquez, Jr., the prison clerk in charge of the medical records disposal project, and obtained the following account from his inmate driver. Rodriquez had assured the traffic gate officers that he had watched the loading of the medical files and since the officers could not probe through them and unloading them in the gate would be a major disruption of gate traffic, he was passed through. Once clear of the prison, Rodriguez and his driver headed toward a secure records disposal site near Battle Creek. When they stopped at a Ponderosa Steak House for a snack, Oliver scrambled out of the truck into a waiting Volkswagen. FBI agents captured him three months later at a relative's house in Los Angeles. Rodriquez went to prison for his part in aiding a prison escape, and the prison disciplined six other employees for rules violation, including the traffic gate officer for improperly clearing the vehicle through the gate. Nevertheless, despite this incident and attendant publicity, the State built the Pittsfield Township Prison with the Board of Supervisors' blessing.

The Health Care Crisis

SPSM's health care system had been on virtual life support for years—underfunded, antiquated facilities and equipment, unqualified inmate nurses and clerical support and definitely too few physicians. Inmates needing sick call or dental attention often had to bribe their way with a carton or two of cigarettes to get by the inmate hospital clerk, so the indigents were generally out of luck. During our counselor days, both Egeler and I had run interference for inmates by calling the Medical Director, Dr. Bartholic, directly or writing a pass to the hospital. Even then, on at least one occasion, a 55-year-old inmate for whom I had paved the way to the hospital, sat on the bench there for two hours and then keeled over dead.

By 1973, we were now in charge but both Egeler and I were well aware of the political reality of Michigan's approaching fiscal calamity resulting from the 1973 oil shock and crash of the State's auto industry. The department was preparing budget proposals to meet the Department of Management and Budget's FY 1974 targets while at the same time trying to improve health care. We were $1.5 million over budget at the time and facing the necessity of layoffs.

In the midst of this, Warden Egeler called to alert me that Dr. Leo Baker had just resigned effective Friday (09-18-1974) to take a similar job at a California prison—this left us with one physician and two registered nurses, both male, for the prison. Dr. Baker complained that the prison hospital was so bad no self-respecting professional would consider working there, so he never had full medical staff and had to use unqualified inmate nurses. (Egeler was using contracts to obtain specialist physicians from Jackson Foote Hospital and three physicians from the University of Michigan led by Dr. Jay Harness to limp by.) I immediately called Ken Franklin, legal advisor to the Governor, and asked for an appointment with Governor Milliken to make a personal appeal. The Governor listened intently, made some executive office funds immediately available, and was unwavering in his support for later appropriation requests. However, of even greater significance, he appointed a "blue-ribbon" committee from the medical community, including Michigan's three university hospitals and the Michigan

192

Department of Health, to develop a professionally endorsed plan. This would also provide political influence with the legislature. The committee published a landmark work titled, *The Key to Health Care in a Padlocked Society*. I could not have asked Governor Milliken for more, but it took twelve years for the approval of construction of a new hospital at SPSM to muddle its way through the legislature. Significant improvement of healthcare services in both equipment and staff had come almost immediately however.

We were most fortunate in being able to recruit a brilliant and energetic young physician, Dr. Jay Harness, to implement and manage the committee plan. Besides his inherent missionary zeal, Dr. Harness had the additional incentive of working off his military obligation by helping this "medically underserved" population of prisoners. His charisma, coupled with improving the working environment by repairing, remodeling, and repainting, as well as, the addition of much new modern equipment, was effective in recruitment of physicians and other professional staff. Early on, Dr. Harness pointed out that the Civil Service barriers that prevented female professionals from working in male prisons created a major staffing problem because the pool of registered nurses was predominately female. Since we were already working on a case-by-case review of gender barriers for custody positions, we agreed to move now to the nurse positions. Egeler would study the work environment for undue risks for women—Deputy Director Brown would order inmate clerks and nurses with a history of predatory violence toward women transferred to Marquette. At least two "serial killers" of women were also moved. Corrections Commissioner, Dr. Duane Waters, chipped in as a volunteer doctor— the department named the new SPSM hospital after him.

So healthcare at SPSM made great strides within a couple of years despite occasional setbacks and a legislative process that made every bit of that progress seem like trying to jog uphill knee-deep in molasses.

Flight to Freedom

On Friday, June 6, 1975, Warden Egeler called me to report an escape by helicopter from inside SPSM. I immediately contacted Governor Milliken's press secretary, George Weeks to say, "George, you aren't going to believe this, but a black and white helicopter just dropped into the yard at Jackson Prison and picked up a prisoner." The movie *Breakout,* based on just such a plot, was playing in local theaters at the time, but this was no movie. Facing a dull news weekend the media were ecstatic—what a story. One reporter wrote:

> I don't think up until last Friday that you could have found a single, doggone thing good to say about Dale Remling (the escapee.) Most would have concluded that the poor devil deserved to be locked up for life. But, you'd never have gotten that vote Friday night. The truth is that dramatic, spectacular escape touched something in us. There was something metaphorically grand in it all. All of us today are trapped in dull little prison cells of lives, and we can't help but exclaim in admiration when we see a man seize events and work out a plan that makes him his own master. It literally gave him wings above the dull plain of ordinary humanity and sent him soaring into an impossible zenith of everyman's aspirations and dreams.[1]

Folks were cheering for the bad guy, and I must admit it was a fascinating story. To begin with, the principal in this plot was a colorful character. A prison buddy said this about him, "I knew Cowboy Remling as well as anyone can know another in here and we used to sit and have long talks with each other. He talked about escaping from here quite a lot. And, his reasons were not to rob, kill, and rape, but to get a hamburger, a bottle of cold beer and a woman. Yes, mostly ... a woman, that was what it comes down to." The FBI described him as "a con man par excellence" who had served time for check forgery, aircraft theft, robbery, theft of horse saddles, and theft of several hundred hogs in Nebraska (where eleven family members were taken hostage and locked in a reeking old stock-hauler while their hogs were stolen.) However, everyone who knew him seemed to agree with his old neighbor's assessment that he was very charming, "a guy you just couldn't get mad at."

It turned out that the brazen but complex escape plan had been hatching for two years. It began when Remling persuaded one

---

[1] *Jackson Citizen Patriot,* June 7, 1975.

Gertrude, a mother of ten, to become his main collaborator, apparently through inducement of romance and riches. He was a handsome thrice-married devil and concocted a convincing tale that $60,000 was cached in Nebraska, obtained from his sale of rustled hogs. With Gertrude's help, they gathered a "couldn't shoot straight" gang of seven. This was comprised of a carnival barker friend Gene, Gertrude, her nineteen-year-old son, a son-in-law, and two young women.

The first plan called for friend Gene to be the helicopter pilot. They were not deterred by the fact that Gene knew nothing about flying one. He had, after all, taken a flying lesson or two one time at the airport in Ionia. This plan went awry though, when he crashed a stolen helicopter along I-94 east of the prison. Apparently, darn it, there is more to flying one of those things than you'd think!

Then came plan number two, highjacking a helicopter with pilot. The other gang members would obtain a get-away vehicle and rent a motel in Lansing to hole up in if necessary. Gene reserved a helicopter in Plymouth's Mettetal Airport for a "business trip to Lansing" and by 10:15 Friday morning, they were in the air. Ten minutes later Gene opened his briefcase and produced a lethal-looking survival knife. He put this at the throat of the pilot and ordered him to fly to Jackson Prison. At 11:05, they landed in the prison yard and Remling jumped aboard. They were out of the prison in twenty seconds.

Remling ordered the helicopter down five miles from the prison where a getaway car was waiting. Squirting the pilot with mace to incapacitate him, and pulling wires to disable the radio, Gene and Remling jumped from the helicopter and ran for the car. As Remling stopped to change from prison clothes, he heard the helicopter start up; realizing the car would be tailed from the air, he waved his accomplices on and fled into the woods where he spent a miserable night fighting mosquitoes. Police arrested most of the gang within hours; they caught the getaway driver at a police roadblock. Gene and Gertrude fled to Kansas, however, where they joined a carnival. Boasting about their part in the escape was their undoing—they were snitched out and arrested two weeks later. The *Jackson Citizen Patriot* reported:

> But strangely, the man who has stolen airplanes, hogs and bamboozled the town of Sidney, took his capture last Saturday in a Leslie bar calmly. He

grinned at his State Police captors and later told reporters "there was no use for me to have tears. The Trooper had a cannon on me and I didn't have it on him.

He was drinking a cold beer at the time. He, along with Gene and Gertrude, were charged with the Federal crime of aircraft piracy, which carried a 20-year minimum term, but several of the gang agreed to turn state's evidence for immunity. Investigators were satisfied that the $60,000 of hog money Remling used for bait never existed; the hog scam had been discovered years before when an attempted sale was botched for lack of proper vaccination papers.

Remling returned to farming near a small village in mid-Michigan after serving his federal and Michigan sentences. He has remained off police blotters since.

The Murder of Dr. Cynthia Miller

A particularly traumatic event became known on Sunday, July 18, 1976. Dr. Harness called me at home to report that Cynthia Miller, a bright young doctor who recently transferred from SPSM to DeHoCo Women's Prison, had been found murdered in her car on the shoulder of I-696 near Southfield. Sunday's *Detroit Free Press* reported "Investigators know that Dr. Miller withdrew $5,000 in $100 bills from her account and then drove off without telling anyone where she was going. About 45 minutes later, she was found dead in her car with two gunshot wounds in her head." In the *Michigan Free Press*, a weekly, reporter Juan Montoya wrote, "I feel in danger of my life," Dr. Cynthia Miller had confided to a friend." Investigators began looking for possible enemies wishing to harm the Doctor. One inmate kite signed "Thomas" and containing threats was in Miller's property, but the prison number and name did not match anyone in the system. However, homicide investigators following a tip, checked the cell of inmate Larry Wells, a lab worker in the prison infirmary at SPSM, and discovered letters from Dr. Miller that indicated that a romantic liaison existed between them during her employment at SPSM. Later, police uncovered a "last will and testament" bequeathing all of her estate to Wells along with records showing $3,000 she deposited into his account. While this fraternization was extraordinary and would have

196

been the basis for firing the doctor, no direct connection between Wells and her murder was apparent. However, a seemingly unrelated incident, the escape of a minimum-security inmate named Wingard three weeks earlier, was soon connected to the Doctor's murder as well as to inmate Wells. Confusing the matter further, Wingard himself had had an illicit tryst with a prison nurse, Gail Oliver, at about the same time.

Investigators received a tip that Oliver, no longer employed by the prison, was in downtown Jackson in the company of Wingard. The police discovered that Oliver helped Wingard escape from the SPSM Trusty Division and, abandoning her husband and children, had now gone "on the lam" with him. Prosecutors finally established what had ultimately happened: Cynthia Miller stopped to meet Wingard on the shoulder of I-696, delivered the $5,000 she had withdrawn from her bank account only moments before, and when she had done this, he killed her. The investigators theorized that Wingard, who knew both Dr. Miller and inmate Wells, might have convinced her that he could put in a "fix" by bribing an official to get her heart's desire out of prison. This theory was supported to some extent by the evidence that Dr. Miller had helped pay for an unsuccessful appeal of Wells' case the previous year.

As fugitives, now wanted for murder as well as prison escape, Wingard and Oliver fled from Michigan. About all we know about their activities after that is that they stole a motor home in a southern state, and were apprehended a year or two later in Alaska. Subsequently, Wingard received a life sentence for Dr. Miller's murder, and Oliver served several years for her part in the crimes.

How did Cynthia Miller, a brilliant 29-year-old University of Wisconsin graduate and gifted physician, allow herself to become entangled in the web of illicit romance and intrigue that took her life? What possessed Gail Oliver to abandon her family for a doomed and ill-conceived adventure with a cold-blooded killer? We will never know the answers to these questions.[2]

---

[2] Information about the Cynthia Miller murder from police/corrections reports in my files.

A Sad Loss

In March of 1977, Warden Egeler and his wife were enjoying a break from the prison routine in Roscommon near the Au Sable—his favorite spot on Earth—when he began to feel chest pains. It was a weekend, before the time of 911 or trained EMTs, so they decided to get on the road home. Egeler was young, tough and a former athlete—a member of the 1951 Michigan State University National Champion swim and dive team—so he did not recognize his danger. Telling his wife that he would ride more comfortably stretched out on a pad on the bed of their pickup they started back to Jackson. Upon arriving at Saint Johns, she stopped to check on Egeler and found him dead. He was only 48.

CHARLES E. ANDERSON
Photo courtesy of the Michigan Department of Corrections

Chapter Eleven
Charles Anderson Becomes Warden

CHARLES ANDERSON, SUPERINTENDENT OF THE RECEPTION and Guidance Center at SPSM and a former Deputy Warden, succeeded Egeler as Warden in March 1977, a position he filled until his voluntary resignation on June 22, 1980. His 40-month tenure came during particularly difficult times at SPSM. Extremely austere budgets, forced unpaid leave days, and shortages in custody staff were wearing on everyone and demoralizing to staff. Federal courts and the Michigan legislature had recently established new due process rights and complex procedures for hearing inmate disciplinary cases, and these were particularly vexing to corrections officers.

Warden Anderson brought his concerns about this issue to the Corrections Commission on April 10, 1980. He objected to the requirements of the Central Office Hearings Division, especially to the constrictive time limits which resulted in obviously guilty violators escaping penalty on a mere technicality. Also, SPSM staff viewed the recently established Corrections Legislative Ombudsman as hostile and biased. Getting no satisfaction from the Ombudsman's office, in February 1980, 27 corrections officers and inmates at the SPSM Reception Center sued the Ombudsman, Leonard Esquina, for defamation of character and unsupported allegations of drug trafficking and homosexual attacks in prison. Their attorney said Esquina's report did not identify specific guards or prisoners, so all were suspect through innuendo, and that he violated state statute by not giving the accused a chance to respond to the charges before issuing his report. It seemed to the staff that they were under siege.

The prison system had been severely overcrowded since 1973, but this problem was compounded in the November 1978 general by enactment of an initiative petition entitled "Proposal B," abolishing special parole and increasing time which had to be served.[1] It passed by a staggering 3 to 1 majority. This was bad news, not only because of the immediate impact of Proposal B, which was marginal at first, but because of the political explosiveness of such an overpowering declaration of public sentiment. It would embolden hardliners to continue tightening the screws on prosecution, sentencing, and parole. Indeed, the cumulative effect would ultimately triple the prison population.[2]

---

[1] Proposal B passed with the most overwhelming majority of any issue or candidate on the ballot in November (74% for.) It eliminated "good time" for 78 crime categories from homicide to possession of burglar's tools.

[2] Johnson, Kime, *Can We Build Our Way Out?* A background paper prepared for The Citizens Research Council of Michigan, November 1989, p 9.

Conned to Perfection

The next unfortunate event involved a confidence man named Westlake. He was a non-violent individual whom we all knew well from an earlier stay at SPSM. He had worn out his welcome then because of various schemes that tended to get employees in trouble, and because he had earned the enmity of other prisoners. Therefore, we stashed him at the Michigan Reformatory where he weaseled a transfer to a minimum-security dormitory.

One day Dale Foltz, Warden at the Reformatory, called to give me a heads up on Westlake's recent escape from the dormitory, because it had potential to become an embarrassing news story.

Warden Foltz said, "Director, remember when Westlake escaped from the Dormitory a few days ago? Well it seems that one of our employees helped him get to Toledo on his way to Florida so he could claim his lease on a ship to recover sunken treasure."

My first thought was, "What possessed an employee to aid and abet a prison escapee—a crime that could get them five years?" Then I realized, Westlake must have another con-game going. Because I knew Westlake was a charming master of the grifters' art, and that was the only way this story made sense.

A word here about confidence men, or "con-artists" as they are called in prison; I received my introduction to the world of con games years before from an infamous confidence man by the name of Van Buskirk. Although he did not claim his was an honorable profession, in his view confidence men were morally superior to sneak thieves, robbers, and murderers because they only took what the "mark" willingly gave them. Furthermore, the con will never succeed unless the mark has larceny in his heart, making him in effect a co-conspirator.

This is so because whether it involves a simple car trunk sale of fake Rolexes or a carefully planned, incredibly complex get-rich-quick scheme, the mark must always believe that he is getting something for relatively nothing—that he is taking advantage of some kind of shady deal. And Van Buskirk's eyes fairly sparkled each time he told about the "sting" when the con came down, a thrill he said was like that of a big game hunter bagging a trophy stag. The sting is better still if the mark does not recognize what went wrong, but blames some third party for queering the deal. That would prove to be the case in Westlake's latest scam.

"So this fugitive inmate without any money is going to lease an ocean-going salvage ship?" I asked Foltz. Well, it seems Westlake actually had arranged all the paperwork for that lease from the Reformatory before he went to the dormitory. However, he was short on cash and hoped the employee would help him out. Which he agreed to do. He would give Westlake money and help him get to Florida. Why? Because as a stockholder in Westlake's company, he would be rich when the venture succeeded.

Warden Foltz and I had a chuckle at that, and then he told me the rest of the story: Being bright and having a lot of time on his hands, Westlake started reading books from the state library. He chanced upon stories of sunken treasure in the sailing ship boneyard off the Maryland coast, about which much had been written. The books even included ocean charts. He researched everything about this subject, and then about diving and recovery ships. He had even managed to reserve one of these ships for rental in Florida and had impressive documentation to prove it.

Westlake became a virtual walking encyclopedia on the subject and then began to dream of an actual expedition to dredge up these riches. Or so he would say: I think all he saw from the beginning was an opportunity for a con. In any case, he then formed a corporation including a Board of Directors (families of other inmates,) stockholders (both inmate families and employees,) all given gilded stock certificates complete with impressive official-looking seals, which he surreptitiously printed in the prison print shop. Inmate families and some of our employees invested $500 or more each in company stock. This was completely illegal, of course, and in violation of both inmate and employee rules.

I asked Warden Foltz a rhetorical question: "How could our employees fall for such a scheme from that guy? Don't they read prisoner files?"

Nevertheless, we both knew the answer. As Foltz said, "I know Director, but this guy is really slick—he painted a picture of instant wealth, as only he can do. And by the way, guess what he named his corporation?"

"What?"

"The Stingray Corporation!"

A week or two later, Warden Foltz called again, "Director, you're not going to believe this, but I called the employees who bought into Westlake's scam and whose jobs we were trying to save, and they got in my face telling me that I was violating their rights—that I couldn't tell them how to invest their money."

Therefore, the victims still did not get it--it was not Westlake's fault. He had indeed pulled a classic "sting"—a perfect "con."

Sadly, the employee who aided and abetted Westlake's escape received a felony conviction and others received unpaid suspensions.

A Yard Party Gone Awry—What Were They Thinking?

Memorial Day each year signaled the advent of good weather coupled with a three day weekend—a cause for celebration in the prison. Staff planned recreation and sports activities and the kitchen staff put out special meals. Inmate entrepreneurs prepared to market their specialties—alcohol and recreational drugs being in great demand. The home brewers were bringing out their "spud juice," made with potato peelings and a touch of yeast, most likely from a handful of raw bread dough. This would have been contained in a salvaged gallon or half-gallon open topped jar. The jar would be stealthily buried somewhere in the acres of yard, with a screen or mesh over the top, and would be located so the sun would provide brewing heat. Juice men claimed that within three or four days their product would "work" to 3% alcohol. The strained works then sold for a dollar or two a glass.

However, an inmate with a "mule," either staff or visitor, would order real liquor, vodka, or whiskey, which would bring $25 or more per drink on the yard. (Several officers and two prison chaplains had lost their jobs for attempting to smuggle in whiskey in recent years.) This contraband was hard to stop, and on that Memorial weekend in 1979, one scheme went horribly amiss.

Three inmates had discovered two gallons of alcohol stored in the special activities counselors' office and hatched a scheme to steal it and make cocktails for Memorial Day. They mixed it with Hi C fruit drink bought in the inmate store, making an attractive, potent drink that they sold for $25 on the yard. Unfortunately the stolen alcohol was actually very toxic duplicating machine fluid (50% Methanol and 50%

Isopropanol—wood alcohol and rubbing alcohol.) Apparently, the miscreants ignored the skull and crossbones symbol on the containers.

Very ill prisoners began showing up at the prison hospital. Prison Medical Director, Kenneth Cole, soon diagnosed methanol poisoning as the cause and commenced emergency treatment. But the antidote for wood alcohol is ethyl alcohol, and the largest supply of that readily available to Dr. Cole was vodka (50% ethyl alcohol) which he quickly requisitioned. As soon as the prison grapevine carried this information the number of prisoners claiming exposure to wood alcohol ballooned from some 80 to 150, so the number of those actually poisoned is unknown. However, one inmate died, several suffered long-term neurological damage, and 42 were hospitalized (22 of these in various hospitals around the State.)

It became immediately necessary to segregate and then transfer the three guilty entrepreneurs, otherwise there would be additional fatalities when poison survivors caught them in the yard. However, two gallons of duplicating fluid clearly marked with skull and crossbones, far more than needed in the special activities office for duplicating, should have been under lock and key. A clear instance of harm through incompetence.

A Stonewall of Shame

August 1978 provided another bad memory. It started when my secretary, Sandy Bosnak said, "Director, you have an urgent call from Warden Koehler (at Marquette..." This usually unflappable Warden sounded grim and worried on the phone. "Director, we had to remove a paralyzed inmate from the transfer bus that just arrived from Jackson. He claims officers injured him in Jackson's segregation unit. Marquette doctors say his neck is broken and he will have to be airlifted to the University of Michigan Hospital." The thought of a paralyzed man being hauled out of segregation at four in the morning, manacled to a chain with 40 other inmates, and forced to ride ten hours on the transfer bus while unable to attend to normal toilet needs, elicited a feeling of instant outrage. How could it possibly be true?

The investigation was difficult and took some six months to conclude. Initially those involved stonewalled both the police and the internal investigators, offering a multitude of alibis. "Yes, the officers had to subdue inmate Goldman to break up a fight with another inmate, so perhaps he was injured when placed in a hammerlock." "Yes, he had lain on the concrete slab in the "adjustment" cell for several days but they thought he was malingering." They carried him out of segregation, put him on the security chain and then carried him on the bus because he refused to walk—no one apparently considering the possibility that he was simply unable to.

A hall-boy in the segregation unit may have given the most accurate account. He said that Goldman was a troublemaker, as most in segregation are, and one of the officers, who considered himself the enforcer, set out to teach Goldman a lesson. In the fracas, the officers took Goldman down and an officer proceeded to put the boots to him, including kicking him at the base of the neck. When confronted, the officer demanded a polygraph, which he flunked convincingly. Our efforts to fire him failed but he did get a long suspension and transfer to a minimum-security unit. His supervisor and fellow officers who contributed to the cover-up received shorter suspensions without pay.

Goldman eventually recovered from his quadriplegic condition and received a $450,000 settlement. It would have been more if not for the fact that he was serving a long prison term and had no substantial earnings loss to be factored into the amount. The Attorney General's Office asked for reimbursement from the officer who was most liable, but that was uncollectable. This shameful incident, stonewalled from start to finish by officers, supervisors, and health care staff at SPSM, was very troubling to all of us, and especially to Warden Anderson.

Prison can be a dangerous place

A spate of violence broke out in SPSM during 1979 and 1980. There were eight homicides in just two years, whereas during former years the prison averaged about one a year. During this same period, there were some dozen stabbings per month—in fact, there were 19 in a 35-day period in early 1980. Warden Anderson and Deputy Director Brown organized an institutional safety task force to address the violence. A number of predatory and violence-prone inmates were identified and either transferred or segregated, and by mid-summer this seemed to stem the violence.

Another Change of Wardens

After 40 months of crisis management, and faced with unsolvable budget issues and overcrowding, Warden Anderson looked longingly at the Trusty Division Deputy Warden position being vacated by Jerry Hansen's retirement—a much less demanding job with nearly equal pay. He was 48 and said he planned to retire soon and work in the private sector. I fully understood Warden Anderson's decision to leave, but very much regretted his departure.

BARRY MINTZES
1980-82

Photo courtesy of the Michigan Department of Corrections

Chapter Twelve
A Final Showdown at SPSM

WE CONTACTED EXPERIENCED WARDENS DALE FOLTZ, GARY WELLS, and Richard Handlon regarding the SPSM Warden's job but they were not interested. However, Barry Mintzes, Warden of the Kinross Correctional Facility, accepted the appointment in June 1980. He had been the department's youngest warden at its youngest prison. Mintzes had started his career at SPSM as a clinical psychologist and had served as an Administrative Assistant to me in the central office. A somewhat controversial charge of insubordination having to do with grooming regulations had occurred under Warden Egeler, but Egeler later became Mintzes' most ardent advocate, and Mintzes justified that by proving to be bright, creative and hardworking.

Warden Mintzes came with a solid understanding of the inmate disciplinary process, having worked in liaison with the Central Office Hearings Division and legislative committees. Therefore, he was able to provide helpful clarification and training for prison staff.

But there was no shortage of problems to deal with. When the budget situation became even more difficult as Michigan slid into an even deeper recession in 1980, Mintzes developed a staffing process to maintain a critical complement of officers using as little overtime as possible. This had been necessary and was professionally done, but it became a major irritant to corrections officers and shift supervisors—to officers because they were accustomed to enhancing their earnings with overtime, and to shift supervisors who wanted more flexibility in shift assignments.

Then, in an example of the unintended consequences of good intentions, the legislature passed the "Prison Overcrowding Emergency Powers Act" in 1980. This law authorized the Governor to reduce prison sentences by 90 days across the board when the prison system reached its rated capacity. This created a surge of prisoners eligible for release to reduce crowding—which it did, at least on the short run. However, at SPSM, with its population of nearly 6000 prisoners, the repeated shuffling of outdate with resulting changes in security classification created an administrative headache with its massive increase in paperwork.

Nevertheless, we had to deal with crowding. Prisoners were coming in with no place to put them, and the Federal Court had little sympathy for our plight. For example, in the *Jackson v. Johnson* case in 1980, I spent an unhappy day in Federal Court: Judge Joiner was upset over an Attorney General delay in entering into a consent decree that would assure that inmates, such as the plaintiff, would be moved from punitive segregation as soon as their segregation sentences were served. That is whether any cell was available or not. He also ordered $2,500 attorney fees for the plaintiff. In addition, Judge Joiner said to me in open court, "Director Johnson, I advise you to get competent representation!"

Anyway, SPSM's new Warden had plenty to occupy his attention in the summer of 1980. Mintzes also took leadership of the newly formed "task force to reduce violence" begun under Warden Anderson. The good news was that the spate of violence beginning in 1979

208

continued to abate. However, in spring of 1981, rumors that an increasing number of inmates were stashing weapons were of concern. Moreover, although these rumors were not supported by hard evidence, Warden Mintzes and his staff planned a pre-emptive strike with a mass lockdown and search of the entire prison, and this took place on the Wednesday prior to Memorial Day 1981. To reduce overtime cost for such a labor-intensive undertaking, Mintzes had mobilized all civilian staff to assist—everyone understood since Warden Bannan's time that all had security and custody responsibility.

During a shakedown all prisoners are locked in their cells. To avoid being caught for possession they throw any weapons and any other contraband out through the bars onto the base floor. Staff then tallied this debris prior to disposal. The tally this time reassured staff by showing that the rumors had been wrong: there was no unusual quantity of weapons.

Mutiny on the Holiday

From the corrections officers' perspective, 1981 was an unstable and unpredictable time. They faced changing leadership, loss of income enhancement from overtime as we tightened the screws on labor costs, and disciplinary due process requirements remained a major irritation.

In mid-May 1981, I began to hear rumors of some kind of "job action" being planned by the correction officer's union (MCO). "Job action" normally means a strike or at least an informational picket line at the prison. I got no response to my concern from the MCO office, which was unusual and worrisome, so I alerted Governor Milliken and all wardens. We were expecting and preparing for a strike.

On Thursday, May 21, 1981, the corrections officer's union issued an "instructional memo" to its membership as a follow-up to a *"resolution on understaffing"* adopted by its Central Committee five days before:

> The resolution incorporates the concept of doing whatever is necessary to resolve the serious staffing problems facing our membership. Have officers and stewards begin to spread the word—verbally, shift meetings, regular meetings, special meetings, etc. Bring your membership along slowly. Tell

them the whole union is doing the same things: must be united. Start with the strongest shift—your strongest union members will usually get the ball rolling. Tell them not to worry about legalities—Central (we) is handling that with the attorneys ... Meet with your administration and inform them of the resolution and that the (union) will do whatever is necessary ...You do not have to tell them specifics, only that we are united in our effort ...

The union presented the resolution to Warden Mintzes at SPSM on that same day, and by evening, we were receiving tips about what this memo had set in motion. We expected an illegal strike, so we readied the department's emergency strike plan, and the next morning, when it appeared the officers were about to lockdown Jackson to prepare for the strike, I called the Governor's Office to trigger the emergency plan. I fired off the prerequisite telegram to the union, which was not returning calls. In it, I advised the union's Executive Director "Any action which caused an unwarranted interruption of inmate programs and activities could be dangerous." Jan Baugh of the Attorney General's Office prepared a restraining order to be entered with the local Circuit Court the instant it was certain a strike had occurred.

At 9:15 a.m. on Friday, May 22, Union President Fryt informed Jackson's Deputy Warden Elton Scott that the union was taking control of the prison with the intention of locking down the inmates and conducting a cell-to-cell search, and that, by the way, they were mobilizing all off duty officers as well. This action explained a tip we had received earlier: Two officers reported that they had attended a meeting in Ann Arbor where union officers complained about unsafe working conditions at SPSM and had been assured by the prosecutor that they had a constitutional right to use whatever means necessary to protect them from harm. Therefore, they refused to heed the Warden's warning that the action was illegal and that all officers participating in such a mutiny would be guilty of gross insubordination.

As the officers tried to lockdown the prison, and supervisors attempted to regain authority, the prisoners had other ideas. They did not intend to miss the holiday events of the Memorial Day weekend while locked in their cells with officers rummaging through their belongings—especially after having gone through the indignity of such a mass cell search just two days before. They overpowered the guards conducting the lockdown in cellblock three and took their keys. This gave them access to adjoining cellblock four, and they promptly overpowered the guards there, taking over both blocks.

Before noon, a full-scale riot was underway, involving about half of the 1000 inmates who were unlocked. Soon fires were set in the captured cellblocks and a food service area. They looted the canteen and vandalism was widespread. The disturbance spread to the north-side prison where inmates burned a temporary dormitory to the ground. While some prisoners attempted to protect property and save medical records, chaos reigned for several hours. As soon as word of the inmate seizure of cellblock three spread, the staff mutiny ceased and the officers assumed disturbance control assignments under the normal command structure. They quickly formed gun squads and forcefully retook the cellblocks. By mid-afternoon, the rioting inmates were contained in the north yard and fire fighters from surrounding communities were putting out the fires. By 9:00 p.m., we had secured all prisoners in cells.

Then, just as we thought we could relax, we received word that the Michigan Reformatory had "blown up" as inmates were going back to their cells from night yard. Inmates soon controlled most of the Reformatory and fires were raging. Armed riot squads were called in from two nearby prisons and Warden Foltz called the Michigan State Police for assistance. Deputy Director Brown and Corrections Commissioner Leduc, who had come to Jackson with me earlier, immediately left for Ionia while I stayed to deal with the media frenzy that had built up at Jackson. It would be 3 a.m. before the Reformatory was back under control.

The remainder of the weekend was spent assessing damage, treating the injured and getting food to locked up inmates. Then, during a planning meeting in Lansing on Tuesday, Warden Mintzes received a call that a second riot had broken out in the medium security Jackson north-side compound. This was a disturbance planned by the prisoners, and we learned later that while supervisors had been warned about it they had taken no precautions. Before officers regained control, inmates burned six temporary housing units along with the food service facility. Some 1000 or so inmates were then locked up — in some cases, two or three to a cell because of housing lost to the fires.

Even though we now had the Jackson and the Ionia prisons locked down, things were not yet all quiet in the prison system. That evening, Marquette's Warden, Ted Kohler, notified us that a major disturbance had broken out there. Inmates had destroyed the vocational school, the textile industry, and a counselor's office, and a number of prisoners barricaded themselves in two cellblocks while trying to wreck the locking systems. Gun squads rescued officers trapped in cellblocks, though in one instance six inmates had protected an officer and escorted him to the yard. The prison regained control by 12:30 a.m.

These disturbances cost $5 million in property losses, $4.2 million for overtime pay for the department, and an unknown amount for the Michigan State Police. While there were no fatalities, more than 30 officers and 50 inmates had been injured. Immediately several investigations were launched: one by a House and Senate joint committee, and one by a Governor's task force; and I ordered a massive internal investigation.

Within a week, we were under a circuit court order preventing any lifting of the general lockdown of the three prisons—at the same time as we were defending ourselves in Federal District Court for having any lockdown at all. By August, more than 80 lawsuits were filed in Federal Court. Preparing reports, interrogatories, and testifying in connection with these consumed much of the time we really needed for rebuilding and repairing, as well as designing better security and training—and, not least, restoring staff esprit de corps.

We charged 30 officers with insubordination and three supervisors with failure to act. Inmates received more than 100 criminal warrants and several hundred were charged with rule violations. A Deputy Warden lost his job and we demoted two supervisors. The Office of State Employer advised me, "You can't fire a union president." I replied, "Watch me!", and fired him anyway; the firing was upheld on appeal.

Need I say that 1981 had been a bad year?

DALE E. FOLTZ
1982-87
Photo courtesy of the Michigan Department of Corrections

Changing of the Guard Once More

In April 1982, Warden Mintzes decided that returning to private practice as a clinical psychologist held great appeal; a move made especially inviting by the crush of litigation following the 1981 riots that was imposed on top of the burden of trying to rebuild the prison and reorganize the staff.

Dale Foltz, Warden at the Michigan Reformatory, and previous Deputy Warden at SPSM under Warden Egeler, was our first choice to replace Mintzes, even though in 1980 he had declined to leave the reformatory for SPSM. Foltz would become the last SPSM Warden, since he assisted in the subdivision of the prison into the smaller institutions under separate wardens that would replace it.

213

Robert Brown Jr.
Former Director Michigan Department of Corrections
Photo courtesy of Robert Brown Jr.

Chapter Thirteen
Breaking Barriers

WHEN I BEGAN MY PRISON CAREER AT SPSM , the civil rights movement was not yet on the public's radar screen, and in Michigan, as in many states in the early 1950s, discrimination based on race and gender was commonplace; both for inmates and staff. To be sure, things began to change during the 1960s, fitfully and grudgingly, but

215

irrevocably—but changed only for inmates and minority male workers—women were left out of the picture.

Of course, the struggle for racial integration in the department had not been easy; black officers and professional staff originally had to endure a good deal of intimidation and abuse. However, because they had prevailed back then many were now in high-level positions. Charles Anderson had been the first black Warden of SPSM, and Robert Brown became the first black Deputy Director of the Central Office Bureau managing the prisons, and then Director of the Department itself. However, women had not even been able to get on the first step of the ladder leading to some of those jobs.

When I became Director, department policy and Civil Service Rules still prohibited women from working inside male prisons and from supervising male parolees or probationers. This policy effectively locked women out of 90% of the Department's well-paying jobs since that was the proportion of male offenders in the system.

Why were women left so far behind? I think it was because discrimination against women was given an official legitimacy that racial and ethnic discrimination never had. Where racial and ethnic discrimination existed, it was always a dirty little secret, unofficial and denied; but discrimination based solely on gender was the official policy of the State and was justified on noble grounds. The policy makers believed they were morally right—that this particular form of discrimination was necessary to protect women from the obscenity and harsh behavior of male criminals. Therefore, it became part of both the corporate and institutional culture. What followed from this was that any challenge to that policy was a challenge to fundamental beliefs, cherished professional judgment, and the history and culture of the organization. This made it more difficult to abolish discrimination for women than for other groups.

The injustice of excluding women from the work place, solely based on their gender, is self-evident. For years, women at SPSM worked alongside male officers at the information desk and in the inmate visiting areas, as well as searching female visitors, and they did all this on clerical pay. With Director Harrison's authorization, I appointed the first women officers to fill these positions at SPSM but Civil Service rules prevented them from working inside the prison. In addition, since corrections officers working in "contact" positions inside the walls or in housing units received premium pay, this prohibition resulted in denying women many better paying positions. This was patently unfair and called for reform.

Moreover, reform began. The road to achieving it was rocky and difficult—more so for the plucky women who pioneered in this all-male domain than for the management team. However, there was enough pain to go around. Resistance and sly insubordination by staff, cruel social, and job isolation of women officers by their male counterparts, sexual harassment, and set-ups for failure, proved to be troubling barriers. The forces opposing this change were formidable. There were lawsuits from inmates, unions, and staff, and the resistance, directly or covertly, led to some brutal assaults and even the murder of a fine officer at Jackson, Josephine McCallum. The reaction to these events by opponents to the change was mostly to say, "We told you so." However, my SPSM team of Warden Egeler and Deputy Director Brown had been steadfast and wholehearted in their support.

The first step in abolishing male-only positions was simply to request that Civil Service remove the gender restriction, justifying each change as we went. However, that was the easy part. There were questions as to how far we should go and how fast we should proceed. Were there actually special risks for women that we should understand and accommodate? Were the constitutional rights of prisoners a valid issue here? (Privacy and religious challenges were soon raised by some,) and how would the courts balance these rights against the employment rights of women? What kind of preparation should existing staff have for the changes that would be needed?

The answers to these and many other questions were unknown because no one had traveled this road before us. However, we were fortunate in selecting incremental implementation as the best strategy for the time. Initially, this allowed us to assign women to the jobs where we were most certain of success and where they would face the least resistance from both staff and inmates. Female nurses went to the prison hospital, female corrections officers were assigned to visiting rooms, towers, gate control, and similar positions. At the beginning, this strategy did not disadvantage women because we always had more positions to fill than available female candidates. Later this was no longer true because female officers would need a full range of job experience for promotion and access to the better paying assignments entitled by seniority. It continued to be a learning experience for all concerned.

There was a mixture of good news and bad news from integrating women into the workplace at SPSM. An unexpected benefit was that from the outset the majority of inmates appeared to welcome the addition of women officers, and responded favorably—by most accounts they toned down the cursing and use of obscenities in the presence of females. Women repeatedly told me that they found dealing with inmates much less a problem than dealing with the hostility of male staff. However, there was also a problem, especially at SPSM, of sexual harassment from some inmates, involving verbal abuse and some touching. This brought to our attention the fact that we had no specific rule against sexual harassment, even though that had always been among the most offensive and intimidating aspects of prison life—especially for timid inmates. Of course, we had to insist that inmates respect officers, but now we had to ask why we had been so insensitive to this harassment problem for inmate victims before the advent of women officers. To remedy this omission we created a class of infractions termed "sexual misconduct," which prohibited unwanted behavior of a sexual nature. This was just one example of the positive impact of female staff on our awareness.

Another problem was that because we had started without women in male institutions, we had no reservoir of experienced women from which to select a manager. We asked Civil Service for authority to set up a management trainee cadre to fast-track women and minorities. They denied our request because it amounted to pre-selection, a no-no in their business. Therefore, we decided to find talented women employees and fast track them without a trainee cadre. We sent them to prison camps, as well as, to maximum security—wherever we could get them management experience. They probably wondered what they ever did to deserve such godforsaken assignments, but we could not tell them lest we be charged with practicing pre-selection.

The women we chose were the trailblazers. Unspoken but understood by all of us was the realization that they needed to be not just good, but very good. Because all eyes would be on them, with detractors hoping they would fail and even tripping them up if they could get away with it. However, they met the challenge; they were indeed very good.

Pam Withrow
Former Warden Michigan Reformatory and Warden of the Year in
North America *Photo courtesy of Pam Withrow*

However, theirs was often a tough lot. I recall a meeting with one, Pam Withrow, who was then an Assistant Deputy Warden at SPSM during a very trying time. She had been working long hours under frustrating circumstances and wanted to accept a two year assignment at the National Institute of Corrections Academy at Boulder. What Pam did not know, and I could not tell her, was that she would soon get a Warden's appointment that would be a piece of cake compared to her present job—an appointment she could not have if she went to NIC. I remember telling her that it was impossible to do the whole job she was trying to do at Jackson—to just do her best, because "no, she could not go to NIC." She did not like my decision but reluctantly accepted it and went back to Jackson. A few months later, in her new Warden's job, our relationship became much less frosty. Years later the National Association of Wardens and Superintendents honored her as "Warden of the Year" in North America, and she retired with the distinction of having had the longest tenure of any warden in the 130-year history of The Michigan Reformatory, the state's oldest penitentiary.

We knew that the changes in policy and culture we were contemplating inevitably carried risks. Nevertheless, while none of us foresaw all of the problems, most of the doomsayers' prophecies never happened. A placement I was particularly concerned about was in the huge five tiered cellblocks at SPSM where officers were often alone on the tiers. I thought the major risk for a woman would be in a place where she could be isolated, and these cellblocks clearly provided such places. The offices in the old prison hospital constituted another. In considering these risks, I wondered where chauvinism left off and moral corporate responsibility took over. My concern was never about the ability and competence of women; it was about the threat from male inmates who viewed women as prey or as irrational objects of hatred. After all, women were the victims of many of the most heinous and brutal crimes for which these inmates were serving. Consequently, I ordered some serial killers of women transferred to Marquette, our most secure prison at the time, and I opposed placing women in SPSM's five-tiered cellblocks. The Federal District Court would overrule me on this, but that would come after the 1981 riots when the structure and staffing at SPSM was forever changed for the better. Were my fears justified? To some extent, they were. Officer Josephine McCallum was trapped and killed in an isolated area.

In fact, the funeral of officer McCallum, a promising new employee, brutally ravished and murdered in SPSM by the type of predator I had worried about, remains one of my most painful memories. It is tragic for anyone to lose his or her life to such bestial violence, but our complicity in her death compounded my pain. The policies violated and the procedures ignored, allowing the inmate to be loose, and Josephine to be without appropriate backup on an isolated assignment, need not be cited here. She did everything right, but the indifference, incompetence and perhaps even malice, of male colleagues cost her life. When those who are supposed to protect and

220

care for one another deliberately fail to do so, it is a scandalous tragedy for our profession.

More than thirty years have now passed, and many of the women who survived those early experiences have moved on to well-deserved retirement. They served ably at every rank: as Sergeants, Lieutenants, Captains, Inspectors, and Wardens. Others went on to become Fiscal Officers, Deputy Directors, Corrections Director and to all levels of responsibility and management in the fields of probation and parole. Their courage, competence, and loyalty contributed in full to the benefit of the department and the public it serves, amply rewarding those early struggles.

Photo of remodeled Jackson prison complex. Note 15 Block is missing *Photo by permission iStockphoto LP*

Chapter Fourteen
SPSM Sees Its Final Days

IN EARLY MARCH 1969, WE HAD BECOME AWARE OF a U. S. Supreme Court decision supporting Federal Judge Frank Johnson's ruling in the "jail house lawyer" case against the Tennessee Department of Corrections *(Johnson v Avery, 393 U.S. 483.)* Being practical by nature, we reviewed SPSM's inmate law library and jailhouse lawyer policies in light of the ruling. To our non-lawyer minds "It should be no problem, we'll tweak things a bit and be OK." We had no premonition that this was a harbinger of change in judicial policy towards prisons and prisoners that would lead to a massive explosion in litigation. As the courts abandoned their long held "hands-off doctrine" regarding prisons, a flood of decisions caught us unprepared, confused and with no legal competence to properly analyze and implement the policy and practice changes which would be required. We had no idea that 15 years later, in 1984, Chief Federal Judge John Feikens would good-naturedly tell me that I held the honor of being a defendant in more filings in Michigan's Eastern District Federal Court than anyone else had ever been—there were over 1000 open cases at the time. And SPSM wardens held second place.

How could this be? After all, Amendment XI of the Constitution specifically prohibits lawsuits against states, and SPSM is a state prison. As mentioned earlier, civil rights lawyers in the 1950s had discovered an obscure "Ku Klux Klan Act," passed in 1871 to combat abuses of former slaves by officials of state or local government. The law was seldom used during the first 90 years but in 1961, the U.S. Supreme Court expanded the application of Section 1983 of the act in their decision in *Monroe v. Pape.*[1] This allowed any inmate to file a claim directly with a federal or state court, alleging that a particular employee or official "under the color of law" violated a civil right. And, under this act, the party who prevails is entitled to reasonable attorneys' fees—this provision permitted plaintiff's attorneys to pursue cases which would otherwise not be cost-effective for them. I would learn that to "prevail" was (in my view, too liberally) applied to the plaintiffs suing us, and that $150 per hour was a reasonable attorneys fee. In one complicated case, we won on all issues, but, because we revised a policy directive affecting one of the issues, the plaintiff "prevailed" and the state paid thousands of dollars in attorney fees and costs.

Furthermore, plaintiff lawyers cleverly deduced that though they could not sue the State directly, they could access the State's deep pockets by obtaining judgments and punitive damage claims against its employees acting in good faith "under the color of law." In addition, they found that, though not legally obligated to do so, legislative bodies would appropriate funds to pay these judgments. Such was the case in a jury award of $70,000 against me in the trial of SPSM inmate, Redmond. Fortunately, the case of inmate Darwin Gravitt, who apparently decided to break the bank when he sued me for $91-hundred-billion for allegedly destroying his first prison file to conceal evidence of civil rights violations, was finally dismissed by the Court of Appeals.

Therefore, this act created a hospitable litigation environment for both inmates and their plaintiff lawyers. Inmates with time on their hands could research their prison law libraries and petition the courts,

---

[1] *Monroe v. Pape*, 365 U.S. 167, 81 S. Ct. 473, 5L. Ed. 2d 611 (1961).

hoping for the best—the worst that could happen to them was to be ignored. Plaintiff lawyers could litigate with the certainty of compensation and funding of the judgments and punitive damages awarded.

Of the many court decisions that followed, the Supreme Court opinion in *Wolff v. McDonnell (1974)* caused SPSM staff the most difficulty. It required due process rights all disciplinary proceedings where the prisoner's freedom could be curtailed. These included good time forfeiture, segregation sentences, and decisions that might jeopardize parole opportunities. Shortly after this ruling came down, the Michigan Legislature added statutory requirements: creating a Central Office Hearings Division, with an administrator and hearing officers' independent from the prisons, and requiring that inmates would have automatic rights of appeal to Circuit Courts.

In 1979, the Michigan Court of Appeals piled on by ruling that inmates were entitled to the due process rights enumerated under Michigan's Administrative Procedures Act. This act called for court-like procedures that would require elaborate hearings with witnesses, as well as, taped and transcribed proceedings and cross-examination of prison officials. The department estimated that 40,000 hearings heard annually would cost the State $1.4 million.

While this was occurring in the midst of a recession, SPSM was operating with minimum staff, referred to as the "critical complement," so officers had to try to implement a complicated new disciplinary process while shorthanded. The result was that technical procedural errors frequently resulted in hearing officers nullifying serious misconduct charges, and this meant that many inmates escaped all consequences for their misbehavior. This left officers frustrated and furious. While eventually the legislature modified the requirements and staff learned to deal with them, this had been a difficult decade for SPSM.

A Sample from Thousands of Lawsuits from the 1970s

Reasons for suing SPSM ranged from the ridiculous to the truly troublesome. Between 1974 and 1976, lawsuits doubled, and doubled again to 464 by 1978. In 1979, I reported to the legislature that we now had 951 open lawsuits, claiming well over half a billion dollars. In

1983 alone, inmates filed 1,106 prison conditions lawsuits, claiming $82 billion. They would win few of these, but the long-term cost to Michigan would be over $150 million. An Assistant Attorney General told me that his office would get about half the suits dismissed without going to court. Some were so silly as to be comical. In 1976, an inmate who ate light bulbs sued the prison because officials tried to change his diet. Another who received serious burns from setting his mattress on fire, sued because guards did not prevent him from getting matches.

I spent three days of the Christmas holidays in 1974 as a defendant in a wrongful death trial before the Court of Claims in the alleged suicide of inmate Dr. Clark. His widow sued for $500,000 for the death of her husband, who had plummeted to his death from the fourth gallery of 11 Block. She said it was accidental while we claimed it was suicide. We prevailed.

In 1977, someone threw paint thinner and a match into the cell of Inmate Hunt. The attack left him severely burned and the parole board released him early, assuming him injured so badly he would no longer pose a threat to society. In January 1979, the Detroit police arrested Hunt for armed robbery and murder. He held a rifle in his maimed hands as his brother robbed a tavern. The court dismissed his habeas corpus plea.

On February 17, 1980, Officers Jennie Griffin, Linda Loftis, and Kathleen Leslie filed suit challenging the Department of Corrections' policy that prevented them from working in the big five-tiered cellblocks at SPSM. Their suit prevailed and we were ordered to put them into the cellblocks.

In 1982, inmate Lawrence Kent filed a suit claiming his constitutional rights were violated because the prison allowed female guards to view him performing necessary bodily functions in his cell and to see his naked body in the shower area. He found this humiliating and degrading and said it violated his constitutional rights to practice his religious beliefs, his fourth amendment right to privacy and his eighth amendment right to freedom from cruel and unusual punishment. This reached The Sixth Circuit United State Court of Appeals, which denied his appeal.

226

The Value & Curse of Consent Decrees

Federal Judge Frank Johnson, perhaps the most courageous judge our country has seen, opened my eyes to the potential power and value of a federal court consent decree when he ordered Alabama to correct the horrible conditions in its prisons and mental hospital—he threatened to sell state assets to pay for the measures the legislature refused to fund. The Supreme Court backed him, saying in effect that the court must have the power to enforce its orders. This meant that the federal court could be an important resource in remedying SPSM's previously insoluble problems, because it could mandate funding which the legislature had failed to provide. As it turned out, the consent decrees in Michigan, which did indeed correct a number of intolerable conditions of confinement, also proved to sound the death knell for SPSM, as we had known it. The magnitude and number of the problems to be dealt with meant that the great behemoth that was Jackson must be either closed or dismembered into smaller separate facilities, which could actually be managed. For much of SPSM's existence state regulators assumed that they could not logically apply evolving building codes, with their fire and life safety requirements, to SPSM—problems which would only compound and become more impossible to remedy.

Breaking up the prison was not a new idea. Even before construction was complete, a special committee met in 1933 to consider changing SPSM into two prisons—north side maximum and south side medium. However, in the depth of the Great Depression adding cost was impossible, and the commission prematurely declared construction complete so as to save money by stopping all building.

Much later, in the late 1960s, the department obtained LEAA funds to begin a "Jackson revamp" aimed at reducing the inside prison population by building program space outside the north-side cellblocks and opening them out to the new space. This action, taken during the early 1970s, was successful in removing a thousand or so from the inside prison population. However plans to bring cellblocks One through Five up to fire safety and sanitation codes died for lack of funding. Years later, expanded and modernized, north side cellblocks One through Three and adjacent program space became the Charles E. Egeler Reception and Guidance Center.

227

SPSM's 1981 Memorial Weekend riots—in both the main prison and the north side—had made it more clear than ever that this was not a manageable facility. Restoring order, repairing damage, investigating crimes, processing misconduct (both inmate and staff,) and dealing with hearings and investigations) made return to normal programs and work assignments difficult at best. All the while, lawyers were perched like buzzards over a Serengeti kill—they filed 80 lawsuits before summer's end.

A class action Sec. 1983 suit brought by SPSM inmates in District Judge John Feikens Sixth Circuit Court in 1980 *(Hadix v. Johnson)* was already winding its way toward a consent decree in 1985. The decree would address more than a dozen aspects of prison life, from protection from harm, to food and out of cell activity. It would require revamping the prison into separate autonomous units. By that requirement alone, the consent decree marked the finish of the State Prison of Southern Michigan.

Then, in 1982, the US Justice Department began investigation of SPSM prison conditions under the Civil Rights of Institutionalized Person Act of 1980 *(CRIPA)* Two years later the Justice Department filed a complaint in Judge Enslen's Western District Court, simultaneous with a proposed consent decree covering many of the same issues as in Hadix. To some extent, the Judges Feikens and Enslen merged the two consent decrees. As if this was not enough attention, on June 11, 1984, the National Prison Project of the American Civil Liberties Union filed a Sec. 1983 class action suit in Judge Enslen's court *(Knop v. Johnson)* and on April 16, 1995, the parties entered into a consent decree. Nevertheless, "consent" did not mean that all was harmonious. On August 20, 1987, Judge Enslen entered an order granting plaintiffs' motion for sanctions against the State because it determined that they had filed motions with the intent to harass, delay, or increase the cost of litigation (The Appeals Court reversed the decision May 20, 1988.)

As the crush of prisoner lawsuits hit both the courts and state corrections departments, calls for congressional action intensified. As a result, Congress enacted the Prison Litigation Reform Act (PLRA) in April 1996, specifically intended to limit the use of court-enforced consent decrees. Also to restrict "the ability of Federal judges to affect the capacity and conditions of prisons and jails beyond what is required by the Constitution and Federal law and—shall extend no further than necessary to correct the violation of the Federal right... " Consequently, SPSM's consent decrees ended in 2002, twenty-two years after Hadix was filed.

It is easy to satirize prison litigation by selecting some of its more absurd examples—as I have done earlier in the chapter—or by criticizing Judge Feikens for including Jackson Community College programs as a part of the SPSM consent decree (perhaps a laudable inmate activity but hardly a constitutional right.)[2] However, the history of intolerable prison conditions is a sorry stain on our society. Over the years, prisoners have died or suffered serious harm from staff incompetence or malevolence. These almost universal afflictions have cropped up in prisons throughout history. The power to monitor prison conditions and to grant humane relief to powerless and friendless prisoners, as courageously wielded by Judge Frank Johnson and shown too in the humane generosity of Judge John Feikens, is essential to the prevention and ending of abuses which can so easily occur, hidden behind concrete and steel.

Lord Acton wrote over a hundred years ago, "Power tends to corrupt, and absolute power corrupts absolutely." In prison work, as with policing, the enormous power of the State is in the hands of staff, who often have the power of life and death over their charges. Therefore, preventing misuse of power is a major responsibility of prison management. When that duty is not carried out, or not provided for by the executive and legislative branches of government, the judicial branch must then intervene.

SPSM no longer exists. In its place, stand three independent prisons renovated and upgraded to meet consent decree standards for conditions of confinement, fire and life safety and health care. Seven Block was left untouched and is now promoted as a tourist attraction for anyone interested in seeing the original SPSM reception unit. The cost of the change was not inconsiderable. Physical plant construction costs alone approached $125 million. Renovation, reorganization of physical plant, and razing of deteriorated buildings reduced the number of cells by more than half—from 5,280 down to 2,524. However,

---

[2] *Hadix v. Johnson,* Nos. 99-1413, 99-1457., October 05, 2000-US 6th Circuit.

because everything remains contained within the old perimeter, to the casual observer driving by on Cooper Street, it looks remarkably unchanged.

To sum it all up, the path from the origin of Jackson Prison to its final demise was long and tortuous, but the flaw which would ultimately bring it down was built into it even before its birth. The Board of Control's plan for the new prison was progressive for its time, but by the time Jackson actually came into the world it had morphed into a monster with more than 5000 cells. Many, if not most, of the problems and intolerable practices taking place over the years, some of which have been recounted here, owed their genesis at least in part to that massive size. The place was simply too big with too many people in it to operate in peace and harmony for any length of time. Its size alone provided for the germination and growth of a prisoner and staff culture that would prove to be self-perpetuating and impossible to control. While it was the scene and backdrop for much of my life and career, and while many of the people I met and worked with provide fond memories, I can only find it a good thing that Jackson Prison itself is now also just a memory.

Entrance to State Prison of Southern Michigan at Jackson
Photo courtesy Jackson District Library

Afterword--A Few Miscellaneous Memories

IN SEPTEMBER 1984, I MADE WHAT WOULD BE MY LAST inspection of SPSM. As I passed through the sub-hall gate to the old north yard, it seemed empty to me—the massive fortress like, 15 Block was missing. Although I had witnessed its demolition 17 years before, it remained part of my image of years past.

The King and His Court

Strolling in the north yard toward the old ball diamond, I vividly recalled that summer day in 1956 when our inmate clerk, Ray, came in exclaiming, "Mr. Kohler, Mr. Johnson, you have got to go see Eddie Feigner this afternoon!" "Who is Eddie Feigner?" we asked. "He is indisputably the greatest softball pitcher who ever lived," our exasperated clerk explained. Because of his respect for our pitcher, Whisky Hunter, Feigner had agreed to an exhibition game at SPSM. Our curiosity aroused, we were at the ball diamond at 2 p.m., joined by a dozen or so other staff members. The word was out and inmates

231

The north yard ball diamond
Photos by permission Archives of Michigan

packed the stands. We watched the "King and His Court," a four man team, play flawless softball. Feigner struck out our hitters blindfolded, pitching from second base, and from between his legs. Whiskey Hunter was also on his game and unhittable. The game was scoreless when we decided to return to our offices. Kohler and I agreed with our clerk; we had never seen anyone like Feigner. No wonder; I learned later that he threw a softball harder than any major league pitcher has ever thrown a baseball.[1] His underhand fastball was officially clocked at 104 mph. Moreover, I still remember our clerk's, "I told you so," smirk afterward.

From Prison to a Detroit Tiger, All Star

Then my thoughts wandered to one of our own athletes; a troubled youth who ended up serving a 5 to 15 year sentence for armed robbery, and for whom that ball diamond became his salvation. Ron LeFlore never played an inning of organized ball at any level before prison—he learned the game at SPSM. His speed and natural talent so impressed a fellow inmate, Jimmy Karalla, that he persuaded Tiger manager Billy

---

[1] Matt Schudel, *Washington Post*, February 11, 2007.

Martin to give LeFlore a workout. The Tigers offered him a contract, which became his parole plan in 1973. Baseball historian Don Keko succinctly summarized LeFlore's bittersweet career in his January 2012 blog:

> LeFlore's career ended (1983) . . . He stole 97 bases with Montreal in 1980, signed with the White Sox in 1981, and retired in 1983. His skills eroded quickly and mysteriously. Following the announcement, LeFlore admitted to being four years older than previously thought. As a result, his decline seemed natural. Despite this, baseball helped save LeFlore's life, rescued him from jail, and provided an inspirational story for his generation.[2]

A Chilling Recollection

In my wandering through the north yard, I decided to skip the gym, (located next to the dining room on the east,) because it called to mind the gory murder of Bernard Fancher in 1960. Barney, as we knew him, was the Assistant Athletic Director at SPSM, and was at his desk in the gym office one late afternoon as inmates were coming into the gym.[3] Among them was inmate, Percy Roberson, whom Fancher had fired from his job as gym porter for being loud and abusive. Roberson, visibly angry, crowded through the inmates, and headed toward the office carrying a baseball bat, which he used to smash his way through the door. He then swung at the duty officer, missing him but smashing a glass desktop. As Fancher and the officer tried to flee, Roberson produced a ten-inch prison made stiletto type knife and began slashing and stabbing. Fancher tried to defend himself and received defensive slash wounds on his hands and fingers, and deep stab wounds in his chest and back—Doctors would pronounce him dead at 5:05 p.m.

During the melee, some inmates attempted to block Roberson while others fled to the yard. Sergeant O'Rourke was the first to arrive on the scene and while others transported Fancher to the hospital, he calmly talked Roberson into surrendering his knife and peacefully

---

[2] Don Keko, *Examiner.Com,* Ron LeFlore: from the Jailhouse to the clubhouse, January 2, 2012.
[3] Jackson Citizen Patriot, April 29, 1960, p 1.

accompanying him to the control center. Roberson was soon committed to the psychiatric clinic in Top Six. At age 25, he had several previous psychiatric referrals and was serving life for first-degree murder. This crime was particularly shocking to treatment department staff because it was the first murder of one of their members in the prison's history.

The Prison Auditorium/Theater

The auditorium, still smoke-scarred from the 1952 riot, carried memories of musical performances by the Ruby Jones Quartet and blues legend B. B. King. Back in 1934, it had hosted boxing icon Jack Dempsey. During Warden Bannan's time, a boxing ring was sometimes set up on Friday to entertain paying civilian and staff audiences with semi-pro quality fight cards. Ironically, since the auditorium was also the chapel prior to the building of the new all-faiths chapel, these matches would be followed on Sunday by church services in the same place.

The auditorium saw many varied uses. Movies were shown there, and inmate musicians practiced on the stage during yard time—I especially recalled one very talented musician who really made the blues sing on his alto saxophone. His name was Neely Buchanan, a name which will come up again very soon as I continue my tour.

The Prison Auditorium/Theater *Photos by permission Archives of Michigan*

Prison entrance, sally port and south yard
Photo by permission iStockphoto LP

End of the South Yard Blues

As I passed back through the sub-hall security gates to enter the south yard, an inmate approached me and said, "Director, Buck wants to see you—he's on the first gallery in 11 Block." Thanking him, I went into the block and found Buck lying on the cot in his cell looking wan and wasted. He was but a shell of the husky black man I had known for nearly 30 years. But I had never called him by his prison nickname, "Buck" and I didn't now. As he looked up when I entered, I asked, "how are you doing, Neely ?" He replied, "Not good Director, I have colon cancer and not much time left."

Taking a moment to gather my thoughts, I looked around his tiny barren cell; one of 386 just like it stacked five tiers high facing each other across the "rock" as prisoners call it. I noted that the barred doors were open in at least this little section. A concession so the half-dozen or so terminal cases living there would not feel so trapped during their last days. I guess it was a prison version of hospice.

"I'm sorry to hear that," I said. Then I asked how the family was. He had always been proud of his two daughters who had graduated a few years earlier from Michigan State University. His ex-wife, who divorced him a year or so after he received his life sentence, had

236

remained, as he said, "my best friend" even though she remarried and had gotten on with her life. He brightened a bit saying that his family members were visiting regularly. They were still supporting him—a welcome but not particularly common experience for long-time prisoners.

We chatted about old times; I had always had a warm spot for Neely, who had been a model inmate all those years. I also remembered him because of the alto saxophone that was his one treasure; his haunting melancholy blues seemed always to express the sadness and tragedy prison represents. When I heard him play, if I had a moment, I would step in and visit. The music director told me Neely could have been an accomplished professional saxophone player in the free world—playing the sax in prison was how he spent most of his yard time. On this final visit, I told him I missed his music and asked what had happened to his sax. "I gave it away," he said. Then I asked the question, "Why did you want to see me?" Very apprehensively, and in a barely audible voice, he asked, "Would you talk to Frank for me? I won my case in the Court of Appeals but they are taking it to the Supreme Court—they know I'll win on merit but they also know I'll die before the court decides."

He was referring to Michigan's Attorney General, Frank Kelly. However, to explain this request I must go back to a conversation we had years before at the prison in Marquette. Neely was working on his case in the law library, and said to me, "When I get near the end I'm going to file an appeal based on quick justice. I want you to know I'm not claiming innocence; you know that is not so. I'm not seeking justice—I'm hoping for mercy. After I have a lot of years in I hope the court will grant bond during the new trial and I will be able to die peacefully outside the wall."

What inmates refer to as "quick justice appeals" are those based on sentences imposed immediately after guilty pleas without benefit of counsel. Courts had consistently ruled that a denial of the due process guaranteed by the Constitution existed in these cases, and Neely's was certainly one of them. The first time I had heard about his case—this was years before our Marquette conversation—was on a radio news account about a fugitive from a murder warrant—an escapee from Jackson's Trusty Division, who had been apprehended in Philadelphia and was being extradited. Soon afterward, while Neely was being held in the Ingham County Jail awaiting trial, the rumor began to circulate that there was so much anger in the community the Sheriff might not be able to protect him from a lynch mob. Within 24 hours, he pled guilty, received a life sentence, and was transferred to SPSM.

I was a student intern just starting out on counselor's row at the time, and because Neely's serial number ended in six he was automatically placed on my caseload when he moved from reception to the general population. His was the first admission summary I would do for a first-degree lifer.

The murder occurred during a walk-away escape from the Trusty Division which had turned very bad very soon. An elderly farm couple discovered Neely stealing their car, and in the melee he bludgeoned both to death—thus committing the very crime most feared by those living near a prison. A routine walk-away and attempted car theft by a young homesick offender had turned into a brutal murder. Years later, because this was so out of character with the Neely I had come to know in prison, I asked him, "Neely, how could you do such a thing?" He answered, "Deputy, I have asked myself that question a thousand nights."

Now, all these years later, with Neely on his deathbed, I knew that the family of the victims were still strongly opposed to his ever getting out of prison and that the Attorney General's office had not made the decision to appeal the overturn of his conviction lightly. Talking to Attorney General Kelly would be futile because the wishes of the victim's children and grandchildren would clearly outweigh any sympathy for Neely.

I tried to explain this as best I could and looking him in the eye, I told him, "Neely, there is nothing that I can do to change the Attorney General's decision." The hurt in his face was as if I had struck him. His last hope dashed; the most influential person he knew had let him down. He said, "I understand," but he did not. We shook hands and parted. A few weeks later Warden Foltz would call to tell me that Neely Buchanan had died. He said,"I thought you would want to know."

My career at Jackson had started with Neely so it seems only fitting that my last visit ended with him. However, as I walked away from Neely that day I asked myself why I hadn't at least lied to him, giving him a few more weeks of hope.

The hospital at SPSM *Photo by permission Archives of Michigan*

The Prison Hospital--and Some Positives of Prisoner Behavior

As I left 11 block, I glanced to the east at a dark and foreboding cellblock—the prison hospital. It had been there since 1929 and I had been in it many times but never before noticed how grim it looked. Like the "new prison" itself. The hospital was begun on humanitarian grounds but came to be anything but humanitarian. Because "slow consumption" (tuberculosis) was the prime cause of death in prisons then, the new prison hospital aimed at giving the best treatment available for that disease. The second floor provided both isolation to prevent disease spread and a solarium for fresh air and sunlight. It was very acceptable to use inmate nurses under a physician's supervision in those early years, and individual rooms were better for patients than open cell housing. However, antibiotics largely eliminated TB, and nothing there now met hospital standards.

As I looked at that old hospital, I recalled hearing that in the 1952 riots a phalanx of inmates had blocked their rioting brothers from gaining access to it. Which reminds me that while I have written much about what went wrong in Jackson, including the misbehavior of some inmates, inmates also did many things like that—things that were positive and crucially helpful to all concerned. When we were housing rioters from the streets of Detroit, and again during the 1981 riots at the prison, they spontaneously, and with no direction from prison staff, organized to prevent looting and the destruction of medicine. They also helped provide medical treatment for the injured and chronically ill. Lost in the publicity surrounding the violence, fires, and general chaos of the riots is the fact that most prisoners did not participate and many tried to protect property. Inmates kept rioters from the vocational school and its tools. Moreover, inmate food service and repair crews worked long hours both during and after these emergencies.

Sometimes inmates who might have reason to act out badly when staff gave them good reason to do so showed saving forbearance. One such instance came to mind that day, as I looked across at the industries buildings on the other side of the security fencing recently installed as part of our efforts to reorganize Jackson into separate prisons.

In 1968, the Hall Office Lieutenant had come into my office saying, "The stamp plant is on strike and they want to talk to someone!" "Well that will be me," I said and started on the way. Captain Clint O'Rourke handed his keys to the lieutenant, saying, "I'm going with the Dep." A very good backup I was glad to have. When we got there, tension was high all around—involving both civilian staff and about two dozen inmate metal stamping operators.

"OK, give me a spokesman—I can't talk to all of you," I said. An inmate foreman reluctantly came forward, making it clear he was not the organizer—no doubt fearing segregation as an agitator. The problem was that the Prison Industries office in Lansing had arbitrarily cut their pay nearly in half as a cost saving measure. I promised to pursue the issue and get back with them but in the meantime told them to "get back to work," which they did. Warden Kropp instructed me to take the matter to Director Harrison—who was disturbed that someone in the Central Office had been that insensitive; he cancelled the pay cut and peace restored. Later the Department would implement a piecework compensation system that reduced cost, increased productivity and improved product quality. By hard work and increased skill, some inmates were able to increase their earnings from five-hundred or so a year, to several thousand. That is, they did until

240

several legislators became incensed that prisoners could "have it so good," and cancelled the program.

This incident sticks in my mind because it is an example of the way in which staff and prisoners could work together to solve a real problem. None of us at the time considered taking a hard line, because industries workers are traditionally well behaved and responsible. What could have escalated with serious consequences did not because both sides were reasonable.

After all, Jackson was really a small city with a social structure forged from mutual habitation and necessity. Officers working in huge cellblocks needed reliable co-operation from prisoners, and successful officers became excellent judges of character in preventing and solving conflicts. Captain O'Rourke's calmness in talking a psychotic inmate out of his weapon in the chaotic setting of the Barney Fancher murder is one example, but there are many others.

Everyone who ever worked or did time at Jackson could tell many such stories, but it seems appropriate that the recollections which came to me as I took my last walk around that old prison yard should be the ones with which I conclude this account. Anyway, for me, for now, looking back over all those years, they will suffice.

Acknowledgements

MANY PEOPLE CONTRIBUTED TO BOTH THE HISTORY and the memories contained in this book, some nearly a half-century ago. Others facilitated my gathering of information and photographs. In addition, some provided critical guidance, challenges, and editing. I am listing many at the risk of overlooking some.

William Kime
Photo courtesy of William Kime

William Kime's assistance was indispensible in reviewing and editing this story. He had provided wise counsel and critical analysis to three Michigan Corrections Directors as their Deputy Director of the Department's Program Bureau for 23 years—a role that has continued in my case during an additional 23 retirement years. He is the most knowledgeable person about crime, punishment, and corrections that I know.

BRUCE L. CURTIS, RPA
Bruce Curtis, Regional Prison Administrator, Southern Region MDOC.
The current occupant of the former warden's office, with administrative
responsibilities over the three prisons created from the revamp. (2014)
Photo courtesy of the Michigan Department of Corrections

Bruce Curtis, Regional Prison Administrator, to whom the three
wardens of the subdivided facilities at Jackson report, was most helpful
in clarifying the newly organized facilities and remaining cell count on
the old SPSM site. Also, in explaining how this complies with the
Hadix consent decree. Kimberly Walbrook, Senior Executive
Management Assistant to Curtis, located and scanned photos of
Jackson's wardens that were not available in the State Archives. I
appreciated the quick response and cheerful assistance both provided
after I had struck out on several dead ends.

Three Directors: Bob Brown, Perry Johnson and Gus Harrison
The Michigan Department of Corrections was established in 1937 and we three represent 37 years of that history. Gus Harrison served for 19 years and I credit him with creating opportunities for my career growth and development.
I served for 12 years and was followed by Bob Brown, someone I found to be a very strong team player, who then served for 6 years.
Photo courtesy of the author

The Archives of Michigan proved to be a gold mine of historical information and the staffs were most helpful in finding obscure files. Julie Meyerle, Archivist, was especially helpful over the years and provided guidance locating and scanning key photographs valuable to the book.

I am also indebted to Gail Light, former Corrections Department Public Information Officer, for meticulously preserving newspaper clips about corrections and for review and edit of earlier drafts of this book.

My daughter, Penny Shanks, Executive Director of Clarkston Area Chamber of Commerce, served as my agent and IT resource to solve computer glitches. She was also the format technician and art designer for this book. Julayne Gensterblum, my youngest daughter and schoolteacher by training, edited the narrative and advised on content. Val Henderson, a co-worker of Penny's at the Clarkston Area Chamber of Commerce, and fellow MSU Football fan, for detailed proofing and final format review. I am indebted to each for their help and encouragement.

Ila J. Bacon, daughter of Deputy Warden George Bacon (SPSM Trusty Division in 1959,) prepared an unpublished term paper for her college history class titled, *"The State Prison of Southern Michigan 1837 – 1959* dated April 21, 1959. The paper contained an excellent summary of the history of the old prison and complete information about prison programs at SPSM in the late 1950s. This proved to be a helpful frame of reference for searching the State Archives.

Professor Charles Bright and seven students from University of Michigan's Residential College/Social Science Research Community published a study titled *A History of Jackson Prison, 1920-1975* in 1979. During their research, the students reviewed documents the Department provided, interviewed staff, including me, and searched archives in both Lansing and Ann Arbor. Their work product proved a very useful resource.

In 1996, *The Powers That Punish: Prison and Politics in the Era of the "Big House," 1920-1955* by Charles Bright, published by University of Michigan Press, expanded on the political and social aspects of the students' 1979 work, and I found this helpful as well.

Three Bullets Sealed His Lips (1987), by Bruce Rubenstein and Lawrence Ziewacz, about the murder of Senator Warren Hooper, possibly being carried out by Purple Gang convicts while they were doing time at Jackson Prison, really brought to conclusion the varied stories, rumors and myths circulating among both staff and inmates at the prison. That book and the Attorney General Files from the State Archives were important resources for reconstructing the Purple Gang and Warden Jackson portions of this history. The Rubenstein and Ziewacz book is well done and goes into much more detail than I have given here—it is a compelling story about crime and corruption in Michigan.

246

Acknowledgements

Intemperance: The Lost War Against Liquor, (1979) by Larry Engelmann provided a sound background into prohibition during the Purple Gang heyday.

The Purple Gang--Organized Crime in Detroit 1910--1945 (2000) by Paul R. Kavieff provided an excellent historical perspective to help me understand the context of the Purple gangsters at Jackson prison.

The Purple Gang's Bloody Legacy by Susan Whitall published in The Detroit News Rearview Mirror August 30, 2004 added detail about the lethalness of the Purples.

Warden George Kropp, whose memory was legendary, was a walking encyclopedia of Corrections Department history that I benefited from both as his Administrative Assistant in 1963 and Deputy Warden (1967-69)—and also, as his houseguest while my family finished the school year at Marquette in 1967.

S. J. Gilman, Deputy Director of the Camp Program and my boss while I served as camp supervisor (1959-63,) was another fascinating storyteller. I became his captive audience whenever we rode together on assignments to northern prison camps. Gilman was the Department's Special Investigator working with the state police detectives on the Warden Jackson scandal in 1947 and was a party to the interrogations recorded in Attorney General files I discovered later in the State Archives. When Governor Williams took over in 1948 and appointed Ernest Brooks as Corrections Commissioner, Gilman became Special Investigator for Brooks. He told endless stories about the skullduggery of Pettit and his inmate aristocrats uncovered in the 1947 investigation, and chilling tales about the Purple Gang. Thus, Gilman planted the seeds for this part of the story to be told fifty years later.

Lee McCoy, the front gun in the prison administration building when I first arrived in 1955, and who became my Arsenal Lieutenant in 1967 and retired as Prison Inspector in the 1970s, contributed much prison lore. He was a nephew and namesake, of Leonard McCoy who was the deputy warden under Warden Hulbert in the 1920s. McCoy's father worked for years in 15-block and his brother, Clare, was the prison locksmith during my years at Jackson. Lee McCoy was an expert shooter and great storyteller—I benefited from both: being his teammate and listening to his stories recounting half a century of Jackson history. I am indebted to Lee for parts of that history and an understanding of Jackson prison not otherwise available.

In addition, one final source to mention. I had only been on the job some six months when the Hallmaster told me, "Deputy Cahill wants you to stop at his office." He added, "You may want to stop at the toilet first because you may be a while." I had already heard that the Deputy could "talk your arm off" if he liked you. Even though I was a lowly counselor, he heard that I was a shooter and had been police officer at Michigan State College (now MSU), so I must be OK, and he wanted me to understand prison culture and hazards. It was an interesting afternoon, and, contrary to my preconception, Cahill proved to be not all preachy. Some staff denigrated him because he had only a grade school education, and, yes dammit some in the Lansing office thought him, too tough, but I found that he was respected by both prisoners and guards as being absolutely honest and straightforward—a welcome change from the corrupt Pettit/Jackson times. I wish I had been able to tape-record that three-hour history lesson from the Deputy—however, it was consistent with what I found in later years in the state Archives.

--Perry Johnson
March 2014

Acknowledgements

**In my Michigan State College Police Uniform with daughter
Kathleen**
Circa 1952

Made in the USA
Lexington, KY
19 February 2018